M000233295

# MEXICAN AMERICANS IN
# TEXAS HISTORY

# Mexican Americans in Texas History

## SELECTED ESSAYS

*Edited by Emilio Zamora,*
*Cynthia Orozco, and Rodolfo Rocha*

Texas State Historical Association

Austin

DEDICATED TO

*Jovita Gonzalez, Irene Ledesma, Americo Paredes, and Emma Tenayuca,*
*all luminaries in the history of the Mexican and Mexican American communities*
*in Texas.*

Copyright © 2000 by the Texas State Historical Association. All rights reserved.
Printed in the United States of America.

*Library of Congress Cataloging-inPublication Data*

Mexican Americans in Texas history : selected essays / edited by Emilio Zamora,
Cynthia Orozco, and Rodolfo Rocha.
     p. cm.
     Includes papers presented at the Mexican Americans in Texas History
Conference, held in San Antonio, May 2–4, 1991.
     Includes bibliographical references.
     ISBN 0-87611-174-6 (alk. paper)
     1. Mexican Americans–Texas History–Congresses. 2. Texas–History–
Congresses. 3. Texas–Ethnic relations–Congresses. I. Zamora, Emilio. II. Orozco,
Cynthia. III. Rocha, Rodolfo. IV. Texas State Historical Association. V. Mexican
Americans in Texas History Conference (1991 : San Antonio, Tex.)

F395.M5M485 1999
976.4'046872–dc21

                             99-050292
                             CIP

10  9  8  7  6  5  4  3  2

Published by the Texas State Historical Association in Cooperation with the
Center for Studies in Texas History at the University of Texas at Austin.

This project was made possible in part by grants from the Texas Council for the
Humanities and the Center for Mexican American Studies at the University of
Texas at Austin.

The paper used in this book meets the minimum requirements of the American
National Standard for Permanence of Paper for Printed Library Materials,
Z39.48-1984.

*Front cover:* Alberto and Eva Garcia with their family, Austin 1922. Alberto Garcia
was the first Mexican American doctor in Austin. Eva Garcia was a missionary
nurse. *Photograph courtesy of Martha X. Garcia (shown in the picture sitting on her*
*father's lap).*

# Contents

# Introduction

This anthology includes papers presented at the "Mexican Americans in Texas History" conference, the first scholarly meeting of its kind in the state. The conference, held in San Antonio May 2–4, 1991, drew approximately six hundred participants, including about one hundred scholars representing at least fifteen universities and colleges located throughout the state. The audience heard fifty-two presentations that addressed bibliographic, archival, historiographical, literary, political, gender-related, labor-related, and conceptual topics. The impressive quality of the presentations as well as the stimulating discussions that followed attest to the meeting's success. The event also provided opportunities for the informal exchange of information and ideas, thus contributing to the further development of the history of Mexican-origin people in the United States.[1]

The Texas State Historical Association (TSHA), the oldest academic society in the state, spearheaded the event. This conference, as well as others that focused on African Americans and women, was organized by the TSHA in conjunction with its encyclopedia

[1] One of the earliest conferences on the broader subject of Mexican history in the Southwest was held at Edinburg, Texas, in 1969. It was entitled "The Role of the Mexican American in the History of the Southwest," and it was sponsored by the Inter-American Institute at what was then called Pan American College. Also, professional organizations such as the Texas State Historical Association, the Western Historical Association, and the National Association for Chicano Studies have devoted entire sessions at their annual meetings to Mexican American history in Texas. The San Antonio conference, however, is the first time that scholars devoted an entire conference to the subject.

project on Texas history, *The New Handbook of Texas*, published in 1996. Conference organizers decided that the meeting should address the post-1836 era, the Spanish colonial and Mexican periods having received more attention from scholars. Moreover, 1836 is a marker for a new period of Euro-American domination as Texas became, first, an independent republic and then a member of the United States.[2]

The conference participants represented various backgrounds and interests. Some offered the initial findings of their graduate research, others revisited dissertation topics, while still others shared parts of ongoing research. Most participants were historians of one kind or another, but some came with training in other disciplines, such as anthropology and literary analysis. Age, gender, and ethnic differences among both the presenters and the audience members contributed to the meeting's overall diversity.

Presenters used a variety of designations to identify their subject, including Mexican, Mexicano, Mexicana, Mexican American, Tejano, Tejana, or Chicano. The term chosen often reflected the speaker's decision to reflect popular usage during the time period studied. In some instances, scholars used certain terms interchangeably to illustrate the fluidity of culture and the malleability of social identities in history. Other presenters were less concerned about the utility of using specific group referents that illustrate the social variability of identity; they opted for one term, such as Mexican or Mexican American that rendered a more coherent sense of community. As editors, we have accepted the choices made by the contributing authors, with only minor exceptions. Throughout this introduction, however, we have chosen to use the terms Mexican and Mexican American, giving emphasis to the former term because it has been the most popular self-referent in the community since at least the middle of the nineteenth century.[3]

---

[2] The Mexican Americans in Texas History conference was organized by research associate and *Texas Handbook* writer Teresa Palomo Acosta, with the assistance of Cynthia E. Orozco, another research associate and writer. The following includes selected papers from another TSHA meeting: Nancy Baker Jones and Fane Downs, *Women in Texas History* (Austin: Texas State Historical Association, 1993).

[3] The editors use *Mexican* and *Mexican American* interchangeably as a way to reflect the various usages present during the conference. We agree with Juan

Conference participants were joined by a spirit of collegiality that drew meaning from an often expressed awareness of the meeting being part of a larger historical experience—the Chicano movement. This acknowledgment underscored a constitutive aspect of Mexican American history: the activities of the 1960's and 1970's social movement influenced institutions of higher learning to promote the study of Mexican American history and culture, and encouraged students to embrace "the cause" and capitalize on its scholarly opportunities. Additional factors such as the growth of the Mexican middle class, the relaxation of institutional barriers to mobility, and the work of other advocates of change within the universities also contributed to decisions by departments and faculty throughout the Southwest to sponsor theses, dissertations, courses, and programs on Mexican American history. Over the course of the 1970s and 1980s a core of specialists emerged. An awareness that Mexican Americans helped bring about these developments, and the frequent claim that a key purpose of Mexican American history is to correct the record of a people placed on the story's margins added a special layer of social meaning to the scholarly pursuit of knowledge that was evident at the San Antonio meeting.[4]

In recognition of their pivotal role in this process of correcting and amplifying the historical record, the conference honored scholars Arnoldo De León, Jovita Gonzalez Mireles, and Américo

Gómez-Quiñones that the term Mexican is an appropriate term to identify the base culture even if we allow for "time and economic changes, cultural adaptation, and the impact of domination." The term Mexican American, on the other hand, is also an adequate descriptor because it refers to "cultural and ethnic identification as well as to residency and citizenship status." Juan Gómez-Quiñones, *Chicano Politics; Reality and Promise, 1940–1990* (Albuquerque: University of New Mexico Press, 1990), 7.

[4] Texas has been slow in the production of Tejana and Tejano historians. In 1997, for instance, only one Tejana—Yolanda Romero—had received a history doctorate from a Texas institution. For readings on the Chicano movement, see: Gómez-Quiñones, *Mexican Students por La Raza: The Chicano Student Movement in Southern California, 1967–1977* (Santa Barbara, Calif.: La Causa, 1978); Arturo F. Rosales, *Chicano! The History of the Mexican American Civil Rights Movement* (Houston: Arte Público Press, 1997); Ignacio M. García, *Chicanismo: The Forging of a Militant Ethos Among Mexican Americans* (Tucson: University of Arizona Press, 1997).

Paredes. Some of the key contributions of each are reviewed below. Gonzalez Mireles wrote decades before the liberating influences of the late 1960s and the 1970s. The decision to honor her was a tribute to her historic role as a scholar who labored under patriarchal and racist conditions. Honoring her was also an exercise in recovering history and in recognizing women's work.[5] In its recognition of these and many other major scholars, the conference confirmed and celebrated the existence of a substantial body of literature in Mexican American history. The varied and comprehensive program of scholarly presentations reminded everyone who attended that Mexican American history is on its way to assuming its rightful place of importance in the Texas-based profession. The brief review of scholarship that is presented below underscores how very far the study of Mexican American history has come.

Before the 1970s, few scholars offered a sustained and constructive view of the Mexican community in Texas history. The general tendency was to ignore or misinterpret the historical record, whether in Texas or elsewhere. Specialists of the Spanish and Mexican periods, for instance, generally followed Herbert Eugene Bolton's institutional approach and focused on male political or religious elites. Notwithstanding the work of some borderlanders, such as Carlos Castañeda and his mentor Eugene C. Barker, colonials, Mexicans, and indigenous people from Texas received little psychological relief from a "Spanish fantasy heritage" that the historian Carey McWilliams long ago associated with works on colonial California.[6]

---

[5] Professor Aida Barrera accepted the award as both a distant relative and as the producer of a National Public Radio program about Gonzalez Mireles.

[6] Carey McWilliams, *North from Mexico: The Spanish-Speaking People of the United States* (Philadelphia: J. B. Lippincott Co., 1949). For early and recent conceptual and historiographical essays on Mexican American history, see: Gómez-Quiñones, "Toward a Perspective on Chicano History," *Aztlán*, 2 (Fall, 1971), 1–49; Gómez Quiñones and Luis Arroyo, "On the State of Chicano History: Observations on Its Development, Interpretations, and Theory, 1970–1974," *Western Historical Quarterly*, 7 (Apr., 1976), 155–185: David G. Gutiérrez, "Significance for Whom": Mexican Americans and the History of the American West," *Western Historical Quarterly*, 24 (Nov., 1993), 519–539. Unless otherwise noted, the discussion on the Spanish colonial historiography draws heavily from the following: Gerald E.

Historians never romanticized the Spanish colonial era to the same extent in Texas histories and narratives. In fact, the general tendency among historians was to downplay the Spanish presence altogether in their survey texts; they typically allotted the more than four-hundred-year-old Spanish past a single chapter, at most. Moreover, scholars cast New Spain's rule over Texas as a failure and largely ignored the established civil, military, and religious communities at San Francisco de las Tejas, Los Adaes, Nacogdoches, San Antonio, La Bahia, Laredo, and Nuevo Santander. Even today, it is largely the colonial administration of the frontier and Mexico's inability to maintain control of its northern territories that are showcased in Texas and U.S. history texts. Mexico, for instance, is often presented through a host of civil and military figures depicted as villains, poised against freedom-loving patriots during the Texas insurgency of the 1830s. This depiction of despotic and undemocratic governance serves to rationalize and justify the dismemberment of Mexico between 1836 and 1846. A case in point is the Alamo narratives. As Juan N. Seguín learned, *all* Mexicans were considered "the enemy." Seguín, despite his participation in the insurgency, was suspected of loyalty to Mexico and forced to vacate his position as mayor of San Antonio in 1842.[7]

---

Poyo and Gilberto M. Hinojosa, "Spanish Texas and Borderlands Historiography in Transition: Implications for United States History," *Journal of American History*, 75 (Sept., 1988), 393–416. The following are examples of positive consideration by the eminent borderlanders: Castañeda, "Myths and Customs of the Tejas Indians," in *Southwestern Lore*, Publications of the Texas Folk-Lore Society, No. 9, ed. J. Frank Dobie (Dallas: Southwest Press, 1931), 167–174; Eugene C. Barker: "Native Latin-American Contributions to the Independence of Texas," in *Speeches, Responses, and Essays, Critical and Historical* (Austin: Eugene C. Barker Texas History Center, 1954), 151–162. Barker presented this essay before a meeting of the League of United Latin American Citizens at Harlingen, Texas, in June 1935. The essay later appeared in the *Southwestern Historical Quarterly*, 46 (Apr., 1943).

[7] By the Alamo narratives, we mean such scholarly and popular works as the following: John Myers Myers, *The Alamo* (New York: Dutton, 1948); Albert Curtis, *Remember the Alamo Heroes* (San Antonio: A. Curtis, Clegg Co., 1961); Walter Lord, *A Time to Stand* (New York: Harper, 1961); George S. Nelson, *The Alamo: An Illustrated History* (Dry Frio Canyon, Tex.: Aldine Press, 1998); Willliam W. Lace, *The Alamo* (San Diego, Calif.: Lucent Books, 1998). Although the common inter-

During the 1970s, historians as well as scholars from other disciplines such as anthropology began to offer a broader and fairer portrayal of Texas's colonial past. Often employing the methods of the new social history, they focused on people and their communities. Some of the earlier noteworthy works by Edward Spicer, David J. Weber, Donald W. Meinig, and Juan Gómez-Quiñones led us beyond the traditional focus on institutions and geopolitical concerns in borderlands history; they followed the histories of peoples and their relations with their environment from the colonial period to the twentieth century. More recently, works by Gilberto Hinojosa, Andrés Tijerina, Jesús De la Teja, Donald Chipman, Mario Cerutti, Miguel A. Gonzalez Quiroga, Robert H. Jackson, and Armando Alonzo have continued to construct a more complex and dynamic social and economic history of the Mexican community of Texas. Sadly, authors of general texts on U.S. and Texas history have not yet integrated the new scholarship, preferring instead to use the older borderlands work in a very limited manner.[8]

---

pretation of the battle of the Alamo has presented the Mexican government and the Mexican nation in disparaging terms, some works like the following offer alternative and sometimes challenging views: Carlos Castañeda (trans.), *The Mexican Side of the Texas Revolution* (Dallas: P. L. Turner Co., 1928); Jeff Long, *Duel of Eagles: The Mexican and U.S. Fight for the Alamo* (New York: Quill, 1990); José Enrique de la Peña, *With Santa Anna in Texas: A Personal Narrative of the Revolution*, trans. and ed. Carmen Perry, Introduction and additional trans. by James Crisp (College Station: Texas A&M University Press, 1997). Jesús de la Teja, *A Revolution Remembered: the Memoirs and Selected Correspondence of Juan N. Seguín* (Austin: State House Press, 1991).

[8] Edward Spicer, *Cycles of Conquest: The Impact of Spain, Mexico, and the United States on the Indians of the Southwest, 1533–1960* (Tucson: University of Arizona Press, 1962); David J. Weber (ed.), *New Spain's Far Northern Frontier: Essays on Spain in the American West, 1540–1821* (Albuquerque: University of New Mexico Press, 1979); David J. Weber (ed.), *Foreigners in Their Native Land: Historical Roots of the Mexican Americans* (Albuquerque: University of New Mexico Press, 1973); Donald W. Meinig, *Southwest: Three Peoples in Geographical Change, 1600–1970* (New York: Oxford University Press, 1971); Donald W. Meinig, *Imperial Texas: An Interpretive Essay in Cultural Geography* (Austin: University of Texas Press, 1969); Juan Gómez-Quiñones, "The Origins and Development of the Mexican Working Class in the United States: Laborers and Artisans North of the Rio Bravo, 1600–1900," In *El Trabajo y los Trabajadores en la Historia de México*, ed. Elsa C. Frost, Michael C. Meyer, and Josefina Z. Vázquez (México, D. F.: Colegio de México, 1979; Gilberto

Historians who have interpreted the more recent past have echoed voices of domination and a collective disdain toward the Mexican community in Texas. Walter Prescott Webb, for instance, placed Mexicans on the fringes of a story of a male frontier. Writing in the 1920s and 1930s, he presented Mexicans as representing the antithesis of progress—obstacles to the inevitable sweep of a Eurocentrically defined cultural world. Few can forget his reference to "ditch water" blood among the Native Americans who intermarried with soldiers of the Spanish crown; his exaggerated praise of the Texas Rangers; and his casual treatment of the South Texas race war of the 1910s.[9]

Labor economist Ruth Allen also expressed the popular anti-Mexican ideas of the 1930s (when increased Mexican immigration and economic crisis exacerbated race relations), and encouraged the view of Mexicans as exploitable foreigners who threatened to depress wages and displace U.S.-born workers. Allen embraced the now discredited notion that Mexican workers were so exploitable and devoid of agency that they became the principal cause of working-class disunity in the state. Her characterization of Mexican rural women as listless participants in history may have accurately captured moments of despondency during the difficult times in Texas. It ignored, however, the equally real presence of

Hinojosa, *A Borderlands Town in Transition: Laredo, 1755–1870* (College Station: Texas A&M University Press, 1983); Andrés Tijerina, *Tejanos and Texas Under the Mexican Flag* (College Station: Texas A&M University Press, 1994); Andrés Tijerina, *Tejano Empire: Life on the South Texas Ranchos* (College Station: Texas A&M University Press, 1998); Jesús de la Teja, *San Antonio de Béxar: A Community on New Spain's Northern Frontier* (Albuquerque: University of New Mexico Press, 1995); Donald Chipman, *Spanish Texas, 1519–1821* (Austin: University of Texas Press, 1992); Mario Cerutti and Miguel A. Gonzalez Quiroga (comps.), *Frontera e Historia Económica: Texas y el Norte de México (1850–1865)* (México, D.F.: Instituto Mora, Universidad Autónoma Metropolitana, 1993); Robert H. Jackson (ed.), *New Views of Borderlands History* (Albuquerque: University of New Mexico Press, 1998); Armando Alonzo, *Tejano Legacy: Rancheros and Settlers in South Texas, 1734–1900* (Albuquerque: University of New Mexico Press, 1998).

[9] Walter Prescott Webb, *The Texas Rangers: A Century of Frontier Defense* (Boston: Houghton Mifflin Co., 1935). Webb's comment, "common soldiers in the Spanish service came largely from pueblo or sedentary Indian stock, whose blood, when compared with that of the Plains Indians, was as ditch water," appeared in: *The Great Plains* (Boston: Ginn and Co., 1931), 126.

determined and creative survival strategies fashioned by these working-class women for themselves and their families.[10]

The long-standing omission and misrepresentation of Mexicans in Texas history is especially evident in public school teaching. Even the World War II impulse to reform the curriculum as a gesture of good neighborliness towards Latin America failed to properly introduce students to Mexican history in the state.[11] When the U.S. State Department and the Coordinator of Inter-American Affairs urged the Texas State Department of Education to adopt a policy to teach Latin American history and culture in the public schools, educators did not interpret this directive to mean the history and culture of Mexicans in Texas. Popular interpretations of Texas history that downplayed or disparaged Mexican contributions continued to find their way into classrooms. Consider, for example, the cartoon-like pamphlet entitled *Texas History Movies.* The widely used supplementary reader that became popular beginning in the 1950s caricatured Mexicans as cowardly, ignorant, and deceitful. Mexican women were largely absent in the story.[12]

Few history textbooks offered a critical view of the state's his-

---

[10] Ruth Allen, *Chapters in the History of Organized Labor in Texas,* Bureau of Research in the Social Sciences, Publication No. 4143 (Austin: University of Texas, Nov. 15, 1941); Ruth Allen, "Mexican Peon Women in Texas," *Sociology and Social Research"* (Nov.–Dec., 1931), 131–142. Allen's unflattering depictions of Mexican workers and women are especially perplexing given the impressive amount of historical evidence in her possession that demonstrated that Mexican men and women exhibited a propensity to use community organizations and unions to protest and improve their poor condition. Her research assistants compiled this kind of information through correspondence with Mexican community and labor leaders from Laredo, Corpus Christi, and San Antonio (Ruth Allen Papers, Center for American History, University of Texas at Austin).

[11] See the following for an example of this effort: Edgar Ellen Wilson and Myrtle L. Tanner, *Meet Latin America; Curriculum Enrichment Materials for Elementary and Junior High Schools,* State Department of Education Bulletin No. 465 (Austin: State Department of Education, 1945).

[12] Jack Patton, *Texas History Movies* (Dallas: Magnolia Petroleum Co., 1956). The Dallas *News* published this work in 1926 and 1927. It first appeared in book form in 1928. Joe B. Frantz was a co-author of the 1985 edition which sanitized the story by expunging the more objectionable characterizations of the Mexican historical character.

tory, especially in the area of race relations. Joseph L. Clark's *A History of Texas: Land of Promise*, adopted for use in public schools in the 1940s, for instance, failed to acknowledge Mexicans as a diverse and complex society or as a charter community with historic ties to indigenous and colonial peoples. Clark devoted less than one page to the Mexican presence in Texas. His textbook, aside from providing basic population figures, included a one-sentence description of the contribution of Mexicans as laborers in agriculture.[13]

The Texas edition of *American Journey, The Quest for Liberty Since 1865*, a U.S. history text adopted by the Texas Education Agency in 1992 and used in high schools throughout the state, is an improvement. The text does not offer either an adequate or critical examination of Mexican history, however. It excludes the Spanish colonial period from its introductory section and accords only a few sentences to the Texas war for independence and the war between Mexico and the United States. The authors do not provide an engaging and in-depth examination of the Mexican community. Instead, they offer superficial and isolated references to topics such as the Spanish heritage of the cowboy, unionism, Cesar Chavez, and migration. Here, too, Mexican women are omitted from the discussion.[14]

Theodore R. Fehrenbach, the author of *American Journey*'s section on Texas history, continues with this approach. He devotes two sentences to Mexicans in his discussion of immigration and provides only a two-page treatment of Mexican politics. In this latter discussion, he focuses on three popular, male, elected officials and uses their experiences to conclude that Mexicans have made important strides. Not surprisingly, this narrow biographical approach to the study of a community leads Fehrenbach to downplay or ignore important factors. For example, he glosses over the civil rights content of Mexican politics and disregards the role of

---

[13] Joseph L. Clark, *A History of Texas; Land of Promise* (New York: D. C. Heath and Co., 1940), 506–507.

[14] James West Davidson, Mark H. Lytle, and Michael B. Stoff, *American Journey; The Quest for Liberty Since 1865, Texas Edition* (Englewood Cliffs, N.J.: Prentice Hall, 1992).

race and ethnicity in Mexicans' self-identification and community affiliation. The end result is an ironic de-Mexicanization of the story of Mexican politics.[15]

Past scholarly treatment of Mexican history and the Mexican community in the U.S. and/or Texas was not unremittingly benighted, however. As Arnoldo De León reminds us, some scholars, most notably Paul S. Taylor and Pauline Kibbe, contributed important work. Two of Taylor's excellent studies of Mexican workers during the late 1920s and 1930s focus on Texas. These works on Nueces and Dimmit counties stand as examples of sound scholarship on what David Montejano calls racially defined social relations in Texas agriculture. Kibbe, on the other hand, provided a highly informative and revealing account of the Mexican condition during a highly contentious period, the 1940s. Although her *Latin Americans in Texas* may be faulted for lacking compelling analysis, she provides valuable firsthand observations of the wartime politics of good neighborliness. And more importantly, she critiqued inequality and discrimination with honesty and at the risk of her professional career. Sadly, neither Taylor nor Kibbe examined the role of Mexican women.[16]

---

[15] Fehrenbach, "Spotlight on Texas," 919–982, in ibid. Also see the following for a similarly deficient work used as a text in university courses on Texas History: Rupert Norval Richardson, *Texas: The Lone Star State* (Englewood Cliffs, N.J.: Prentice-Hall, 1965). Richardson's work has undergone numerous revisions in its multiple editions since the 1950s. Its depiction of Mexicans has improved significantly over the years. Richardson and his new co-authors, however, have not made full use of the current literature on Mexicans in Texas and thus continue to commit serious errors of omission and misrepresentation. Rupert Norval Richarson, Ernest Wallace, Adrian N. Anderson, *Texas: The Lone Star State* (Englewood Cliffs, N.J.: Prentice-Hall, 1983). The problem of misrepresenting Mexicans in history is not unique to *American Journey* and *Texas: The Lone Star State.* State-adopted textbooks, according to a recent study, continue to depict Mexicans in a highly biased fashion. Ricardo Jesús Pérez, "A Quantitative Analysis on the Treatment of the Mexican American in State Adopted Texas History Textbooks" (Ph.D. diss., University of Michigan, 1979).

[16] Arnoldo De León, "Our Gringo Amigos: Anglo Americans and the Tejano Experience," *East Texas Historical Journal,* 32 (Fall, 1993); Paul S. Taylor, *An American Mexican Frontier, Nueces County, Texas* (Chapel Hill: University of North Carolina, 1934); Paul S. Taylor, *Mexican Labor in the United States: Dimmit County, Winter Garden District, South Texas,* University of California Publications in

Nonacademic writers have also contributed works of historical value. Some of the most important ones began appearing in
the 1930s, partly in response to the less than favorable representations produced by academics. The works by José Tomás Canales
and Ruben Rendón Lozano, for example, recast Mexican historical figures in a more favorable light. As members of an emerging
middle class who often sought social acceptance on Mexican
terms, Canales and Réndon Lozano may have offered their own
sanitized version of history. Their early attempts to recover their
history, however, also announced to the English-speaking public
the extent to which Mexicans objected to an exclusionary reading
of the past.[17]

José de la Luz Saenz and Alonso Perales, on the other hand,
provided significant accounts and analysis that inform the historical record on such themes as civil rights activity, identity, and
inequality. They too wrote in English and represented the new
leadership of the emerging Mexican middle class. Their works
nevertheless were different. With his World War I diary De la Luz
Saenz documented the Mexican contribution at the war front at a
time when the armed revolt associated with the San Diego Plan of
1915 led many Anglos to suspect Mexicans of disloyalty. He also
offered the civil rights movement of the 1930s and 1940s one of
its most powerful moral arguments: Mexicans earned the right to
expect equal treatment in all endeavors with their major wartime

---

Economics, Vol. 6, No. 5 (1930), 293–464; Pauline Kibbe, *Latin Americans in
Texas* (Albuquerque: University of New Mexico Press, 1946). Another early
notable figure was Carey McWilliams. Although he did not write focused studies
on Mexicans in Texas, his classic *North From Mexico* provided a postwar audience
the earliest book-length synthesis of the Mexican historical experience in the
United States. The Mexican anthropologist Manuel Gamio, on the other hand,
conducted a major sociological study of immigration that also addressed the historical experience in Texas. McWilliams, *North From Mexico: The Spanish-Speaking
People of the United States*; Manuel Gamio, *Mexican Immigration to the United States; A
Study of Human Migration and Adaptation* (New York: Dover Press, 1931).

[17] José Tomás Canales, *Bits of Texas History in the Melting Pot of America, Part 2,
Native Latin American Contribution to the Colonization and Independence of Texas* (San
Antonio: Artes Gráficas, 1950); José Tomás Canales, *La Guerra de Tejas*
(Brownsville: J. T. Canales, 1959); Réndon Lozano, *Viva Tejas, The Story of the
Mexican-Born Patriots of the Republic of Texas* (San Antonio: Southern Literary
Institute, 1936).

sacrifice. Perales, known in civil rights circles as "el defensor de La Raza," brought together affidavits, letters, speeches, and essays that not only documented cases of discrimination and struggles against inequality, but also brought greater visibility and legitimacy to the civil rights movement led by the League of United Latin American Citizens (LULAC), of which he was a founder and one of its most popular leaders.[18]

Other nonacademic authors such as Enrique Santibáñez, Jesús Franco, and Federico Allen Hinojosa offered immigrant or exiled views that partly addressed the themes of life, work, and politics in Texas. Santibañez and Franco spoke from their experience as members of the Mexican consular service. The former was primarily interested in pointing out the suffering occasioned by discrimination and the supportive role that the Mexican consulate played in assisting Mexicans, particularly the Mexico-born ones. Franco wrote a sensitive history of the work of Las Comisiones Honoríficas and the Cruz Azul, the two most important patriotic and welfare organizations in the immigrant communities of Texas. Allen Hinojosa's work belongs to a vast literature by exiles of various political and cultural backgrounds who commented on their experiences in places such as Texas. Like many other such writers, Allen Hinojosa spoke of "los de afuera" as Mexicans who lived outside Mexico's borders yet remained within its historical and cultural traditions. Other writers like Conrado Espinosa, Teodoro Torres, and Hart Stilwell took a literary approach to depict work in the cotton fields, the return to Mexico as myth, and class and racial conflict in the Mexican community of the 1920s, 1930s, and 1940s. Espinosa's short novel describes in detail the oppressive nature of farm work under the hot Texas sun of the 1920s. Torres, on the other hand, reminded his Spanish-speaking readers of their version of the classic immigrant

---

[18] José de la Luz Saenz, *Los México-Americanos y La Gran Guerra y Su Contingente en Pro de la Democracia, la Humanidad y la Justicia: Mi Diario Particular* (San Antonio: Artes Gráficas, 1933); Alonso Perales, *El México Americano y La Política del Sur de Texas: Comentarios* (San Antonio: [s.n.] (s.n.), 1931); Alonso Perales, *En Defensa de Mi Raza*, Vol. 1 and 2 (San Antonio: Artes Gráficas, 1936–1937); Alonso Perales, *Are We Good Neighbors?* (San Antonio: Artes Gráficas, 1948). De la Luz Saenz and Canales were also LULAC founders and leaders.

dilemma—since the Mexico that they knew no longer existed they had to learn to accept an often inhospitable Texas as home. Stilwell suggested that if the violent reaction to the union organizing of the 1930s was any indication, Mexicans would have to continue fighting for their rights to achieve equality and a sense of belonging.[19]

Mexican-origin scholars have also made early important contributions to the study of the Mexican community in Texas. Folklorist Jovita Gonzalez Mireles, for instance, wrote an impressive early social history of Mexican-Anglo relations in South Texas beginning in the late nineteenth century, as well as authoring studies of Mexican folklore in the same region. She was the first Mexicana in the United States to obtain a Master's degree in history. In the 1940s she joined her husband Edmundo Mireles in the writing of Spanish Texas history curriculum for public schools. Her recently discovered historical novel, coauthored with Eve Raleigh, reveals the breadth of her abilities and sensibilities regarding the telling of a South Texas story of race, class, and gender in Mexican history.[20]

Gonzalez Mireles' contemporaries George I. Sanchez and Carlos E. Castañeda also made important contributions to the

---

[19] Enrique Santibáñez, *Ensayo Acerca de la Inmigración Mexicana en los Estados Unidos* (San Antonio: Clegg, 1930); Jesús Franco, *El Alma de la Raza; Narraciones Históricas de Episodios y Vida de los Mexicanos Residentes en los Estados Unidos de Norte América* (El Paso: Compañía Editora, ca. 1932); Allen Hinojosa, *El México de Afuera* (San Antonio: Artes Gráficas, 1940); Conrado Espinosa, *El Sol de Texas* (San Antonio: Viola Novelty Co., 1926); Torres, *La Patria Perdida, Novela Mexicana* (México, D.F.: Ediciones Botas, 1935); Hart Stilwell, *Border City* (Garden City, N.Y.: Country Life Press, 1945).

[20] Jovita Gonzalez Mireles, "Social Life in Cameron, Starr, and Zapata Counties" (Master's Thesis, University of Texas at Austin, 1930); Jovita Gonzalez Mireles and Eve Raleigh, *Caballero; A Historical Novel,* ed. José E. Limón and María Cotera (College Station: Texas A&M University Press, 1996); Aida Barrera, "Sabor del Pueblo—Jovita Gonzalez," Washington: National Public Radio, 1983; Teresa Palomo Acosta, "Jovita Gonzalez de Mireles; An Appreciation," Mexican Americans in Texas History Conference, 1991; Gloria Velasquez-Treviño, "Cultural Ambivalence in Early Chicana Prose Fiction" (Ph.D. diss., Stanford University, 1985); James McNutt, "Beyond Regionalism; Texas Folklorists and the Emergence of a Post-Regional Consciousness" (Ph.D. diss., University of Texas at Austin, 1982). For examples of her folklore studies, see the following: "Folk-Lore

study of Mexicans in Texas. During the 1930s, 1940s, and 1950s, Sanchez directed numerous theses and dissertations, primarily on discrimination and inequality in public education. He also established (at the University of Texas) inter-American programs responsible for sustaining research and publication projects on the Mexican community from Texas. Moreover, Sanchez wrote and spoke on contemporary issues related to education, agricultural labor, and hemispheric relations.[21]

Castañeda, best known for his multi-volume work *Our Catholic Heritage in Texas*, became one of the most prolific and respected borderlanders. His numerous studies of colonial institutions in Texas stand as examples of rigorous and dedicated scholarship. Less known are his contributions in more public settings where he often used his knowledge of history to draw attention to discrimination and inequality as issues of domestic and hemispheric importance. He was intimately associated with LULAC during the 1930s, and in the 1940s he assumed important administrative positions with the Fair Employment Practice Committee, a

---

of the Texas-Mexican Vaquero," *Texas and Southwestern Lore,* Publications of the Texas Folk-Lore Society, No. 6, ed. J. Frank Dobie (Austin: Texas Folk-Lore Society, 1934), 7–22; "Among My People," *Tone the Bell Easy,* Publications of the Texas Folk-Lore Society, No. 10, ed. J. Frank Dobie (Austin: Texas Folk-Lore Society, 1932), 99–108; "The Bullet-Swallower," *Puro Mexicano,* Texas Folk-Lore Society Publications, No. 12, ed. J. Frank Dobie (Austin: Texas Folk-Lore Society, 1935), 107–114.

[21] See the following example of a public meeting and a research project report that Sanchez was instrumental in organizing at the University of Texas: Sanchez (ed.), "First Regional Conference on the Education of Spanish-Speaking People in the Southwest," Inter-American Education Occasional Papers, I (Austin: University of Texas Press, 1946); Lyle Saunders and Olen E. Leonard, "The Wetback in the Lower Rio Grande Valley of Texas," Inter-American Education Occasional Papers, VII (Austin: University of Texas Press, 1951). Américo Paredes, *Humanidad: Essays in Honor of George I. Sánchez* (Los Angeles: Chicano Studies Center Publications, University of California, 1972); Gladys R. Leff, "George I. Sánchez: Don Quixote of the Southwest" (Ph.D. diss., North Texas State University, 1976). Sanchez also penned essays that examined the contemporary condition and history of Mexican Americans: "North of the Border," *Proceedings and Transactions of The Texas Academy of Science, 1941,* 25 (Austin: The Texas Academy of Science, 1942), 77–85; "Spanish-Speaking People in the Southwest—A Brief Historical Review," *California Journal of Elementary Education,* 22 (Nov., 1953), 106–111.

wartime agency that investigated complaints of discrimination.[22]

Castañeda was not unlike his contemporaries Gonzalez Mireles and Sanchez. In offering alternative views on the depiction of Mexicans, they remind us of a claim in the field of anthropology: that natives learn to question unfavorable, Westernized portrayals of their community, using the language of their detractors. Castañeda, Gonzalez Mireles, and Sanchez voiced *both* Latin American (i.e., hemispheric) and Mexican American perspectives. They drew from a broadly defined Latin American heritage while simultaneously interpreting their own reality as Mexican Americans. Gonzalez Mireles went an important step further, evincing a marked gender consciousness.[23]

Gonzalez Mireles, Sanchez, and Castañeda may have initiated the "native" challenge to the unfavorable depiction of Mexicans, but it was Américo Paredes who gave it a more sophisticated and pronounced force. Paredes's first major scholarly contribution was *With His Pistol in His Hand: A Border Ballad and Its Hero.* This finely crafted study of the Gregorio Cortéz story and legend was also a revisionist narrative, critical of Walter Prescott Webb. Of

---

[22] Like Sanchez, Castañeda commented on the condition and historical significance of the Mexican American community: "La Aportación del Mexicano al Desarrollo de Texas," in J. Montiel Olvera, *Primer Anuario de los Habitantes Hispano-Americanos de Texas/First Year Book of the Latin-American Population of Texas* (San Antonio: n.p., 1939), 13–14; Castañeda, "The Broadening Concept of History Teaching in Texas," *Inter American Intellectual Interchange* (Austin: University of Texas, Institute of Latin American Studies, 1943), 97–108; "Statement of Dr. Carlos E. Castañeda, Special Assistant on Latin-American Problems to the Chairman of the President's Committee on Fair Employment Practice, Senate Committee on Labor and Education in the Hearings Held September 8, 1944, on S. Bill 2048, to Prohibit Discrimination Because of Race, Creed, Color, National Origin or Ancestry; "The Second Rate Citizen and Democracy," in Perales (ed.), *Are We Good Neighbors,* 17–20; "The World Today and the New Pan Americanism," Presented before Rotary Club, Houston, Texas, April 13, 1950, pp. 1–6, in Carlos Castañeda Collection (Mexican American Archives, Nettie Lee B enson Collection, University of Texas at Austin). See the essay by Félix D. Almaráz Jr. in this volume for a discussion of Castañeda's works. Also consult other works by Almaráz, Castañeda's biographer, in Arnoldo De León's bibliography in this anthology.

[23] For a discussion on Mexican Americans "speaking back," see Renato Rosaldo, "When Natives Talk Back: Chicano Anthropology Since the Late Sixties," in *The Renato Rosaldo Lecture Series Monograph,* Vol. 2, Series 1984–85" (Tucson: Mexican American Studies and Research Center, 1986).

special significance was Paredes's use of Mexican folklore. Employing the theretofore discredited word of the Mexican community as evidence, he debunked the myth of the super-human, Texas Ranger macho and offered a more nuanced and sensitive portrayal of the Mexican community. Like Cortez, Paredes shot the sheriff (Webb). He did not, alas, manage to kill the hundreds of deputies. Nevertheless, Paredes introduced the theme of resistance. Moreover, he emphasized what José Limón and Emilio Zamora have described as the "Mexicanist" cultural and political tradition among Mexicans in Texas.[24]

Beginning in the late 1960s, the Chicano movement made the academy more mindful of the history of the Mexican community throughout the United States, as well as in Texas. This awakening was part of a larger trend that involved revisionist challenges that broadened the view of history to include previously neglected groups such as minorities, workers, and women. Accompanying this intellectual expansion was the increased participation of Mexican Americans in the academic professions, including history. In many instances, this group acted as a community when it invoked a special responsibility to counter unfavorable depictions and to further the field of study. Professor Paredes himself encouraged this claim as part of an evolving historical tradition. In 1980, for instance, he described the young Mexican scholars attending the annual conference of the National Association for Chicano Studies as the embodiment of his once-distant dreams of a scholarly cadre conscious in and of itself.[25]

Numerous authors have contributed to the development of Mexican history in Texas since the early 1970s. Book-length studies by Guadalupe San Miguel and Emilio Zamora, for instance,

---

[24] Americo Paredes, *With His Pistol in His Hand; A Border Ballad and Its Hero* (Austin: University of Texas at Austin, 1958); Americo Paredes, *Folklore and Culture on the Texas-Mexico Border* (Austin: Center for Mexican American Studies, 1993); José Limón, "El Primer Congreso Mexicanista de 1911: A Precursor to Contemporary Chicanismo," *Aztlán*, 5 (1974), 85–115; Emilio Zamora, *The World of the Mexican Worker* (College Station: Texas A&M University Press, 1993).

[25] The reference to Professor Paredes's commentary is based on personal notes and recollection of Emilio Zamora, co-editor of this volume.

have introduced us to important struggles against discrimination and inequality in the areas of schooling and work. Martha Cotera, on the other hand, provided an early historical work on Mexican women. Her *Diosa y Hembra: The History and Heritage of Chicanas* represents the first Mexican feminist challenge to the profession, to Texas women's history, and to Mexican American history. She and Evey Chapa founded the Chicana Research and Learning Center in Austin to recover and promote Mexicana history. They are also responsible for the inclusion of Mexican women in *The Texas Women's History Project Bibliography*, the first major Texas women's bibliography. To date, Cotera's contributions have not been adequately acknowledged, nor has her work been a subject of critical analysis.[26]

The two best known historians making significant contributions to the history of Mexicans in Texas are De León and Montejano. De León, the most prolific historian since Castañeda, has given the field definition and visibility. With *The Tejano Community, 1836–1900* he provides a comprehensive study focusing on the everyday life experiences of nineteenth-century Mexicans. His *They Called Them Greasers: Anglo Attitudes Toward Mexicans in Texas, 1821–1900* is instructive for its highly rigorous approach and exhaustive analysis of racial perceptions and representations. In addition to authoring studies on cities and towns like Houston, San Angelo, and Benavides, De León has written the only book-length, survey history of Mexicans in Texas, *Mexican Americans in Texas: A Brief History*. Also significant is his collaboration with Robert A. Calvert in producing *The History of Texas*, the best attempt to integrate Mexican history into a basic text. It is one of the most widely used surveys of Texas history.[27]

---

[26] Unless otherwise noted, these and other cited works appear in De León's or Orozco's bibliographies located elsewhere in this anthology.

[27] De León's most recent addition to his long list of publications is a text that he co-authored with Richard Griswold del Castillo: *North to Aztlán: A History of Mexican Americans in the United* States (New York: Twayne Publishers, 1997). Like De León, other historians have produced important studies of urban Mexican populations. These include: Oscar Martínez, *Border Boom Town: Ciudad Juarez Since 1848* (Austin: University of Texas Press, 1978); Mario García, *Desert Immigrants: The Mexicans of El Paso, 1880–1920* (New Haven: Yale University Press, 1981).

Montejano has authored one of the best received studies on the history of the evolution of racially defined social relations in Texas. His *Anglos and Mexicans in the Making of Texas, 1836–1986* was the first synthesis of the post-1836 era in terms of political economy. Montejano's book, with its provocative analysis of social relations, labor controls, and the dismantling of South Texas racial order, has reinvigorated the field. His scholarship and activism have earned him well-deserved recognition from various regional and national professional organizations. His work, as well as De León's, awaits a gendered analysis, however.[28]

This anthology constitutes the first collection of essays and bibliographic works by historians on the post-1836 period in Texas History. Twenty-five presenters submitted their works for inclusion. The editors selected twelve of them, including the conference's keynote address by David Montejano. The selection was based on the quality of the work as well as on the degree to which each essay represented important trends in the historical literature. All along, the editors sought to compose an anthology that would introduce students of history at the high school and college level to the type of work that is currently being done in Mexican American history. With this introduction, we also wish to underscore the importance of continuing to collect, preserve, and promote Mexican American history.

*The Editors*

---

[28] One of the most recent studies on modernization and race relations that draws on the works of Montejano and Zamora is Neil Foley's *White Scourge: Mexicans, Blacks, and Poor Whites in Texas Cotton Culture* (Berkeley: University of California Press, 1997).

# Old Roads, New Horizons:

## Texas History and the New World Order

### DAVID MONTEJANO*

I am delighted to be here before you on this historic occasion. I thank the sponsors for their initiative and work in putting this conference together. I should give you fair warning: I have been known to ruin dinner events with my somber commentaries. At some point I will pick up some appropriate after-dinner jokes and "light" intellectual talk; for the moment I will simply keep my comments to some minimum. For dessert, I offer you an outline of a theme, to be thickened and sweetened at some other time.

During the time that I was preparing these comments, the events of the Middle East and the Persian Gulf War dominated out daily lives. I was one of those who rushed out to get cable television service, so I could see live reports from CNN and Univision. These recent events left a definite imprint on my thoughts about social change, war, and ethnic relations, and I would like to share these with you.

Analogies drawn from what historian Stanley Elkins called "living memory" help identify important areas for historical

*David Montejano is associate professor of history and sociology and director of the Center for Mexican American Studies at the University of Texas at Austin. He is the author of *Anglos and Mexicans in the Making of Texas, 1836–1986* and the editor of *Chicano Politics and Society in the Late Twentieth Century.*

research, and they also help establish some distance from the remembered frame of reference. Using the Middle East as such a reference point, I believe, can help us better understand the situation of the Texas Mexican 150 years ago, and it can also serve as a marker or baseline to measure how far we have come.

## Anatomy of "War Play" and International Conflict

What is fascinating to note is that whether we talk about a war of conquest or a war of liberation, we see similar dynamics at play. The contending parties must dehumanize the enemy and seize the high moral ground. This becomes clear if we compare the recent Gulf War with the Mexican American War of the mid-nineteenth century. The United States war with Iraq over its conquest and annexation of Kuwait may be taken at face value as a war of liberation; the United States war with Mexico and the subsequent occupation and annexation of the Mexican northern frontier may be seen as a war of conquest. In both cases, the leadership and armies of the enemy were portrayed as evil forces.

According to one *New York Times* commentator, "Saddam Hussein was a mailorder despot right out of the Sears catalogue."[1] Antonio Lopez de Santa Anna was similarly portrayed as a tyrant who inspired both fear and respect from the Mexican masses. A Time-Life book entitled *The Texans* noted, for example:

Having acquired great power, he thirsted for more; now he took political differences as personal challenges, an attitude that dictated the violence with which he subdued the liberal state government of Zacatecas and the destruction he planned for Texas. But cruelty and love of power and luxury made him no less effective a general. He was a charismatic leader whom his troops admired and feared.[2]

The Mexican army and citizen-soldiers were likewise seen as cruel and treacherous. Walter Prescott Webb in his history of the Texas Rangers characterized Mexicans as volatile and mercurial, cruel, ignorant, dishonest, superstitious, and wholly unequal to the Texans as fighters. Arnoldo De León provides a summary of the views held by the Anglo Texans during the days of the

---

[1] *New York Times*, Feb. 24, 1991.

[2] *The Old West: The Texans* (Alexandria, Va: Time-Life Books, 1975), 83.

Republic: Mexicans were primitive beings, religious pagans, indolent and carefree, sexually remiss, degenerate, depraved, and questionably human.[3]

In both cases, the presidents of the United States proclaimed a great reluctance to go to war. President Bush, in his State of the Union Message declared:

And the war in the gulf is not a war we wanted. We worked hard to avoid war. . . . But time and again Saddam Hussein flatly rejected the path of diplomacy and peace. . . . The world can therefore seize this opportunity to fulfill the long-held promise of a new world order where brutality will go unrewarded, and aggression will meet collective resistance.[4]

In like manner, President James Polk declared in his Second Annual Message of December 8, 1846:

The existing war with Mexico was neither desired nor provoked by the United States. On the contrary, all honorable means were resorted to avert it. After years of endurance of aggravated and unredressed wrongs on our part, Mexico, in violation of solemn treaty stipulations and of every principle of justice recognized by civilized nations, commenced hostilities, and thus by her own act forced the war upon us.[5]

The similarities in the reasoning of both presidents seem to suggest a collapse of history or time, or what is known popularly as a "time warp." In fact, all effective analogies suggest such time distortions. The praise of President Polk for American patriotism, for example, anticipates the words of President Bush 145 years later:

It is a source of national pride . . . that the great body of our people have thrown no [such] obstacles in the way of the Government in prosecuting the war successfully, but have shown themselves to be eminently patriotic and ready to vindicate their country's honor and interest at any sacrifice. The alacrity and promptness with which our volunteer forces rushed to

---

[3] Arnoldo De León, *They Called Them Greasers* (Austin: University of Texas Press, 1983), 12.

[4] "Transcript of President Bush's State of the Union Message to the Nation," *New York Times*, Jan. 30, 1991.

[5] "James K. Polk, 1845–1849," in *The State of the Union Messages of the Presidents, 1790–1966*, ed. Fred L. Israel (New York: Chelsea House, Robert Hector, 1966), 634–772.

the field on their country's call prove not only their patriotism, but their deep conviction that our case is just.[6]

Either man could have said the following:

The war will continue to be prosecuted with vigor as the best means of securing peace. It is hoped that . . . our last overture . . . may result in a speedy and honorable peace. With our experience, however, of the unreasonable course of their . . . authorities, it is the part of wisdom not to relax in the energy of our military operations until the result is made known.[7]

Which president do you think said the following?

It has never been contemplated by me, as an object of the war, to make a permanent conquest of the Republic . . . or to annihilate her separate existence as an independent nation. On the contrary, it has ever been my desire that she should maintain her nationality, and under a good government adapted to her condition be a free, independent, and prosperous Republic.[8]

The words were those of President Polk, who seemed to have "backed into the future."

Certainly this comparison is more than just an analogy. A thread of continuity links the marshes of San Jacinto with the sands of Dhaharan; what connects these wars of conquest and liberation is a long thread of hegemony of a European-American center over a non-European periphery. Indeed, one can argue that the preeminent position of the United States—its "more commanding position," in President Polk's words—in today's "New World Order" had its origins in the Texas Revolution and the U.S.-Mexico War.

President Polk in his Fourth Annual Message to Congress had noted as much: that one of the "most important" results of the Mexican American War was the demonstration of the country's military strength, which many European and other foreign powers had questioned. The war with Mexico had "undeceived" them. Moreover, the vast additions of Texas, New Mexico, and

---

[6] Ibid.

[7] Ibid.

[8] Third Annual Message, Dec. 7, 1847, ibid.

California—which now gave the country as much territory as "the whole of Europe, Russia only excepted"—had elevated the country to "a more commanding position among nations than at any former period." In fact, emphasized Polk, these acquisitions "will add more to the strength and wealth of the nation than any which have preceded them since the adoption of the Constitution."[9]

Moreover, added Polk, such strength and wealth would make for peace: "The great importance and wealth of the territorial acquisitions" would enable the United States to pursue without interruption "our cherished policy of 'peace with all nations, entangling alliances with none.'"[10]

Since the days of San Jacinto in 1836, the European-American axis has shifted its center from Western Europe to the United States, but this axis nonetheless remains the dominant allied force in the international arena. An Anglo-European core continues to exercise dominion over a non-European periphery.

Reflecting, then, on President Bush's declaration of a "New World Order," one might ask, in complete candor, what really is so "new"? Or as one political scientist put it, "the Administration's proclaimed new world order is remarkably like the old one: The United States still calls the tune."[11]

Perhaps the only "new" aspect is that this latest military action took place in the post–Cold War era, after the collapse of the Warsaw Pact and the crisis of Communism in the Soviet Union. Some have called this the "end of history," meaning that with the decline of Fascism and Communism, Western liberal democracy has won the great East-West ideological struggle. More suggestive than such proclamations about the "end of history," in my opinion, is Hegel's *dicho* that "man learns nothing from History."

### Old Roads: The Texas Experience of War and Conquest

The Middle East analogy also helps us comprehend the depth of the chaos that characterized Mexico throughout much

---

[9] Fourth Annual Message, Dec. 5,1848, ibid.

[10] Ibid.

[11] Richard Ullman, *New York Times,* Jan. 12, 1991.

of the nineteenth century. For Mexico appears much like Lebanon, a nation marked by civil strife and a tenuous sovereignty.

It is ironic that two of the most popular holidays celebrated in San Antonio—Fiesta week commemorating the defeat of Santa Anna at San Jacinto (on April 21, 1836) and Cinco de Mayo commemorating the defeat of the French army at Puebla (on May 5, 1862)—point to this chaotic state of affairs in Mexico.

Except for the twenty-five-year peace of the Porfiriato, Mexico was in a constant state of civil war and threat of foreign invasion from 1810 through 1920. In this period Mexico was racked with provincial rebellions and unending civil war between conservatives and liberals, fought wars with the Spanish, American, and French armies, and suffered the loss of nearly one-half of its territory along with some 100,000 Mexicans; all of which finally culminated in a bloody revolution in the 1910s.

So Lebanon may be an appropriate frame of reference, but Jordan also qualifies if we consider Texas as an occupied "West Bank." Because of a common experience of war and occupation—often called colonialism—such a comparison appears fruitful. In fact, Texan historians have made the analogy explicit. T. R. Fehrenbach describes the situation of the Texas Mexican as being similar to that of the Palestinian, and the work of Webb and J. Frank Dobie likewise touch on the related themes of occupation and of "being the chosen." Indeed, this notion of "being the chosen" is generally cited as a source for Texan chauvinism or what is called "Texanism."

This experience of independence or occupation—they are really the same thing, just flip sides of the same reality—provided a powerful story line for Texan historians: the prevailing image, according to a recent review of the literature, became one of "sure shooting, morally upright frontiersmen against "bloodthirsty and tyrannical Mexicans.[12]

The story of the Battle of the Alamo is the clearest reflection of this type of narration. For much of the twentieth century, the

---

[12] Paul D. Lack, "In the Long Shadow of Eugene C. Barker: The Revolution and the Republic," in *Texas Through Time: Evolving Interpretations*, ed. Walter L. Buenger and Robert A. Calvert (College Station: Texas A&M University Press, 1991), 164.

"heroic democratic struggle for freedom against tyranny" has remained the central theme. The Alamo, however, has not just been seen as a symbol of freedom from tyranny, but also as a reminder of war and conflict with Mexicans. In the 1920s, for example, it had apparently become routine practice in annual celebrations to omit mention of the seven Spanish-surnamed defenders who had died in the Alamo, thus preserving the simplistic appearance of a pure ethnic or nationalist struggle. The IMAX Cinema production "The Alamo—The Price of Freedom" (a film sanctioned by the Daughters of the Republic of Texas, custodians of the Alamo) likewise commits the same omission in its treatment of the Texas Revolution; again we find the stock theme of freedom-loving, patriotic Anglo-Americans fighting against "foreign" Mexican tyranny.

Indeed, for Anglo Texans the lessons of history explained the Mexicans' inferior place in the scheme of things. Texan war memories facilitated the denigration of the Mexican. In the first half of the twentieth century, the story of the Alamo furnished Anglo Texans with the emotional set for being "good Texans." Américo Paredes has summarized the matter well:

The truth seems to be that the old war propaganda concerning the Alamo, Goliad, and Mier later provided a convenient justification for outrages committed on the Border by Texans of certain types, so convenient an excuse that it was artificially prolonged for almost a century. And had the Alamo, Goliad, and Mier not existed, they would have been invented, as indeed they seem to have been in part.[13]

Thus analogies based on "living memory" force us to look for certain evidence: at settlement policies, at population relocations and expulsions, at both institutionalized and random violence, at uprisings like the intifada, at attempts to create a "peace structure" between the occupying force and the "safe" leadership of the occupied communities.

In Texas, identifying a "safe leadership" among the Mexican settlements, a leadership willing to acquiesce to the new sovereignty was a critical question for seventy years after annexation.

---

[13] Quoted in David Montejano, *Anglos and Mexicans in the Making of Texas; 1836–1986* (Austin: University of Texas Press, 1987), 224–225.

During this time there appeared periodic uprisings that questioned the legitimacy of the new order: the Cortina War of the late 1850s, the Skinning War of the early 1870s, the El Paso Salt War of 1877, the guerrilla war of 1915–1916 in South Texas. All of these resistance movements were suppressed, but they underscored the tenuous legitimacy of the Anglo-American order. It was a sentiment that Jovita Gonzalez suggested when she described the invasion of "hordes of money-making Americans" that undermined the Texas Mexican ranch society at the turn of the century.

The distinction between safe and unsafe Mexicans also underscores the various tendencies within the Texas Mexican community, and the need for the Anglo Texan authorities to find a leadership group that would accept the right of the State of Texas to exist.

In the nineteenth century, such support was provided by a conservative landed elite fearful of losing its property and standing in the new order. José Antonio Navarro of San Antonio, Santos Benavides of Laredo, the Canales and Cavazos families of the lower Valley, were among the more prominent intermediaries. In the twentieth century, the supportive group proved to be the League of United Latin American Citizens (LULAC), a middle-class civic organization founded in Texas in the 1920s. LULAC was adamant about fighting discrimination and inequality, but it was also adamant that its membership be loyal, patriotic Americans. The expressed purpose of the League, which in the 1920s saw itself "as a small nucleus of enlightenment" for the rest of the Texas Mexican community, was "to develop the best, purest and most perfect type of a true and loyal citizen of the United States of America."

In exchange for such commitment, LULAC demanded an "opening up" of opportunities for the Texas Mexican; they argued that the Latin American people would be uplifted once they had more doctors, teachers, lawyers, and professionals of all types. The strategy essentially called for an expanded middle class.

Such moderate proposals amounted to little in the 1920s, 1930s, and 1940s. Until World War II, according to C. Vann Woodward, the United States was following a path similar to that of South Africa. Factories, public buildings, schools, restaurants, hotels, parks, neighborhoods, cemeteries, and even churches were all marked by segregation. Indeed it may make sense to speak of a form of apartheid in the South and Southwest, the regions that had large African American and Mexican American populations.

In Texas, and elsewhere in the Southwest, such politics of white supremacy, of exclusion, were gradually weakened after World War II due to the civil rights movements of the 1950s, 1960s, and 1970s, movements organized by veterans and their Chicano offspring. In the 1960s, for example, the major political events revolved around the farm-worker strikes in the Lower Rio Grande Valley and the formation of a populist-nationalist party known as El Partido Raza Unida in the Winter Garden region. The electoral takeover by Raza Unida of Crystal City and Zavala County in 1970 stunned the state, frightened the Anglo residents of South Texas, and prompted Gov. Dolph Briscoe to denounce Zavala County as a "little Cuba."[14]

Such militancy forced the political authorities and institutions to take the moderate proposals offered by groups such as LULAC more seriously. The result was a collapse of *de jure* segregation, and the emergence of an influential middle class in the urban Texas Mexican communities.

## New Horizons: Transformation of the United States

How far have we come? How far have we come from the battles of Texas Independence and the Mexican War? In a century and a half, Anglos and Mexicans in the United States have traveled a long, difficult road from war and conquest to a form of reconciliation and inclusion. The evidence comes from several quarters. For example, the growth in Latino political participation in the Southwest the past twenty years has been dramatic: the number or registered Latino voters doubled from 1.5 million in 1976 to 3 million in 1988, an increase also reflected in the doubling of the number of Latino elected officials (from 1,400 to 3,000 officials). One could draw from "living memory" a number

---

[14] Ibid., pp. 278–287.

of dramatic and significant electoral victories—that of Henry Cisneros as mayor of San Antonio in 1981, or of Dan Morales as state attorney general in 1990, and so on. Such political advances have been built on evident upward economic mobility. The ranks of the unskilled laborers—service laborers and farm workers—declined from 51 percent in 1950 to 29 percent by 1980; likewise white collar ranks increased from 21 percent in 1950 to 36 percent in 1980. To clinch the argument about inclusion, one has only to look at the composition of the volunteer armed forces in the recent Persian Gulf War; some estimates have run as high as 30 percent black and Latino.

The new horizon we see, in fact, points directly to a social transformation of the United States, to a debate over American national culture. The debate essentially concerns the ethnic character of the core, even as it continues to exercise its dominion over the periphery. In other words, what is truly "new" in the "New World Order" is that the Anglo-European character of the core itself is undergoing a metamorphosis.

To be sure, such politics of inclusion, of multiculturalism, are not accepted by all. Recently a sharp reaction to such efforts have become evident, especially on university campuses. In lamenting the turn towards multiculturalism, for example, political scientist Andrew Hacker, writes:

Each year, this country becomes less white, less "European," and less tightly bound by a single language. The United States now has a greater variety of cultures than at any time in its history. This has resulted largely from the recent rise in immigration, for the most part from Latin America and Asia. . . . In addition, some Americans who were born in the United States are saying they can no longer identify with its prevailing culture.[15]

What this reaction means is that the struggle for inclusion continues. And it continues on the terrain of history as well as in politics. A history of inclusion must be developed, one that would undermine the opposed and simple categories of Anglo and

---

[15] Andrew Hacker, "The Transformation of White America," *The New York Review of Books*, Nov. 22, 1990, 19.

Mexican, one that would explore their meanings by peeling away different layers of identity—of ethnic identity, of gender identity, of regional identity, of religious identity, of class identity, and so on—so that in the end Anglo and Mexican become quite clearly social constructions, continually maintained and placed over other competing identities. A history of inclusion would reveal the complexity of historical events like the Texas Revolution and the Alamo, not just by emphasizing that many of the Tejano elite supported the insurrection, but by noting also that many Anglo settlers, described as Tories, supported the Mexican government and Santa Anna. As historian Paul Lack recently put it:

Texans entered into their quarrel with Mexico as a fragmented people, individualistic, divided from one community to another by rivalries for land and other jealousies, bothered by ethnic and racial tensions, and lacking a consensus about the meaning of political changes in Mexico.[16]

The complexity and totality of past experience must become known to us, and must impart important lessons to us as we travel the road of change together. Let me conclude by appropriating the words of President Bush:

The winds of change are with us now. The forces of freedom are together, united. And we move toward the next century, more confident than ever, that we have the will at home and abroad to do what must be done: the hard work of freedom.[17]

---

[16] Lack, "In the Long Shadow of Eugene C. Barker," 153.

[17] "Transcript of President Bush's State of the Union Message to the Nation."

# Part One:
# The Nineteenth Century

This section addresses the period immediately after 1836 when the Mexican community adjusted to political domination, economic subordination, and cultural exclusion brought on by the end of Mexico's rule in Texas and the birth of the Texas Republic. Most histories have addressed the struggle for Texas independence as a war between "Mexicans" and "Texans," ignoring the political loyalties and economic interests of Mexicans living in the contested terrain. Historians from Mexico, on the other hand, have usually focused on the role of the Mexican state and have forgotten the Mexicans residing in Texas.

Today, scholars generally reject the binary categories of "Mexican" and "Texan" and have begun to analyze political ideology, race, nationality, class, and nation/state in order to better understand the revolt.[1] While most studies of the Texas Revolt still focus on pro-independence efforts, authors such as Paul Lack offer a more complex picture of the period. Lack's essay focuses on how male elites fared in the pueblos and ranchos of San Antonio de Bexar and La Bahia during and after the revolt. He underscores the fact that Mexican loyalties were divided and that the fight over San Antonio deserves as much attention as the

---

[1] For varied examples of the new scholarship, see: Jesús F. de la Teja, *San Antonio de Béxar: A Community on New Spain's Northern Frontier* (Albuquerque: University of New Mexico Press, 1995); Stephen L. Hardin, *Texas Iliad: A Military History of the Texas Revolution, 1835–1836* (Austin: University of Texas Press,

famous battle of the Alamo. He also argues that race played a significant role in the struggle for independence and that the fighting had a profound impact on the lives of ordinary Mexicans.

Mexican scholar Miguel Gonzalez Quiroga studies the role that Mexican elites played during a period of intense economic growth in the binational region of northern Mexico and South Texas. Historian Jerry Thompson has addressed the issue of Mexican military and political participation during the Civil War, but until now no one had examined the manner in which economic change affected established Mexican communities along the Texas-Mexico border.[2] With his preliminary and focused study of Mexican merchants, Gonzalez Quiroga demonstrates that Mexicans were very much a part of the story during the middle 1800s. Moreover, while historians have focused on the intense conflict that occurred during that time, he reminds us that economic exigencies encouraged the bridging of an ordinarily impassable racial divide.

Roberto Calderón addressed the role of mutual aid societies and other organizations in Laredo in the late nineteenth century. Laredo was a major center of economic and political activity with a Mexican population that exceeded 90 percent. Like in Brownsville and El Paso, Mexicans claimed a highly stratified society and much political influence. Consequently, electoral participation was greater and organization life was far more complex than in the Mexican communities of inland towns and cities such as Corpus Christi, San Antonio, and Houston. While other scholars have studied *mutualistas* in such places, Calderón is the first to call attention to "electoral mutualistas." He also introduces a

1994); Paul D. Lack, *The Texas Revolutionary Experience: A Political and Social History* (College Station: Texas A&M University Press, 1992); Gerald E. Poyo and Gilberto M. Hinojosa (eds.), *Tejano Origins in Eighteenth-Century San Antonio* (Austin: University of Texas Press, 1991); Ana Caroline Castillo Crimm, "Success in Adversity: The Mexican Americans of Victoria County, Texas, 1800–1880," (Ph.D. diss., University of Texas at Austin, 1994); David Urbano, "The Saga of a Revolutionary Family: The Martín De León Family of Texas," (Master's thesis, University of Texas at San Antonio, 1990).

[2] Jerry Don Thompson, *Vaqueros in Blue and Grey* (Austin: Presidial Press, 1974); Jerry Don Thompson, *Mexican Texans in the Union Army* (El Paso: Texas Western Press, 1986).

same-gender tradition in the membership of the benevolent organizations and is the first to study Mexican American women in organizational life before 1900. While the author does not offer an in-depth examination of a given mutualista or focus on one across time, he does credit these organizations for contributing significantly to the vibrant social, cultural, and political life of a border town.[3]

---

[3] One of the best-known and most recent studies of mutual aid societies in an urban setting is: Julie Lenninger Pycior, "La Raza Organizes: Mexican American Life in San Antonio, 1915–1930, As Reflected in Mutualista Activities," (Ph.D. diss., University of Notre Dame, 1979).

# Occupied Texas:

## Bexar and Goliad, 1835–1836

PAUL D. LACK*

The story of the Texas Revolution has been told and re-told in narrow military terms, but the impact of this war on the people has scarcely been explored except for accounts of predominantly Anglo civilians who fled eastward before the armies under Gen. Antonio Lopez de Santa Anna. Moreover, the experience of Mexicans who lived in the war zone at the inception of hostilities has been ignored by traditional scholarship. The residents of the San Antonio River valley from Bexar to La Bahia and southward to Refugio felt the brunt of war as early as October 1835 and withstood its ravages for almost a year as their lands were occupied and re-occupied by the contending armies. The predominantly Anglo military force that first sided with the Federalist cause and then fought for independence often impressed their food, animals and other property, looted their possessions, and destroyed their homes. In the end the Tejanos' sacrifices, whether given voluntarily or under compulsion, never satiated the appetite of the force of occupation which at times sought to exact vengeance on them for real or alleged support of the defenders

*Paul Lack is professor of history and vice president for academic affairs at the McMurry University, Abilene, Texas. He has written extensively on Texas history. His major publications include: *The History of Abilene: Facts and Sources* and *The Texas Revolutionary Experience: A Political and Social History, 1835–1836.*

of Centralism or Mexico's sovereignty. The war left a core of uncompensated losses, mutual suspicion, and festering hatreds that poisoned relations between Mexicans and Anglos during the period of the Republic and beyond.[1]

The approximately three thousand Tejanos who lived in the region of Bexar and Goliad were caught in the middle of a destructive war. Military victory and control over the area changed sides four times in less than a year, leading to continuous suspicions about local residents. Resident Mexicans were participants as well as victims. They served on the battlefields and acted politically, but without complete unity or a majority voice in the Texas Revolution, the Texas Mexicans lost control over their destinies.[2]

Initially, *Bejareños* were prominent in the opposition to the Centralists of Mexico who under Santa Anna overturned the Federalist Constitution of 1824. This Federalist structure of government had promoted a high degree of local autonomy and been responsive to the economic needs and political influence of both Mexican residents and Anglo settlers in Texas. The prestige of the town of Bexar was considerable because the political chief over the province of Texas resided there. Federalism promised a future of progress as immigration to Texas fed population and

---

[1] For a fuller discussion of the background and causes of the war see Paul D. Lack, *The Texas Revolutionary Experience* (College Station: Texas A&M University Press, 1992), 3–37.

[2] The use of terminology in writing about the 1835–36 period presents many problems and requires definition. Names originating from national identities (e.g., Texan, Mexican) can be misleading because the question of nationhood was in flux for Texas during this entire period. Tejano is a convenient term adopted by historians to signify a Texas resident of Mexican origin (as opposed to a resident of U.S. origin or a person from some other part of Mexico), but many historians object to it because Tejano was not used with that meaning by people at the time. The term Anglo is problematic because it was seldom used by the people to describe themselves (they more often used "American"). Further, in the Goliad-Refugio-San Patricio area many of the residents were Irish colonists who most likely would have objected to being called "Anglos."

Since this matter cannot be resolved here to the satisfaction of all scholars or political elements, the best that can be done is to define terms and to be as specific as possible. *Tejano* will be used to refer to residents of Mexican origin who lived in Texas at the time of the outbreak of hostilities in 1835. In some cases

trade growth. In the minds of many Bejareños defense of the Constitution of 1824 signified adherence to the liberal cause of limited, decentralized government and increasing prosperity.[3]

Thus, Tejanos led the way in resisting the new Centralist order. In May 1835 an independent company of troops from Bexar under Juan Seguín traveled to Coahuila in a failed effort to help Federalist Coahuila-Texas governor Augustín Viesca save his crumbling authority. Moreover, Mexican Texans volunteered in substantial numbers in the fall of 1835 when the Texas cause still held to the possibility of restoring the 1824 Constitution. As many as 160 Tejanos participated in the October–December 1835 siege of Bexar, service for which, as local resident Sam J. Smith wrote in 1874, "they got no pay or credit."[4] According to the best estimate, ninety-two of these men were residents of the Bexar municipality, a majority being from the town of San Antonio. They served in a variety of capacities, as scouts, raiders, and soldiers in the battles or skirmishes at missions San José and Concepción and in the attack that captured the town from Centralist forces in early December. Acts of valor occasionally gained Tejanos recognition. One veteran of the campaign extended plaudits to the community as a whole: "Our army owe[s] many thanks to the brave inhabitants," for they "ranked

---

*Bejareño* will be substituted to identify a Tejano resident of the town of Bexar (San Antonio). Other terms such as "Mexican resident of Refugio" are used for reasons of specificity. "Anglo" signifies a person who had come to Texas, presumably from the United States (and with due apologies to the Irish), before October, 1835. "U.S. volunteer" refers specifically to those who enlisted in the war but are known to have come to Texas after the outbreak of hostilities.

[3] Jesús F. de la Teja and John Wheat, "Bexar: Profile of a Tejano Community, 1820–1832," in Gerald E. Poyo and Gilberto M. Hinojosa (eds.), *Tejano Origins in Eighteenth-Century San Antonio* (Austin: University of Texas Press, 1991), 1–24.

[4] Sam J. Smith to Edward Miles, Sept. 21, 1874, and Juan Seguín to the Comptroller of the State, Dec. 5, 1874, José Almeda folder, Republic Pension Applications (cited hereafter as RPA), Comptroller of Public Accounts (Texas State Archives; cited hereafter as TSA). Juan Seguín recalled that "no muster rolls were made while we were besieging Bexar," but an unsigned statement in the muster roll files described the roll of the Mexicans as "being misplaced." Adjutant General Military Rolls, Texas Revolution, 1835–1836 (TSA). See also Fane Downs: "The History of Mexicans in Texas, 1820–1845" (Ph.D. diss., Texas Tech University, 1970), 233–234.

themselves on the side of liberty, and fought bravely with the Texan forces."[5]

This level of participation may have been greater had not the town been placed under martial law by the Centralist force of occupation commanded by Martín Perfecto de Cos.[6] Bejareños nevertheless supplied goods, ammunition, and even confidential communications to aid the insurgents in the loosely conducted siege of October and November. Word came also of continued dissatisfaction by Bejareños with the politics and policies of General Cos, who established a pass system to control civilian movements, impressed goods, animals, and labor, and conscripted citizens into two local militia companies.[7]

Hearing these reports, members of the Texas army came to expect more from the Bejareños. As a result, Gen. Stephen F. Austin issued a "Proclamation to the Inhabitants of Bexar" in mid-November that amounted to an invitation to join the army or make peace, promising fair treatment and amnesty.[8] Few Bejareños had a reasonable opportunity to respond to Austin's proclamation because they lived under Centralist martial law. Nevertheless, after this pronouncement the predominantly Anglo leaders of the Texas insurgency generally considered residents who remained in town to be either enemies or potential spies,

[5] Juan N. Seguín, *Personal Memoirs* (San Antonio: Ledger Book and Job Office, 1858), 7–8; W. B. Travis, [certificate], Feb. 22, 1836, Antonio Cruz folder, Audited Military Claims (cited hereafter as AMC), (TSA); An Act for the relief of María Jesusa García, Feb. 1, 1844, María Jesusa García folder, Audited Civil Service Records (TSA); William B. DeWees, *Letters from an Early Texas Settler to a Friend* (Louisville, Ky: Morton & Griswold, 1852), 159.

[6] Martín Perfecto de Cos to Angel Navarro, Oct. 15, 23, Nov. 17, 1835, Angel Navarro to [Martín Perfecto de Cos], Oct. 20, 25, 1835, Bexar Archives (microfilm), Reel 167 (Center for American History, University of Texas at Austin).

[7] David B. Macomb to ———, [Oct. 5, 1835], John Holmes Jenkins (ed.), *The Papers of the Texas Revolution, 1835-1836* (10 vols.; Austin: Presidial Press, 1973), II, 50; [S. F. Austin] to José Ma. Gonzales, Nov. 18, 1835, ibid., 450; J. W. Fannin Jr. to Stephen F. Austin, Nov. 18, 1835, ibid., 457; [affidavit], Macedonia Arocha folder, RPA; Joseph E. Field, *Three Years in Texas* (Austin: Steck Co., 1935), 18–19; Paul C. Lack, *The Texas Revolutionary Experience* (College Station: Texas A&M University Press, 1992), 165–168.

[8] [S. F. Austin, Proclamation to the Inhabitants of Bexar, ca. Nov. 18, 1835], Jenkins (ed.), *Papers*, II, 452–454.

and tensions between Bexar civilians and the Texas army increased.[9]

Relations also worsened because of growing demands by the Texas army for supplies. It had but a meager commissary and little cash to make purchases. Even officers who attempted to respect private property had difficulty in establishing ownership of the corn, beans, and beef they needed, or in evaluating the needs of the population, or in paying for these products.[10] Members of the Texas military quickly resorted to impressment of goods. Responding to queries regarding dealings with Mission Espada, Austin ordered his regimental commanders to use persuasion, give certificates of credit, and keep an accurate accounting. Otherwise, they were instructed to follow "the Law of necessity, and take what you want." However oppressive this statement may seem, in these matters Austin showed more restraint than others. He ordered goods to be purchased and sought to organize impressment procedures so as to prevent the haphazard ravaging of local residents. Austin also resisted the movement for a more concerted scorched earth policy.[11] Nevertheless, much property was taken without any form of payment.[12] Obvious tensions and conflict existed by November.

This antagonism became evident when the besieging forces stormed the city and battled house-to-house between December 5

---

[9] F. W. Johnson et al., [to S. F. Austin], Nov. 6, 1835, Jenkins (ed.), *Papers*, II, 338–339; Military Affairs Committee Report, Dec. 6, 1835, ibid., III, 102–104.

[10] James Bowie and J. W. Fannin Jr. to [Stephen F.] Austin, Oct. 22, 23, 1835, Jenkins (ed.), *Papers*, II, 190–191, 202–203; Stephen F. Austin to Antonio de la Garza, Nov. 16, 1835, ibid., 433.

[11] [Receipt by Estevan F. Austin], Nov. 11, 1835, Luis Gonzáles folder, AMC; [Receipt by Juan N. Seguín], Feb. 4, 1837, José María Arocha folder, ibid.; S. F. Austin to Juan Seguín, Oct. 24, 1835, Jenkins (ed.), *Papers*, II, 206; S. F. Austin to James Bowie and Capt. Fannin, Oct. 24, 1835, ibid., 208; S. F. Austin to Patrick C. Jack, Nov. 17, 1835, ibid., 444–445.

[12] S. F. Austin to the Provisional Government of Texas, Nov. 30, 1835, Jenkins (ed.), *Papers*, III, 42. A week after his resignation Austin reminded the provisional government of its responsibility "to ascertain the amount of property thus [by compulsion] made use of, and to provide for a Just compensation." Nevertheless, over four years later Josefa Jimenez still had not settled the account for the corn "that during the storming of Bexar was taken from her by the volunteer army of

and 10. One of these units shot a boy who tried to escape from a captured dwelling and arrested three women and a priest. Another company stormed a stone house and shot inside, eliciting "screams of women & children."[13] Turning houses into strongholds involved forced entries, tearing holes out of walls and ceilings, and reinforcing doors and windows with dirt and furniture. These tactics left the city in heaps of ruins, and the siege stripped the countryside nearly bare. Col. J. W. Fannin, who had found provisions abundant when he arrived in October, soon reported to Austin that "we have nearly consumed all the corn near here."[14]

Although Goliad was not in the center of hostilities, the Tejanos of this region also experienced the traumas of militarization. Several factors influenced Mexican residents there to make a different response to the insurgency than had the Bejareños. Descendants of soldiers had prominent voices in Goliad in contrast to the more trade-conscious residents of Bexar. The leading family of the area, headed by Carlos de la Garza, favored the Centralist cause from the outset. Further, the military leadership of the insurgent forces in Goliad did nothing to court the favor of Mexican residents and much to alienate them. The occupation differed in that the insurgency triumphed there very early in the war (on October 9) and held the post with a garrison that seldom exceeded one hundred. Moreover, in contrast with Bexar, where Cos ruled the town and Austin exercised less than strong authority over the surrounding countryside, in Goliad commander

---

Texas," as her claim read. These contributions burdened both poor and affluent. In 1840 a congressional resolution awarded Erasmo Seguín $3,004 for the oxen, mules, corn, beans, beef, and other supplies he had furnished in 1835. [Power of attorney by Josefa Jimenez], Antonio Cruz folder, AMC; Receipts, Erasmo Seguín folder, ibid.

[13] Mag Siffs, account of Taking of San Antone, n.d., Jenkins (ed.), *Papers*, III, 391; Herman Ehrenberg, *With Milam and Fannin* (Dallas: Tardy Publishing Co., 1935), 82. Other civilian casualties occurred as a result of firing from the Centralist side. M. L. Cummins (ed.), "The Storming of San Antonio de Bexar in 1835," *West Texas Historical Association Yearbook*, 22 (Oct. 1946), 114.

[14] Alwyn Barr, *Texans in Revolt: The Battle for San Antonio, 1835* (Austin: University of Texas Press, 1990), 68–71, 76–80, 83; J. W. Fannin to [Sam Houston], Nov. 18,1835, Jenkins (ed.), *Papers*, II, 459.

Phillip Dimmit asserted absolute control over both resources and civil authorities.

Several specific developments created tensions between Goliad Tejanos and the occupying force. Dimmit's conduct gave the local conflict an Anglo vs. Tejano flavor. He purged the occupying forces of nearly all Mexican recruits by having them stationed in Bexar. Even though a sizable body of Centralist supplies fell into Texas hands with the capitulation of the presidio at La Bahia, Dimmit immediately began impressing the property of local citizens. Nothing seemed to escape the hands of his army. Between October and November the insurgents forced numerous contributions, including cattle and horses, carts and teamsters, corn, wagon wheels, a rifle, a string of ponies, even a crow bar.[15]

Dimitt aggravated the situation further by ignoring the local Mexican government officials. Alcalde Miguel Galán, who had initially attempted to serve in the Texas army but was rejected, enumerated the sufferings of the Goliad residents. The soldiers, he wrote, are "breaking into houses, ravaging the corn without the consent of property owners, killing cows randomly without making an effort to know who they belong to, impressing servants without the consent of their masters, and then letting them loose without supervision. . . . [or] paying them for their labor," and making other Tejano residents work on fortifying the plaza.[16]

The citizens of Goliad responded in several ways. As Dimmit himself explained, "immediately after the place was taken," they began to seek refuge in the countryside. According to another account, all but twenty persons left town; "the people are afraid

---

[15] Noah Smithwick, *The Evolution of a State* (Austin: University of Texas Press, 1985), 18; Receipt by P. Dimitt, Oct. 10, 1835, C. E. Vasquez folder, AMC; receipt by P. Dimitt, Oct. 15, 1835, Domingo Falcón folder, ibid.; Receipt by P. Dimitt, Nov. 26, 1835, Antonio Vasquez folder, ibid.; Receipt by P. Dimitt, Nov. 28, 1835, Carlos de la Garza folder, ibid.; Receipt by P. Dimitt, Nov. 29, 1835, Jertrudio Mendez folder, ibid.; Receipt by P. Dimitt, Dec. 4, 1835, Ignacio Cantú folder, ibid.; Receipt by P. W. Humphries, Oct. 17, 1837, Erasmo Seguín folder, ibid.

[16] P. Dimitt to S. F. Austin, Oct. 27, 1835, Jenkins (ed.), *Papers*, II, 233; Certificate by P. Dimitt, Nov. 26, 1835, Andrew Guzmán folder, AMC; Roberto Galán to Stephen Austin, Nov. 13, 1835, Stephen F. Austin Papers, Transcriptions Series IV (Center for American History, University of Texas at Austin; cited hereafter as CAH).

to come [back] as they do not want to be made hewers of wood and Drawers of water."[17] In early November the Tejanos sought to rectify their situation politically. Many enthusiastically welcomed Governor Viesca, who arrived in Goliad on November 11 while in flight from the Centralist powers. As a legally constituted Federalist leader, he seemed like a potential savior to those suffering from the local despotism of the army. His own refusal to receive Viesca "in an official capacity" incited what Dimmit called "insubordination, . . . discontent, a spirit of opposition." Thirty-one Tejano residents of La Bahia attended a public meeting which adopted resolutions against military usurpation by the local commandant.[18] Dimmit promptly declared martial law. This policy brought an additional set of protests, mostly directed to Austin and seeking Dimmit's ouster. Despite these objections, he remained as commander of the fort and garrison.

The fate of the Goliad civilians worsened between December and February with the arrival of additional U.S. volunteers, who tended to be militantly anti-Mexican. Even though some Goliad Tejanos professed support for the Federalist cause (which had not yet been officially abandoned by the provisional government of Texas) and extended hospitality to the occupational force, their refusal to leave rural sanctuaries and to serve the Anglo Texas troops accelerated the conflict.[19] Once again press gangs rounded up every yoke of oxen, team of mules, or stray horse they could find, and camp-weary soldiers roamed the countryside in search of those who supported their enemy. The pattern of distrust and antagonism undoubtedly increased the numbers who followed the de la Garzas in supporting the Centralists.[20]

---

[17] P. Dimitt to S. F. Austin, Oct. 17, 25, 1835, Jenkins (ed.), *Papers*, II, 146, 217; John J. Linn to Austin, Nov. 11, 1835, ibid., 379.

[18] P. Dimitt to Stephen F. Austin, Nov. 13, 1835, Jenkins (ed.), *Papers*, II, 384–385; A. H. Jones to J. W. Fannin, Nov. 12, 1835, ibid., 390–391; A Record of the public meeting held in Goliad on Nov. 12, 1835, Records of Citizens Meetings and Committees of Public Safety (TSA).

[19] J. W. Fannin to J. W. Robinson, Feb. 16, 1836, Jenkins (ed.), *Papers*, IV, 351; Hobart Huson (ed.), *Dr. J. H. Barnard's Journal* ([Refugio, Texas]: n.p., 1950), 8, 13.

[20] Receipt by A. C. Horton, Mar. 18, 1836, José María Hernandez folder,

When hostilities came to the La Bahia-Refugio region in March 1836 many Tejanos fought alongside the Centralists. Whether they welcomed or opposed the forces from Mexico under Gen. José de Urrea, the coming of the war into their homeland devastated their lives. Some noncombatants died in the guerrilla-like fighting around Refugio during March 11–13. Mexican residents also lost equipment, horses, cattle, and other property, especially those who resided in the town of Refugio, which the Georgia Battalion and other forces under Maj. William Ward burned on March 13. That same fate befell La Bahia, as Fannin set it ablaze just before beginning his tardy retreat. General Santa Anna later argued that the Texas brand of warfare which had "reduced [the Tejanos] to the most dreadful situation" justified the execution of Fannin and his men.[21]

The winter of 1835–36 in Bexar likewise saw the continued deterioration of relations between local residents and the insurgents. Press gangs, in particular, continued to come into conflict with Tejano farmers over rights to the local food supply.[22] Moreover, although merchants like Francisco A. Ruiz and José A. Navarro sold a variety of goods on credit, the burden of supplying the army had exhausted the area economy by January. Even cattle were in short supply, prompting officers to attempt to employ vaqueros at twenty dollars per month to drive in beef from the range. A promise of employment on credit hardly helped local residents. According to the acting governor of the provisional Texas government, "the unfortunate inhabitants [were] reduced

---

AMC; Certificate by A. C. Horton, Sept. 17, 1836, Manuel Zepeda folder, ibid.; Receipt by Thos. K. Pearson, Dec. 5, 1835, M. Lopez folder, ibid.; Affidavit of Esteban Cisneros, Oct. 9, 1857, Esteban Cisneros folder, Unpaid Claims (TSA); Ehrenberg, *With Milam and Fannin*, 119–20.

[21] Antonio Lopez de Santa Anna to David G. Burnet, May 23, 1836, Jenkins (ed.), *Papers*, VI, 361; John Joseph Linn, *Reminiscences of Fifty Years in Texas* (New York: D. & J. Sadlier & Co., 1883), 125–126.

[22] J. C. Neill to the Governor and Council, Jan. 6, 1836, Communications Received, Records of the General Council (TSA); Ehrenberg, *With Milam and Fannin*, 112–114; Receipts by F. W. Johnson, Dec. 16, 25, 1835, Juan José Casillas folder, Yginio Cuellar folder, AMC; Receipt by Juan N. Seguín, Feb. 12, 1836, María Jesusa de Treviño folder, ibid.; Certificate by Juan N. Seguín, n.d., Antonio Cruz folder, ibid.

by the war, from opulence and ease, to penury and want."[23]

Other problems such as "loose [military] discipline" led to tensions.[24] Full-scale civilian rule was not restored, and frequent changes in army command accelerated the pattern of military disorder. Col. James Bowie, in particular, interfered with private property, preventing citizens from carting their goods to the country. He also abrogated civil government by releasing prisoners from jail, creating a dispute with local authorities that culminated in an armed parade of tumultuous, "disorderly," and drunken troops.[25] Political factors also led to growing disenchantment, as the Texas cause changed from federalism within the Mexican nation to independence, which boded for Tejanos a permanent minority status in an Anglicized nation.

Despite a general trend of recruits from the United States replacing most of the volunteers who had lived in Texas at the outbreak of hostilities, some of the soldiers from Bexar remained militarily active in scouting and related duty. Through the first six weeks of 1836 army leaders paid little attention to recruiting locals or preparing the town for defense. The prospect of renewed war persuaded many Bexar residents to evacuate in advance of the arrival of Santa Anna's army. At the time those units began arriving in late February, most Bejareños were providing for the welfare of their families. Few of them joined or re-enrolled in military service until after the conclusion of the battle at the Alamo. War weariness, dissatisfaction with the goal of

---

[23] Ehrenberg, *With Milam and Fannin*, 98; Resolution providing for the troops at Bejar, Jan. 16, 1836, Provisional Government Letterbook (TSA); James W. Robinson, message to the Council, Jan. 14, 1836, Jenkins (ed.), *Papers*, IV, 25; Receipt by F. W. Johnson, Dec. 26, 1835, Receipt by Robt. Morris, Jan. 1, 1836, José Antonio Navarro folder, AMC; Certificate of payment, Dec. 13, 1836, Francisco Antonio Ruiz folder, ibid.; Walter Lord, *A Time to Stand* (New York: Harper, 1961), 57.

[24] J. C. Neill to Sam Houston, Jan. 14, 1836, Communications Received, Records of the General Council (TSA); James Bowie to H. Smith, Feb. 2, 1836, Jenkins (ed.), *Papers*, IV, 59; G. B. Jameson to Sam Houston, Jan. 18, 1836, ibid., 238.

[25] W. Barrett Travis to Henry Smith, Feb. 13, 1836, Jenkins (ed.), *Papers*, IV, 328; J. J. Baugh to H. Smith, Feb. 13, 1836, General Correspondence, Army Papers (TSA).

Texas independence (officially declared on March 2, 1836), and their earlier losses of private property combined to reduce the Bejareños' support for the cause of resisting the Centralists.[26]

During March and April 1836 Mexican residents of Bexar suffered from scarcity of food and high prices.[27] Nevertheless, over one hundred Tejanos showed support for the cause of independence by volunteering for military service in the spring of 1836.[28] Others cooperated with the Centralist military forces left by General Santa Anna, did their best to secure family and property on area ranches, or fled in advance of the armies toward the Louisiana border. Whether they joined this pall mall rush eastward known as the "Runaway Scrape" like the families of Juan Seguín and Antonio Menchaca, or persevered closer to home, the Bejareños continued to experience many privations.[29]

Even the truce and evacuation of Centralist forces following the battle of San Jacinto did not end the occupation experience.

[26] Lack, *Texas Revolutionary Experience*, 118–121, 194–197.

[27] Antonio Lopez de Santa Anna to the Inhabitants of Texas, Mar. 7, 1836, Jenkins (ed.), *Papers*, V, 20–21; Juan José Andrade to [unknown], Apr. 20, 1836, ibid., 506; Francis Antonio Ruiz, "Fall of the Alamo," James M. Day (comp.), *The Texas Almanac 1857-1873: A Compendium of Texas History* (Waco: Texian Press, 1967), 356–357; José Enrique de la Peña, *With Santa Anna in Texas* (College Station: Texas A&M University Press, 1975), 59.

[28] They served either in the unit led by Seguín that fought at the battle of San Jacinto or among those commanded by Salvador Flores and others whom Houston assigned to guard fleeing civilians. Seguín, *Memoirs*, 7–12; José Antonio Menchaca, "Reminiscences, 1807–1836," Typescript, Part I, 7, Part II, 3–4 (CAH). Among those who gathered at Gonzales in early March, General Houston sent a company of 25–40 under the command of Salvador Flores to defend families that had remained on their farms. Another body of about 30 soldiers escorted civilians from Bexar to Nacogdoches. One source gave the size of the Flores company as 25. Affidavit by Domingo Díaz, Dec. 22, 1858, Clemente García folder, Court of Claims records (Archives Division, General Land Office, Austin). Seguín estimated this unit at "more than forty men." Juan Seguín to the Comptroller of the State, Dec. 5, 1874, José Almeda folder, RPA. In another letter a few days later, Seguín placed the number who served in the spring of 1836 at 71 (not counting the 46 in his command with Houston). These included 28 under Flores and 43 with Deaf Smith and others escorting Anglo families or in similar duty. Juan Seguín, et al., to Stephen H. Darden, Jan. 12, 1875, *Texana*, 5 (Spring, 1967), 82–84.

[29] Downs, "Mexicans in Texas," 246; Augustín Bernal affidavit, Nov. 28, 1874, Augustín Bernal folder, RPA. Seguín, *Memoirs*, 17.

Many Tejanos stayed on the move. A significant number from both Goliad and Bexar fled south with the retreating Mexican army rather than face the revenge-minded and undiscriminating "Texas" military, swollen with more U.S. recruits. Others slowly reoccupied their residences, but their pre-war existence did not return. Worries about renewed military clashes kept many refugees in their rural homes, leaving Bexar depopulated. Dire conditions encouraged some to plunder the retreating army of Vicente Filisola. Capt. Juan Seguín's small company that arrived in early June was insufficient to guard even against attacks from irregulars, outlaws, or Native Americans who threatened the entire area.[30]

The region from Bexar to Goliad remained insecure for months despite being under military rule. Army measures continued to be harsh toward Mexican residents. Initially, at least, the commander presented an image of restraint. Gen. Thomas J. Rusk (who replaced Sam Houston after the San Jacinto engagement) ordered Col. James Smith, head of a force dispatched to relieve Seguín, to "be careful on going to San Antonio to prevent any unnecessary interruption to the citizens there. Such conduct as entering their homes and taking their property you will certainly forbid [as] improper." According to reports that reached Mexico that summer, the soldiers did exactly what the General had forbidden. Perhaps in response to this treatment, several townspeople joined others who had earlier sought Centralist protection. Some of them drove their cattle southward, thus depleting the local beef supply.[31] Violence directed along racial lines by Anglo soldiers and reluctance among many of the Mexican residents to support the fledgling government of the Texas Republic created fundamental conflicts. A cycle of mutual mistrust further worsened army-Tejano relations.

---

[30] Huson (ed.), *Barnard's Journal*, 34; Edwd. Burleson to T. J. Rusk, May 5, 1836, General Correspondence, Thomas Jefferson Rusk Papers (CAH); Juan N. Seguín to Thomas J. Rusk [June 7, 1836], ibid.; [Vicente Filisola], *Evacuation of Texas* (Waco: Texian Press, 1965), 48; James Smith to T. J. Rusk, June 8, 1836, Jenkins (ed.), *Papers*, VII, 75–76.

[31] Thos. J. Rusk to James Smith, June 8, 1836, Jenkins (ed.), *Papers*, VII, 74; José María Ortiz to the Governor of the Department of Coahuila and Texas, Aug. 1836, Guerra y Marina, Archivo General (CAH).

When Seguín departed the town on June 21, he ordered the people of the region to herd their stock eastward, out of potential enemy use, as a demonstration of loyalty to the new republic. Their reluctance to implement this order convinced some military leaders of the need for reprisals against Mexican residents. A month later Rusk threatened "to give Bejar a shake."[32] Impressments of private property continued to occur, and the army also functioned in a quasi-police role. Residents protested about these policies, but Rusk only expressed "eternal regret . . . that the distress of War should fall upon families of women and children" and promised that "in no case will they be injured by our Troops." His letter to Bexar judge Miguel Arciniega held out little hope for relief: "Bejar being the frontier . . . must be for some time the Theatre of War and as such will be exposed to many hardships & inconvenience."[33]

The problems of the people of Goliad and Refugio were if anything worse. Perhaps a majority departed southward with the retreating Mexican armies in May 1836, but according to one account, its leader impressed so many draft animals and carts that other civilians had no means of flight. One Mexican officer observed that the Tejano residents objected to having their property taken and to being forced to choose between fleeing or staying in their homes without protection. They "became quite angry with us and insulted us, saying that we were fleeing as cowards from a handful of adventurers."[34]

Those who remained behind, regardless of their sympathies in the war, soon learned that the doomsayers had been right: the Texas army arrived on the scene in a vindictive mood. Additional Anglo Texas and U.S. recruits increased the size of this force

[32] Juan Seguín "TO THE INHABITANTS OF BEXAR," June 21, 1836, Jenkins (ed.), *Papers*, VII, 224; Thomas J. Rusk to [Sam Houston], July 20, 1836, ibid., 505.

[33] T. J. Rusk to Miguel Arciniega, Aug. 5, 1836, Jenkins (ed.), *Papers*, VIII, 133.

[34] José Urrea to the Secretary of War and Navy, June 15, 1836, Jenkins (ed.), *Papers*, VI, 493–496, VII, 160–161; Vicente Filisola, *Representation*, in Carlos Castañeda (trans.), *The Mexican Side of the Texas Revolution* (Dallas: P. L. Turner Co., 1928), 185; de la Peña, *With Santa Anna*, 185.

from four hundred to two thousand. It quickly set out to discourage resistance.[35] A soldier noted to Rusk that army arrests and thefts of property convinced many of the "old settlers" of Goliad that "they wood all be killed and they think that you are after them as hard as you can march."[36] Official army policy was harsh enough, yet soldiers acting out of control also stole goods and attacked Tejanos without respect to whether they had supported the Centralists. Area merchant John J. Linn believed that new recruits from the United States operated from a "creed [of] the total extermination of the Mexican race and the appropriation of their property to the individual use of the exterminators."[37]

Initially, Rusk received criticism for failing to control his men, but his policy soon became purposeful. Throughout the Victoria-Goliad-Refugio-San Patricio region the people were to be removed and their land despoiled of its most valuable property, cattle. On June 19 Rusk informed the secretary of war of the Republic of Texas of having issued orders "to all the Families Mexicans and all to fall back at once and clear the country." He offered residents of the area a grim choice—to flee to Mexico or to a part of Texas out of the war zone and to drive out their herds or surrender them to his army.[38] Ironically, enforcement was most rigorous in Victoria, where sympathy for the insurgency had been greatest. Meanwhile, Centralist supporter Carlos de la Garza disregarded the soldiers who brought the removal orders to his ranch and thus defied Rusk's policy. The Texas military nevertheless continued its depopulation policy for the remainder of the year.[39]

---

[35] S. Sherman to Rusk, May 23, 1836, Rusk Papers; Tho. J. Rusk to M. B. Lamar, May 17, 1836, Jenkins (ed.), *Papers*, VI, 314–315, J. M. Burton to Thos. J. Rusk, May 30, 1836, ibid., 414.

[36] H. Teal and H. W. Karnes to Thos. J. Rusk, June 2, [1836], Jenkins (ed.), *Papers*, VI, 502.

[37] Robert W. Shook (ed.), "A Letter from John J. Linn," *Southwestern Historical Quarterly*, 72 (Oct. 1968), 240; Linn, *Reminiscences*, 200; Smithwick, *Evolution of a State*, 102.

[38] Thomas J. Rusk to A. Somerville, June 19, 1836, Jenkins (ed.), *Papers*, VII, 203.

[39] Hobart Huson, *Refugio A Comprehensive History* (2 vols.; Woodsboro,

Elsewhere, many Tejanos attempted to save their birthrights and demonstrate their worthiness by enlisting in the army of the Texas Republic.[40] Service may have helped to advance their cause individually, but as a whole the government's policy toward persons of Mexican descent had become capricious by the summer of 1836. Those who survived the 1835–1836 ordeal of war and military occupation, which was characterized by harsh material exploitation and ruthless denial of liberty, confronted a future of continued anti-Mexican prejudice. Racism did not originate in the 1835–1836 period. Historian Arnoldo De León has shown that North Americans brought with them to Texas prejudices against persons of darker color and that these views developed into a fuller revulsion against Mexican culture.[41]

The policies of the army from the beginning of the insurgency through the summer of 1836 indicate a quickened pace of racial antagonism. The war both caused conflict with ethnic dimensions and weakened the political need for restraint. Persons of Mexican descent in Texas did not speak with one voice, act with one purpose, or suffer to an equal degree. Many accepted the outcome of the war by holding military or political office under the Republic of Texas. But in general their status declined rapidly along with their influence and property. For Tejanos the Texas Revolution represented a revolutionary experience—not one filled by the romance of a selective historical memory but by hard, bitter, and destructive conflict.

---

Texas: The Rooke Foundation, 1953), I, 398; Henry W. Barton, "The Problem of Command in the Army of the Republic of Texas," *Southwestern Historical Quarterly*, 62 (Jan., 1959), 304; Thos. J. Rusk to J. W. E. Wallace, July 16, 1836, Jenkins (ed.), *Papers*, VII, 466.

[40] Columbia *Telegraph and Texas Register*, Dec. 17, 1836; Discharge papers by Secretary of War William J. Fisher, May 15, 1837, Martin Flores folder, AMC.

[41] Arnoldo De León, *They Called Them Greasers* (Austin: University of Texas Press, 1983), 1–23.

# Mexicanos in Texas During the Civil War

MIGUEL GONZALEZ QUIROGA*

The Civil War arrived at a time when Mexicanos in Texas were confronting the growing power and hostility of Anglos. Racial conflict between them which arose in the post-1816 years abated to a tenuous and temporary truce as the War of Secession stepped up the tempo of economic activity and improved employment opportunities for both groups. Historians have given little attention to this brief interlude in the historical experience of Mexicanos, although it represents a time of relative prosperity in a century largely marked by economic decline and setbacks in race relations.[1]

To better understand what occurred during the war, it is necessary to examine conditions Mexicanos faced on the eve of the conflict. At the start of the 1860s they were largely concentrated

*Miguel Angel Gonzalez Quiroga is a professor of history at the Universidad Autónoma de Nuevo León, Monterrey, Mexico. He has been serving in the 68th Congress of the State of Nuevo León since 1997. His publications include: (co-edited with Mario Cerutti), *Frontera e Historia Económica: Texas y el Norte de México, 1850–1865* (1993); "Nuevo León," in Donald S. Frazier (ed.), *The United States and Mexico at War* (New York: Simon and Schuster, 1998).

[1] The Mexican experience in Texas in the nineteenth century is best described by the following: Arnoldo De León, *The Tejano Community, 1836–1900* (Albuquerque: University of New Mexico Press, 1982); David Montejano, *Anglos and Mexicans in the Making of Texas, 1836–1986* (Austin: University of Texas Press,

in the central, southern, and western part of the state, particularly in Bexar County and the Lower Rio Grande Valley. Mexicanos increasingly assumed a subordinate position largely because of the major losses in land ownership they suffered as a result of wars and violent racial conflict. Their decline was also evident in the positions they increasingly filled in a racially defined labor market. Mexicano workers were displaced from specialized and skilled fields of work and converted into what Arnoldo De León calls a "general labor pool" that supplied agriculture and urban-based industries.[2]

Conflict characterized their relationship with the Anglo majority. After the signing of the Treaty of Guadalupe Hidalgo in 1848, and throughout the 1850s, hostility towards Mexicanos prevailed in Texas. Numerous predominantly Anglo communities from East Texas, for instance, openly objected to their settlement in the area. Mexicans also confronted problems in parts of Central and South Texas. They were expelled from Seguín in 1854 and from Austin in 1855. In 1854, delegates from nine counties representing slavery interests met in Gonzales to form vigilante committees to prevent the flight of slaves to Mexico. It was assumed that Mexicanos were aiding the slaves in their escape. In 1856 Anglo residents from Colorado County reportedly discovered such a conspiracy and quickly expelled an untold number of Mexicanos from the area. A similar expulsion occurred in Matagorda County that same year. Shortly thereafter,

---

1987). The heightened economic activity generated by the Civil War is described in James A. Irby, *Backdoor at Bagdad: The Civil War on the Rio Grande* (El Paso: University of Texas Press, 1977); Le Roy Graf, "The Economic History of the Lower Rio Grande Valley, 1820–1875" (Ph.D. diss., Harvard University, 1942).

[2] According David Montejano, the land in Cameron County, which had belonged to Mexicanos at mid century, was largely owned by Anglos in 1892: ". . . forty six non-Spanish-surnamed owners owned over 1.2 million acres of land, nearly four times as much as the acreage owned by Spanish-surnamed owners." Arnoldo De León and Kenneth L. Stewart note that 33.8 percent of the Mexicanos in 1850 were farmers and stockraisers. This presumably land-owning figure declined to 9.3 percent by 1900. Montejano, *Anglos and Mexicans in the Making of Texas*, 72; De León and Stewart, *Tejanos and the Numbers Game: A Socio-Historical Interpretation From the Federal Censuses, 1850–1900* (Albuquerque: University of New Mexico Press, 1989), 31–35.

an undetermined number of Mexicanos were stripped of their possessions and forced to flee to the other side of the border. Further south, in Uvalde County, authorities decreed in 1857 that Mexicanos could not travel in the area without an official pass from the county government.[3]

Mexicanos also suffered racial violence. In 1855, unknown persons lynched twelve of them near the Nueces River. In the same year, the violent harassment of Mexican cartmen began in Goliad County. This culminated in the famous Cart War of 1857 which resulted in the killing of an estimated seventy-five Mexicanos in Central Texas. Anglos perpetrated this violence to eliminate the freighters from the lucrative commercial trade between San Antonio and the Gulf coast. The 1850s clearly did not represent a period of good fortune for Mexicanos in Texas.

The Civil War dominated the following decade and although Texas was never an important area of conflict it contributed units for the fighting in the East and suffered brief occupation in the Rio Grande Valley. The state did, however, serve as an important conduit for provisions and war material needed by the besieged South. With the Union blockade of Confederate ports and the occupation of New Orleans, Texas became an especially important funnel for southern cotton. Cotton normally crossed into Mexico at various points between Brownsville and Eagle Pass and sailed unmolested towards Europe.

Northeastern Mexico played a critical role in this war trade. Matamoros's strategic importance as a way station for European goods is well known. Less well known is that the northern Mexican states of Chihuahua, Coahuila, Nuevo León, Tamaulipas, Zacatecas, Durango, and San Luis Potosi provided the South with large quantities of hides, flour, salt, sugar, coffee,

---

[3] The discussion on anti-Mexican sentiments and violence is drawn from the following: Montejano, *Anglos and Mexicans in the Making of Texas*, 28–29; David J. Weber (ed.), *Foreigners in their Native Land, Historical roots of the Mexican Americans* (Albuquerque: University of New Mexico Press, 1973), 153; Jose Reséndiz Balderas, intro., *Informe de la Comisión Pesquisidora de la Frontera del Norte al Ejecutivo de la Unión* (1874; reprint, Nuevo León: Archivo General del Estado, 1984), 72–74; Litha Crews, "The Know Nothing Party in Texas" (M.A. thesis, University of Texas, 1925), 48; Arnoldo De León, *They Called Them Greasers, Anglo Attitudes*

lead, powder, and rope.[4] Maintaining cordial relations with Mexico consequently became an important concern to the Confederacy. As we shall see, this concern would affect the way Mexicanos in Texas were treated. To appreciate this development, we must first examine the Mexicans' view of the struggle, their participation in the armies of the North and the South, their socioeconomic situation, and the employment opportunities which opened up for them as a result of the commercial frenzy which seized the state.

Jerry Thompson, the well-known Civil War historian from South Texas, has argued that Mexicanos in Texas were largely indifferent towards the war because they had been excluded from the political discourse. Moreover, they held little patriotic sentiment for the Confederacy, and were hardly moved to defend slavery. When Texas counties decided on the question of secession, Mexicanos were largely excluded from voting, even in the southern districts where they were in the majority.[5]

Mexicano immigrants reinforced the community's general indifference since they were primarily interested in obtaining work rather than fighting. A recruiting officer visiting several communities in the Lower Rio Grande Valley discovered this among numerous Mexicans who claimed exemption from military service on the grounds that they were not U.S. citizens.[6] The case of

---

*Toward Mexicans in Texas, 1821–1900* (Austin: University of Texas Press, 1983), 82–83; Paul D. Lack, "Slavery and Vigilantism in Austin, Texas, 1840–1860," *Southwestern Historical Quarterly*, 84 (July, 1981), 1–20.

[4] Annie Cowling, "The Civil War Trade of the Lower Rio Grande Valley" (M.A. thesis, University of Texas, 1926); James A. Irby, "Line of the Rio Grande: War and Trade on the Confederate Frontier, 1861–1865" (Ph.D. diss., University of Georgia, 1969); James A. Irby, *Backdoor at Bagdad: The Civil War on the Rio Grande*; Graf, "The Economic History of the Lower Rio Grande Valley, 1820–1875"; Ronnie Tyler, *Santiago Vidaurri and the Southern Confederacy* (Austin: Texas State Historical Association, 1973); Tom Lea, *The King Ranch* (Boston: Little Brown & Co., 1957); Robert W. Delaney, "Matamoros, Port of Texas During the Civil War," *Southwestern Historical Quarterly*, 58 (Apr., 1955), 473–487; Mario Cerutti and Miguel González Quiroga, "Guerra y comercio en torno al Rio Bravo (1855–1867), Linea fronteriza, espacio económico común," *Historia Mexicana*, 40 (Oct.–Dec., 1990), 217–297.

[5] Jerry Thompson, *Vaqueros in Blue and Gray* (Austin: Presidial Press, 1976), 9–11.

[6] Corpus Christi *Ranchero*, Apr. 30, 1863.

Vicente Hernandez reflected and reinforced this view in 1864. Hernandez, born in Zacatecas and a resident of Bexar County, was taken before the court for failing to report to the army under the recruiting law then in force. He could not serve in a foreign army, he argued, because he had pledged loyalty to Mexico to which he would one day return. The prosecutor argued that for-eign-born persons should also serve, but the judge decided in favor of Hernández, adding that the government could not extend such a requirement to citizens of Mexico, a country with whom it was necessary to cultivate good relations as it was the only nation helping the Confederacy.[7]

Notwithstanding the indifference that most Mexicanos in Texas displayed toward the war, some enlisted and participated in the struggle. Thompson estimates that three thousand Mexicanos served in the Confederacy and nine hundred in the Union Army.[8] Seventy-five percent of the unionists were from south of the border, particularly from Tamaulipas, Nuevo Leon, and Coahuila.[9] Although the origins of the Mexicano confederates is unclear, some were also natives of Mexico. One Confederate company, for instance, consisted of sixty-two Mexicanos, only three were born in Texas.[10]

Most Mexicanos probably joined for economic reasons. The promise of an eleven- and thirteen-dollar monthly salary plus a uniform and a rifle was a sufficient stimulus for Mexicanos.[11] The prospect of receiving wages on a regular basis also attracted the

---

[7] San Antonio *News*, May 14, 1864. The judge reportedly stated that it was "inexpedient to force aliens into the army as it might exasperate other nations toward us, that it was particularly so with regard to citizens of Mexico, which gov-ernment had afforded us every facility for obtaining munitions of war, which we so much needed, whilst other nations had shown an unfriendly disposition; and that we were still dependent upon her, and therefore should cultivate friendly relations with her."

[8] Thompson, *Mexican Texans in the Union Army* (El Paso: Texas Western Press, 1986), 28.

[9] Ibid., 42.

[10] Thompson, *Vaqueros*, 27.

[11] Ibid., 16. Thompson notes that Mexicanos were offered up to one hun-dred dollars in gold, and fifty acres of land for single men and 150 for married ones.

poor from Mexico and South Texas. This is confirmed by the fact that recruits usually deserted when the military failed to pay their salaries on time. According to Thompson, it was for this reason that one-third of the Mexicanos who enlisted in the Union Army deserted.[12]

Some Mexicano inhabitants of the border area defended the Confederacy under the leadership of Santos Benavides of Laredo, while others joined the ranks of the Union. The majority of the Mexicano population of the Lower Rio Grande Valley avoided the fray but lived under the constant threat of losing their homes or their lives. A large undetermined number of them abandoned their lands and sought refuge below the Rio Grande.[13] With the general confusion generated by the war, many others were victimized by pillage and plunder and lost their possessions.[14]

The Mexicano population outside the border area was spared most of the violence. Nevertheless, inflation, another wartime curse, affected them as well as the Anglo population. According to one Civil War historian, the federal blockade drove up the price of consumer products between 1861 and 1864. The cost of beef, for example, increased from two to twenty-five cents a pound, while rice rose from eleven cents to six dollars, sugar from eight cents to seven dollars, and coffee from sixty-five cents to thirty dollars. Wartime inflation in these basic consumer items created severe hardship for the poorer sectors of the population.[15]

---

[12] Thompson, *Mexican Texans*, 27. Other reasons for desertion included discrimination in the military, a lack of patriotic sentiment among the Mexican recruits, and their ambivalence toward the nature of the conflict. *Vaqueros*, 6–7, 48.

[13] *Informe de la Comisión Pesquisidora de la Frontera del Norte*, 37. The Mexicanos who fled Texas found little security below the border where a regional conflict emerged. Two bands, the Rojos and the Crinolinos, battled for control of Tamaulipas. Serious fighting occurred in Reynosa, martial law was declared in Matamoros, and a steady flow of refugees crossed into Brownsville. *San Antonio Weekly Herald*, Nov. 2, 1861.

[14] *Informe de la Comisión Pesquisidora*, 39–40. The commission complained that the abandoned ranches of the Mexicanos were raided by Anglo outlaws who robbed cattle and other property. Special mention was made of the Wright brothers, Billy Mann, and Patricio Quinn.

[15] Bill Winsor, *Texas in the Confederacy, Military Installations, Economy and People* (Hillsboro, Texas: Hill Junior College Press, 1978), 51.

Surging prices were a perpetual concern as evidenced by one San Antonio newspaper which cried out for action against merchants and speculators who were making huge profits at the expense of a hungry population. Ordinary people responded. In February 1863, for instance, a mutual aid society was established to provide food to the poor at a low cost. The association bought food items directly from merchants in Mexico. Flour, a basic article which cost forty dollars per hundred pounds, could be bought from the association for sixteen dollars. Another mutual aid society followed suit by selling beef at five to fifteen cents a pound. Although these cooperative efforts were meant for the general citizenry of Bexar County, especially for the working classes, we do not know to what degree the large and poor Mexicano population benefited. The work of such cooperative institutions no doubt kept hunger at bay and allowed Mexicanos as well as Anglos to weather the crisis.[16]

A more welcomed development occurred when increased war trade improved employment opportunities throughout South Texas. The inflated demand for labor was especially evident in the transportation of goods to and from Mexico. In the 1850s, Mexicanos had occupied a prominent place in trade as employees of merchants and transport firms or as freighters. They were recognized for their ability to handle animals and for their honesty in business transactions.[17] Anglos had largely displaced Mexicano teamsters after the Cart War of 1857.[18] This would change during the war years.

In order to move cotton to Mexico and to international markets, commercial routes were established across Central and South Texas. San Antonio became a key army supply center and when coastal routes were threatened by the proximity of Union

---

[16] *San Antonio Weekly Herald,* Feb. 21, 1863, May 2, 16, 1863.

[17] Arthur J. Mayer, "San Antonio, Frontier Entrepot" (Ph.D. diss., University of Texas, 1976), 378; August Santleben, *A Texas Pioneer, Early Staging and Overland Freighting Days on the Frontiers of Texas and Mexico,* ed. I. D. Affleck (New York and Washington: Neale Publishing Co., 1910), 116.

[18] De León and Stewart, *Tejanos and the Numbers Game,* 33–34; Miguel Gonzalez Quiroga, "Mexicano Freighters in Texas, 1850–1870," unpublished paper.

forces, many producers and merchants sent their cotton to Matamoros by way of the Alamo city, Laredo, Piedras Negras, and
Monterrey. Army supplies, on the other hand, returned by the
same routes. All of the towns in the region, especially Brownsville,
Laredo, and San Antonio grew as a consequence.

The border town of Laredo experienced exceptional growth.
Immigrants, particularly from Mexico, arrived in large numbers
as the local booming economy drew them into the production
and movement of goods, foodstuffs for soldiers, and feed for
draft animals.[19] According to the *Texas State Gazette*, the Laredo
labor supply was insufficient in 1864 to transport the cotton
across the border. Moreover, the cost of moving cotton across the
river was ten times higher than before the war, indicating a corre-
sponding increase in wages.[20]

Archival materials left by entrepreneurs operating in South
Texas indicate that merchants and agents of the Confederacy
actively recruited Mexicano workers.[21] Employers continually
expressed concern about meeting the increasing demand for
workers and teams, carts, and wagons to haul goods. The labor
problem could not be resolved by relying on conscripts because
they were too few. Slaves, on the other hand, might escape.
Consequently, Texas merchants fixed their sights below the Rio
Grande.[22]

One of these merchants, the Spaniard José San Román,
based his operations in the Brownsville-Matamoros area and
employed hundreds of Mexicano freighters to haul goods on
both sides of the border. Two of his associates or agents, Joseph
Kleiber of Brownsville and John Vale of Roma, were charged with

---

[19] Gilberto M. Hinojosa, *A Borderlands Town in Transition: Laredo, 1755–1870*
(College Station: Texas A&M University Press, 1983), 87.

[20] *Texas State Gazette* (Austin), Aug. 10, 1864.

[21] Of particular value are the José San Román Papers, John Twohig Papers,
Jean B. Lacoste Papers, Joseph Kleiber Papers, and the John Z. Leyendecker
Papers (Center for American History, University of Texas at Austin).

[22] They were not always successful because transport might also be scarce in
Mexico. James Irby explained that toward the end of 1862 the *carretas* of the interior were expropriated by the Mexican government for use in the resistance to the
French invasion. This, of course, was another reason why Mexicano freighters
would wish to go to Texas. James A. Irby, "Line of the Rio Grande," 100.

obtaining transport for cotton and war supplies. Among the documents left by San Román are bills of lading, i.e., documents prepared by the freighter which inform us not only of the merchandise that was shipped but also give the carrier's name and sometimes his place of origin. A review of these documents for the 1864–1865 period reveals that all the workers were Mexicanos and that most were from the interior of Mexico, particularly from Tamaulipas and Nuevo Leon.[23]

Many Mexicano workers traveled to the interior of Texas where work was abundant. Some transactions between San Román and business associates in the interior of Texas suggest that workers traveled inland in response to recruitment overtures. One such business deal involved John Lang of Houston who reported sending an agent to Matamoros or Roma in search of carts and cartmen. He had 450 bales near the Colorado River and needed to haul them to the border. Lang asked San Román to recruit the needed Mexicano drivers and to offer them an advance payment for their services.[24]

Another communication—this one originating in Mexico—helps explain why many Mexicanos traveled north. Eugenio Serrano of Santa Isabel informed San Román that he had sent his son to Texas with a train of wagons because the profits were greater and there was less risk of having his goods seized by authorities.[25] The northward migration of freighters seeking higher earnings often reached levels that depleted labor supplies in Mexico. In November 1862, for instance, the Confederate agent at Monterrey, Juan Quintero, reported a scarcity of *carretas* in the city because many of the teamsters had gone to Texas.[26]

Prominent merchants in San Antonio such as the Vance brothers, Jean Baptiste Lacoste, and John Twohig also encouraged the immigrant flow. They employed the services of other merchants or agents situated on the Rio Grande such as John

---

[23] This observation is based on a review of such documents in the San Román Papers, Box 2573.

[24] Lang to San Román, Feb. 19, 1863, San Román Papers.

[25] Serrano to San Román, Jan. 7, 1863, ibid.

[26] Irby, "Line of the Rio Grande," 100.

Leyendecker of Laredo, a brother-in-law of Santos Benavides. With extensive contacts among the Mexicano community of both sides of the border, Leyendecker served the firm of Attrill-Lacoste of San Antonio in recruiting Mexicano freighters and arranging other transportation needs.[27] Another agent, Daniel Murphy, managed Twohig's operation in Monterrey. In September 1863, he received a request for thirty carretas and their drivers to transfer cotton from San Antonio to that city.[28] In the same manner, Friedrich Groos, a future Alamo city banker, worked out of Piedras Negras for John Twohig, one of the biggest merchants of Bexar County. Expense reports which Groos sent to Twohig between March and August 1863 reveal the names of cart drivers contracted to haul freight between the border and San Antonio. All but one of the twenty-seven cart drivers were Mexicanos, further suggesting a significant economic recovery for at least one class of workers.[29]

The wages received by the drivers further underscore the importance of the war trade in stimulating the economy. Throughout the 1850s they were paid one dollar for carrying one hundred pounds over one hundred miles. This rate remained in effect until 1861. During the war, as commerce increased and transportation grew scarce, the rate increased. By 1863 the going rate was between five and six dollars. In May 1864, Twohig paid his drivers up to 10 percent of the value of the freighted cotton.[30] Arthur Mayer claims that in 1864 a freighter could command between six hundred and fifteen hundred dollars (depending on the size of his wagon) to haul cotton from San Antonio to Matamoros. He could make even more if he returned with merchandise from the coast.[31]

---

[27] Lacoste to Leyendecker, Jan. 24, 1863, Leyendecker Papers.

[28] S. L. James to Murphy, Sept. 25, 1863, Twohig Papers.

[29] Twohig Papers, Box 3N1.

[30] May 21, 1864, Twohig Papers. A San Antonio newspaper announced that the freighters who did not possess their own teams or wagons would receive forty dollars per month plus board. Payment would be made in Confederate currency and those reaching Brownsville would be given merchandise for the return trip. *Semi Weekly News* (San Antonio), July 27, 1863.

[31] Mayer, "San Antonio," 501–502.

The wartime economy brought another welcomed result in the deference that was now visibly extended to Mexicano freighters. This took various forms that further enhanced earnings. For instance, they could now negotiate advances and payment in specie rather than in Confederate bills which devaluated rapidly.[32] Moreover, they were exempt from military service since freighting was considered strategically important.[33]

Although beyond the scope of this study, the wartime economy improved employment and earning opportunities in other sectors besides transportation, particularly in those areas dedicated to the production of war goods. Urban based industries that expanded as a result of increased economic activity no doubt provided new and better-paying jobs shared by Mexicano workers. Moreover, when Anglo males enlisted or were recruited into the army they vacated jobs which became available to Mexicanos.[34]

What does the preceding discussion tell us about the Mexicano condition during the War of Secession? Preliminary data suggests they did not do badly. With the exception of those who lost their possessions or their lives, Mexicanos in Texas prospered because employment was readily available and well remunerated. Many were able to withstand the pressure of rising prices in the urban areas because they were partially insulated by consumer cooperatives and rising wage levels which resulted from the increased economic activity of the period. Darlis Miller also discovered that the wartime prosperity had a significant positive impact on the Mexican community of New Mexico.[35]

---

[32] Joseph Kleiber became aware of this when a group of freighters he had sent to Bexar County with a cargo of coffee returned and demanded payment in specie rather than the Confederate money they were offered in San Antonio. He was forced to give them two thousand dollars in silver coin. Kleiber to James Hale, Feb. 18, 1862, Kleiber Papers.

[33] *San Antonio Weekly Herald*, Apr. 25, 1863; Thompson, *Vaqueros*, 55; Cowling, "The Civil War Trade," 40–41.

[34] One such area of employment was the army. Although the topic is beyond the scope of this paper, it is clearly a promising area of research as the following archival collection indicates: Adjutant General, Civil War Records, Confederate State Records, Reports of Hired Persons (Texas State Archives).

[35] Darlis A. Miller, "Hispanos and the Civil War in New Mexico: A Reconsideration," *New Mexico Historical Review*, 54 (1979), 105–123.

Another consequence was improved race relations. This occurred because attention was focused on the sectional conflict rather than on race and other sources of conflict. Moreover, Mexicanos served a critical need, and it was not desirable, nor even possible, to maintain the level of tension and hostility which characterized the 1850s. The competition for Mexicano workers would have been unthinkable in the previous decade.

War has a way of bringing people closer together, but often for strategic purposes rather than humanitarian reasons. Anglos and Mexicanos in Texas became temporary allies during the course of the conflict. In Arizona during this same period, a war against the Apaches also united them—at least until their common foe was vanquished.[36] The racial oppression of Mexicanos became especially visible once again after the Civil War, although it seemed less intense.

This paper also reinforces an insight offered by other historical works regarding the ambivalent nature of Mexico-U.S. relations. In times of war calls are made for laborers from Mexico to supply labor needs. The enthusiasm for this labor force diminishes after the conflict, only to resurface during a new crisis. This cycle began during the Civil War, some fourteen years after the signing of the treaty of Guadalupe Hidalgo.[37]

---

[36] James E. Officer, *Hispanic Arizona, 1536–1856* (Tucson: University of Arizona Press, 1987), 311.

[37] For a review of Mexican immigration and the issue of a reserve labor pool, see: Jorge Bustamante, "The Historical Context of Undocumented Mexican Immigration to the United States," *Aztlán*, 3 (Fall, 1972), 257–281; Juan Gómez-Quiñones, "Mexican Immigration to the United States and the Internationalization of Labor, 1848–1980; An Overview," in *Mexican Immigrant Workers in the United States*, Anthology No. 2, ed. Antonio Ríos-Bustamante (Los Angeles: UCLA Chicano Studies Research Center Publications, 1981), 13–34.

# Unión, Paz y Trabajo:

## *Laredo's Mexican Mutual Aid Societies, 1890s*

ROBERTO R. CALDERÓN*

This study examines the world of *mutualista* organizations, or mutual aid societies, the most common organizational form that appeared at the turn of the century in Mexican communities of the Southwest. With a few notable exceptions, existing scholarship has tended to abbreviate mutualista history. In spite of their acknowledged centrality to organized community life, little is known about the specific contributions of mutualistas in important cities, regions, or periods in U.S. history. Mutualistas led civil rights efforts long before the more recent Mexican American legal defense organizations appeared on the scene. They emerged in response to circumstances in the Southwest. One of the most important formative influences in the spread of mutual aid societies, however, originated in Mexico. Their membership was comprised of immigrant and U.S.-born Mexicanos.[1]

* Roberto R. Calderón is assistant professor in the Division of Bicultural-Bilingual Studies, University of Texas at San Antonio. His publications include *South Texas Coal Mining: A Community History; Directory of Organizations for Immigrant Rights, 1996; Mexican Coal Mining Labor in Texas and Coahuila, 1880–1930*; and the anthology, *Nuestra Voz: Memories of Our Education.* This article was made possible by a grant from the University of California Institute for Mexico and the United States.

[1] "Union, Paz y Trabajo," or unity, peace and work, was the motto or *lema* of a mutual aid society from Laredo, Sociedad Hidalgo Para Auxilios Mutuos. All Spanish translations in the essay are the author's.

One prominent Mexican scholar observed that by the second quarter of the twentieth century more Mexican cooperatives and mutualist groups were found in the United States than Mexico.[2] This suggests, at minimum, a highly dynamic formative history during the late nineteenth century, particularly in Texas, the preferred destination of Mexican immigrants and the site of the largest concentrations of Mexicans during the late nineteenth and early twentieth centuries. Significant points of entry and concentration such as Laredo provide a basis for examining early mutualista history.[3] This essay represents the first such examination in Laredo from 1880 to 1900, though the emphasis lies in the activities of the 1890s. It seeks to demonstrate that Mexican organizational life was dynamic and instrumental in helping members and the community survive and challenge the difficult conditions they faced. As such, it contributes to the growing body of knowledge on the history of Mexicans in the United States.

This essay culls heretofore unused scattered evidence of organizational life in the Texas-Mexico border town of Laredo in an attempt to assess the nature of mutual aid societies and their role in the larger context of Mexican organizational life. It raises important questions that must be addressed in order to understand the historical experience of Mexicans in the United States. For instance, how did class, race, gender, and religion interact in the formation and development of organizations in the Mexican

---

At least two unpublished studies have attempted to write the history of mutualistas in some detail. Both studies focus on the early twentieth century to the almost complete neglect of the nineteenth. This pattern still holds with most published accounts within Chicano historiography. Mexican mutual aid society history in the nineteenth century remains relatively unknown. Kaye Lynn Briegel, "Alianza Hispano-Americana, 1894–1965: A Mexican American Fraternal Insurance Society" (Ph.D. diss., University of Southern California, 1974); Julie Leininger Pycior, "La Raza Organizes: Mexican American Life in San Antonio, 1915–1930 as Reflected in Mutualista Activities" (Ph.D. diss., Notre Dame University, 1979).

[2] Manuel Gamio, *Mexican Immigration to the United States* (New York: Dover Press, 1971), 132; Pycior, "*La Raza* Organizes," 25–26.

[3] Mario T. García, *Desert Immigrants: The Mexicans of El Paso, 1880–1920* (New Haven: Yale University Press, 1981), 2–4; Arnoldo De León, *Mexican Americans in Texas: A Brief History* (Arlington Heights, Ill.: Harlan Davidson, 1993), 53, 58–59.

community? Moreover, how did mutual societies reflect, accommodate, distill, and referee competing views in attempts to assist their membership; and how did the community survive and challenge trying conditions?

A detailed approach is necessary given the lack of such information in Mexican American historiography. It informs the lived experience of a community in need of such documentation and serves as a substantive basis for interpretation. This study addresses circumstances surrounding the founding of the numerous organizations which appeared in Laredo. Attention is given to women's participation and cultural and political activities normally associated with the mutualistas. These activities included music recitals, theatrical works, and annual celebration of patriotic holidays, as well as public meetings, civic programs, and disputes involving organizations and newspapers in the community and along the border region.[4]

The antecedents to mutualistas began in Mexico and, according to the Mexicanist James D. Cockcroft involved "elements of nonelite groups—small farmers, artisans, workers, mestizos, professionals."[5] Mexico's liberal 1857 Constitution, which guaranteed artisans and workers the right to associate, strengthened this tradition. Between 1853 and 1855 artisans organized the first mutual aid societies in Mexico, and the 1860s witnessed a proliferation of these artisanal and workers' organizations as well as the establishment of regional alliances.[6]

---

[4] For a general discussion of mutualistas in the late nineteenth and early twentieth century Texas, see Arnoldo De León, *The Tejano Community, 1836–1900* (Albuquerque: University of New Mexico Press, 1982), 177, 194–195; Emilio Zamora, *The World of the Mexican Worker in Texas* (College Station: Texas A&M University Press, 1993), 86–109. For similar coverage on southern California mutualistas, see Richard Griswold del Castillo, *The Los Angeles Barrio, 1850–1890: A Social History* (Berkeley: University of California Press, 1979), 135–138; and Albert Camarillo, *Chicanos in a Changing Society: From Mexican Pueblos to American Barrios in Santa Barbara and Southern California, 1848–1930* (Cambridge: Harvard University Press, 1979), 119, 147–154.

[5] James D. Cockcroft, *Mexico: Class Formation, Capital Accumulation and the State* (New York: Monthly Review Press, 1983), 80.

[6] For a discussion of the origins and late-nineteenth-century history of mutualism and cooperativism in Mexico, see Moisés Gonzalez Navarro (ed.), *Historia*

Throughout the last three decades of the nineteenth century, mutualism in Texas exhibited an all-inclusive, Mexicanist, approach to organizing.[7] Central to mutualismo were the values of fraternalism, reciprocity, and altruism. These values prescribed a code of moral behavior often represented in specific rules of conduct printed in mutual aid societies' constitutions.[8] Until the end of the 1920s, according to historian Emilio Zamora, these values formed the unifying cultural basis through which Mexican mutualista members undertook "moralistic and nationalistic political action that was intended to set things right."[9]

Mutual aid societies offered their members and families multiple forms of assistance and civic participation. They offered members burial and illness benefits, legal aid and emergency loans, and assistance in finding employment. They established newspapers, libraries and private (mostly primary) schools. Curricula at these private schools was in Spanish, although some used English as the medium of instruction as well as a subject of study. Schools also offered evening classes in a variety of subjects. Middle-class mutualistas often promoted bilingualism among their members and children. Mutualistas also sponsored activities for the general public. These included dances, patriotic and anniversary celebrations, lectures, and theatre and musical performances. They also promoted participation in the political process by fielding and endorsing candidates, supporting specific campaigns, soliciting votes, and urging Mexican Nationals to legalize their status to become voters.[10]

---

*Moderna de México. El Porfiriato. La Vida Social* (México, D.F.: Editorial Hermes, 1973), 344–360.

[7] Zamora, *The World of the Mexican Worker*, 86–89. Zamora focuses his analysis on the post-1900 period. A Mexicanist viewpoint within mutualismo characterized the period prior to 1900 in particular. By the 1920s social divisions had begun tearing this initial consensus apart.

[8] Pycior, "*La Raza* Organizes," 24–25; Zamora, *The World of the Mexican Worker*, 86.

[9] Ibid., 86, 88–92.

[10] Pycior, "*La Raza* Organizes," 41–81; Zamora, *The World of the Mexican*, 86–109; De León, *The Tejano Community*, 177, 194–195; Roberto R. Calderón, "Mexican Politics in the American Era, 1846–1900: Laredo, Texas" (Ph.D. diss., University of California, Los Angeles, 1993), 842–870.

Included in the ranks of early mutualistas were tailors, carpenters, bricklayers, and small-scale merchants. Reflecting early industrial development, artisans in these organizations endorsed the liberal and republican ethos of a society of small and equal producers.[11] By the 1870s and 1880s, as Mexico's economy developed and large-scale industrial production expanded and concentrated a waged labor force, mutual aid societies began to address workers' issues such as strikes in the mining, textile, and railroad industries. The interdependent development of regional economies along the Mexico-United States border encouraged the migration of these workers who brought to northern Mexico and the Southwest their tried and tested organizational and political traditions.[12]

Laredo has always claimed a Mexican majority. In 1890 Mexicans constituted about 75 percent of a population that exceeded 11,500. Most were poor, occupying the lowest-paying and least-skilled jobs in Laredo and in the farms outside the city. Anglos represented a more privileged segment of the community as members of an economic elite who had intermarried with Mexicans. Typically, Mexicans who intermarried with Anglos belonged to the merchant-rancher Mexicano elite. Landowning Mexican elites derived part of their wealth from rental income. They comprised between 1 to 3 percent of the city's Mexican population in the late nineteenth century. By 1900 Laredo had a

---

[11] Calderón, "Mexican Politics in the American Era," 821–822.

[12] The mostly urban-based workers' associations assumed two major forms, mutual aid societies and cooperatives. Moderate leaders espoused liberalism and Christian humanism while radicals, influenced by the ideas of socialist thinkers such as Proudhon, Fourier, and Bakunin, put forth "radical ideologies" like utopian socialism and workers' internationalism but particularly anarchism. For an assessment of these issues within the Mexican labor movement, see Gonzalez Navarro, *Historia Moderna de México,* 344–360; John M. Hart, *Anarchism and The Mexican Working Class, 1860–1931* (Austin: University of Texas Press, 1987), 43–59. For assessments of the transborder impact of Mexican organizational, cultural, and political traditions in the United States during the late nineteenth and early twentieth century, see: Zamora, *The World of the Mexican Worker,* 55–85; and Juan Gómez-Quiñones, *Mexican Nationalist Formation: Political Discourse, Policy and Dissidence* (Encino, Calif., Floricanto Press, 1992), 211–287; Gómez-Quiñones, *On Culture* (Los Angeles: Chicano Studies Center Publications, University of California, 1980), 8–19.

pattern of residential segregation with Mexicans residing throughout the city while Anglos clustered in small, separate areas. The vast majority of Mexicans were members of a mixed urban-rural industrial and agricultural working class. Seasonal labor and migratory work patterns were common and unemployment haunted the landless Mexican worker.[13]

Organizational life reflected the community's ethnic and class makeup. Mexican organizations were numerous, largely comprising working-class memberships and leaders. The most common organizational form was the mutual aid society. Mutual aid societies were typically all-male, although some mixed and all-female organizations were also present. Other organizations included Masonic orders, religious organizations, and groups associated with the Mexican consular office.[14]

Laredo's organizations were either entirely Mexican or entirely Anglo with the exception of a few such as the status-conscious Casino Mexicano which claimed a mixed membership drawn from the city's elite. The mixed organizations included working-class Mexicans, although the leaders were usually local elites. Between 1880 and 1900 at least thirteen Mexican mutual aid societies appeared in Laredo. Some of them survived into the 1920s. Four were all-women mutualistas with both married and single members. Six were comprised of mostly working-class members and leaders. Three of them were primarily electoral mutualistas, i.e., they organized primarily to rally partisan electoral support and to encourage Mexicans to seek citizenship and become eligible voters.[15]

The earliest organizations to appear in Laredo were the Sociedad Unión Mejicana, the Sociedad de Obreros Igualdad y Progreso, the Club Azul Independiente Méjico-Tejano, and the

---

[13] "Laredo, As It Appears to the Annual Statistical Editor of the Galveston News," *Laredo Times*, Sept. 3, 1890; Arnoldo De León and Kenneth L. Stewart, *Tejanos and the Numbers Game: A Socio-Historical Interpretation from the Federal Censuses, 1850–1900* (Albuquerque: University of New Mexico Press, 1989), 86–89.

[14] Calderón, "Mexican Politics in the American Era," 828–842.

[15] This discussion is based on a review of the following Laredo newspapers during the 1880s and 1890s: *Laredo Times, El Correo de Laredo*, and *El Horizonte*.

Sociedad Unión Democrática. The Sociedad de Obreros appears to have been the only one that continued into the 1890s. It claimed thirty-two charter members, all Mexicans. Its first president and secretary were Clemente Rodríguez and Rito Landeros, respectively. The founders acknowledged their working-class origins and association with other like-minded organizations in Mexico: "all [present] in common accord resolved to adopt as fundamental principles the contents of the statutes in various other workers circles of Mexico."[16]

Another two mutualistas were founded in the 1910s: the Sociedad Unión de Jornaleros, and the Sociedad de Conductores y Obreros Unidos. The latter was originally organized under the auspices of the American Federation of Labor, but it separated from the Federation and continued operating as an independent union within the circle of mutualista organizations.[17]

Laredo's mutual aid societies emerged around the same time that other such organizations were appearing for the first time along the international border and in inland Texas cities. El Paso, for instance, produced its first mutualista, the Sociedad Mutualista Mexicana "La Protectora," in 1888. Brownsville, on the other hand, produced its first mutual aid society, the Sociedad Mutualista Miguel Hidalgo, in 1881. San Antonio and Corpus Christi recorded some of the earliest mutual aid societies. San Antonio's Mexican residents established the Sociedad Benevolencia Mexicana in 1875 while in Corpus Christi they formed the Club Recíproco in 1873. Mexicans in Corpus Christi may also have founded their first women's mutualista in Texas

---

[16] *Reglamento General Reforma de la Sociedad de Obreros Igualdad y Progreso* (Laredo: Gate City Printing Office, 1891), 1–4. The other founding members were: Trinidad G. Ayala, León Bernal, Pedro Camacho, Rafael Cárdenas, Florentino Castro, Margarito de la Cruz, Anastacio de la Rosa, Victor de la Rosa, Jesús De León, Agustín Fuentes, Pablo Gómez, Donaciano Gonzalez, Eusebio Guevara, Felipe Hernández, Bartolo López, Antonio Martínez, Ignacio Méndez, Secundino Orozco, Lugardo Pérez, Timoteo Rangel, Ramón Rodríguez, Andrés Ruiz, Pedro Salinas, Bernardino Sánchez, Epigmenio Sánchez, Carlos Tovar, Félix Villegas, and Marcial Zárate.

[17] *Reglamento General de la Sociedad "Unión de Jornaleros"* (Laredo: "X Y Z," 1915), 1–2, 24; *Reglamento General de la Sociedad de "Conductores y Obreros Unidos"* (Laredo: Compañía Publicista Idar, 1923), 2–3.

when they formed the Sociedad Mutualista de Beneficiencia de Señoras y Señoritas. Although more research is needed before we can posit geographic and chronologic patterns in the development of mutualistas, the available evidence minimally suggests that concerted drives to form such organizations began to bear fruit at least by the middle 1870s.[18]

José María Vela, Webb County tax assessor and collector and founding member of the Sociedad de Obreros, headed the Club Azul in 1884. The Club Azul was loyal to a political faction led by Democrat Raymond Martin. Vela, a strong Martin partisan, may have influenced the organization to support Martin and oppose the *reformeros* (reformers) which included disaffected Democrats and local Republicans. The Sociedad Unión, on the other hand, refused to make any electoral promises when the reformers approached them during the 1884 elections.[19]

The Sociedad Unión was aligned with the local Democratic Party. The editors of the newspaper *El Horizonte*, brothers José and Fernando López Montalbo, referred to its members as "Democrats," who represented the popular masses and the Texas-Mexican people. One the Sociedad Unión's aims, according to the editors, was "the close union of the Texas-Mexican element" in both Encinal and Webb Counties.[20]

The Sociedad Unión Democrática recruited 581 voters in 1884, more than half the number needed to win at the polls. The list of voters included mostly workers and artisans, although it

---

[18] José Amaro Hernández, *Mutual Aid for Survival: The Case of the Mexican American* (Malabar, Fla.: Robert E. Kreiger Publishing Co., 1983), 65; Pycior, "La Raza Organizes," 37; De León, *Tejano Community*, 195–196; Calderón, "Mexican Politics in the American Era," 843–847; García, *Desert Immigrants*, 224. The apparent geographic pattern suggested by the appearance of the earliest mutualista organizations in the inland cities of San Antonio and Corpus Christi is unreliable because of the lack of comparative information. The primary sources of information, Spanish–language newspapers, were available to record the earlier founding of mutual aid societies in San Antonio and Corpus Christi. Newspapers did not appear in Laredo and El Paso until the 1880s.

[19] Jerry D. Thompson, "Guarache Party Makes Its Debut," *Laredo News*, Apr. 4, 1986; "Aviso," *El Horizonte*, Oct. 11, 1884; "Oficina," ibid., Mar. 28, 1884.

[20] "La Democracia Triunfante," *El Horizonte*, Oct. 11, 1884; De León, *The Tejano Community*, 199.

also carried the names of elite Mexicans and Anglos such as Luis R. Ortiz, José María Rodríguez, Atanacio Vidaurri, Anacleto Vidaurri, Charles W. Macdonnell, Herman Poggenpohl, Raymond Martin, Thomas Ryan, and W. H. Adams. The *reformeros* were less successful. They tried to stage a street march but drew a mere thirty to forty supporters. The embarrassed reformers retired to a local tavern while the Democrats marched eight hundred strong with music blaring and blue colors flying. Reformeros included prominent Mexican Democratic and Anglo Republican politicos such as Santos Benavides, Juan Benavides, and Charles Cushman Pierce. They were known as the *Huarache* Party, while the opposition was called *Las Botas*.[21]

The Sociedad Unión Democrática dissolved as an electoral mutualista by the early 1890s. The Bota Democrats, however, continued to win in local and regional elections. Incumbency had its privileges and organizational advantages. Not until late 1894 did the opposing coalition of Democrats and Republicans, the Huaraches, manage to organize a successful challenge which involved the formation of a new, and eventually powerful, electoral mutualista, the Club Independiente.[22]

The Independent Club, as it was named in the English-language press, succeeded in organizing a disciplined group of immigrant and native-born Mexican workers. The organization elected college-educated Mexicans to the leadership, and within ten months its membership had increased to nearly 1,350.[23] The Sociedad Unión México-Tejana, the successor to the Sociedad Union Democrática, was unable to muster the strength to stop the growing influence of the opposition. The Club Independiente

---

[21] "La Democracia Triunfante," *El Horizonte*, Oct. 11, 1884; Thompson, "Guarache Party Makes Its Debut." Although the supporters of the Sociedad Union Democratica took the initiative with the earlier and more impressive gatherings, the reformers managed to organize their own well-attended public meetings a day before the election.

[22] "The Independent Club. Unwritten History on Its Charities and Humanities. Its Officers and Objects," Laredo *Times*, Aug.28, 1895.

[23] This made the Club Independiente the largest electoral mutualista in Texas during the nineteenth century. Calderón, "Mexican Politics in the American Era," 880–881.

successfully drew into its ranks important figures such as labor and mutualista leaders Nicasio Idar and Emilio Flores as well as the popular mutualista, the Sociedad de Obreros Igualdad y Progreso. The Club Independiente thus brought to an end the political hegemony of the Bota Democrats in city politics.[24]

Mexican women organized at least four mutualistas in the 1890s: Sociedad de Hidalgo, Sociedad Josefa Ortíz de Domínguez, Sociedad Unión Mexicana de Señoras y Señoritas, and the Sociedad Dorcas Industrial de Señoras. Mexican Methodist Church members formed the latter. Easily the most resilient and active of the four, the Sociedad Josefa Ortíz de Domínguez persisted at least through the early 1900s.[25]

Women's organizations were an integral part of the community as *Fiestas Patrias,* or patriotic holiday celebrations, indicate. Three groups participated in the 1895 commemoration of Mexican independence, or *El Diez y Seis de Septiembre.* They marched in a well-attended parade and their official orators took to the podium during the evening program.[26]

These associations participated in other public programs hosted by sister organizations. In 1906, for instance, the Sociedad Josefa Ortíz de Domínguez participated in the first anniversary celebration of the AFL-affiliated Unión Obrera Federada No. 11,953. The Unión Obrera Federada, one of the largest unions of Mexican workers in the Southwest, was involved in organizing Laredo and its vicinity. The friendly ties between both organizations suggests that the Sociedad Josefa Ortíz de Domínguez supported efforts by labor to organize. Although the Unión Obrera Federada called on women to join its ranks, few did so.[27]

---

[24] Calderón, "Mexican Politics in the American Era," 870–917.

[25] Ibid., 847–848.

[26] "Official Programme," *Laredo Times,* Sept. 16, 1895; "Speeches on Church Plaza," ibid., Sept. 17, 1895.

[27] *El Defensor del Obrero,* Sept. 30, 1906; Emilio Zamora, *El movimiento obrero mexicano en el sur de Texas, 1900–1920* (México, D.F.: Secretaría de Educación Pública, 1986), 95–121. Mexican women in San Antonio during 1915–1930 period also participated in the city's mutualistas. According to Pycior, "Of the nineteen traditional mutualist associations active, seven allowed women to join and hold office, two formed female auxiliaries, and two had almost entirely female membership." Pycior, "La Raza Organizes," 77.

Women's organizations often took the lead in hosting community-wide events. In 1895, for instance, the Sociedad Dorcas organized a *Cinco de Mayo* celebration commemorating the 1862 defeat of French forces in Puebla. The festivities were so successful that the group staged the event again two weeks later at the popular Market Hall. Unlike the more secular patriotic celebrations sponsored by other mutualistas, this program included religious activities such as prayers by the pastor of the Mexican Methodist Church, Alfredo R. Cárdenas. It also included poetry and musical recitals, oratory, singing, and a dramatic dialogue titled "La Libertad y Sus Hijas." At least fourteen women participated in the program.[28]

Four of the mutualistas, the Sociedad de Obreros, the Sociedad Hidalgo Para Auxilios Mutuos, the Sociedad Ignacio Martínez, and the Unión Mexicana Hijos de Juárez, were composed entirely of Mexicans. The last three were new additions to the local mutual aid network of the 1890s.[29]

The Sociedad Hidalgo began it history with an impressive fund-raising project that involved a theatrical production staged by a dramatic group composed of men and women. The proceeds were used to support the 1891 Diez y Seis de Septiembre celebration. The association applied the remainder of the funds to the improvement and beautification of the San Agustín Plaza.[30]

Like most mutual aid societies, the Unión Mexicana recorded its beginnings in the organization's founding documents. According to the organization's treasured story, fourteen men met at the home of José Treviño on December 26, 1891. They agreed that another mutual aid society was needed and proceeded to

---

[28] "A Nice Entertainment Will Occur in Market Hall Tonight, A Repetition of a Fifth of May Program," *Laredo Times*, May 17, 1895; "Grand Entertainment," ibid., June 26, 1895; "Grand Concert," ibid., June 29, 1895.

[29] *Reglamento General de la Sociedad Mutualista Hijos de Juárez* (Laredo: Tipografía Bravo's Mexican Publishing Co., 1916), 37–38; *Reglamento General de la Sociedad Mutualista Hijos de Juárez* (Laredo: Tipografía Bazaldúa, 1924), 1–2 48–49: Zamora, *El movimiento obrero*, 103–104; "Junta Patriótica," *El Correo de Laredo*, Sept. 8, 1891.

[30] "El Teatro," *El Correo de Laredo*, Aug. 15, 1891; "La Función Teatral," ibid., Aug. 18, 1891; "Función Teatral," ibid., Aug. 23, 1891; "Teatro," and "No Hay Que Olvidar," ibid., Aug. 26, 1891; "La Sociedad Hidalgo," ibid., Aug. 29, 1891.

elect officers and adopt a statement of purpose. They sought to offer their membership services such as health, death, and life insurance policies, a credit fund, and employment assistance. They also sought to uplift or rejuvenate the community by establishing a public library and by promoting a public discourse on the principles of mutuality and reciprocity, the basis for prescribing "uplifting" moral behavior within the organization in the community.[31]

Mutual aid societies collaborated fully in community affairs. In 1895, for example, when the Sociedad Unión Mexicana Hijos de Juárez celebrated its fourth anniversary in the hall of the Club Independiente, other mutualistas sent orators or delegates who posted their organizational banners. On other occasions, the Sociedad Mutualista reciprocated with its own orators and delegations.[32]

The Sociedad de Obreros hosted some of the most popular city celebrations. On April 5, 1895, it commemorated its tenth anniversary with a function that filled the local Market Hall with hundreds of well-wishers. Four months later, the mutualista had occasion to celebrate the construction of its own hall. The dedication ceremony included local officials and representatives from other organizations. As tradition would have it, festivities included oratory that lauded the organization for its exemplary conduct and called on other mutual aid societies to continue promoting the community's well-being.[33]

Mutualista leaders used their public programs to recruit new members as well as to expound on public issues such as workers' rights. One of their favorite recruiting techniques was to speak about the benefits of mutual support, which attracted the poor. They noted that mutuality represented the basis for well-being and community development. On numerous occasions pronouncements on behalf of mutual support were couched in terms of organizing more specialized associations or unions and

---

[31] *Reglamento General de la Sociedad Mutualista Hijos de Juárez* [1916], 1–3; *Reglamento General de la Sociedad Mutualista Hijos de Juárez* [1924], 1–3, 12–18.

[32] *Laredo Times,* Dec. 27, 1895; *El Defensor del Obrero,* Sept. 30, 1906.

[33] *Laredo Times,* Apr. 6, 1895.

of waging strike actions. The Sociedad de Obreros was notable for making this connection. In 1895, for example, some of its members joined with local carpenters in a special meeting to discuss the low wages that workers earned in local jobs. They agreed on a minimum wage and subsequently struck an employer that presumably refused to accept their demand. The organization's leadership continued to support workers' rights. In 1906, during the anniversary celebration of the Unión Obrera Federada, Aureliano Ramos spoke in support of the right to form unions and to challenge employers.[34]

Mutualista cooperation extended beyond the border and included sister organizations from Nuevo Laredo. This was particularly evident in co-sponsored Fiestas Patrias and anniversary celebrations. Occasionally, however, differences between the societies would surface. Seemingly calm and friendly relations revealed ongoing tensions on at least one occasion in 1891 when the Sociedad de Obreros Hijos del Trabajo Alianza y Fraternidad and the Sociedad Concordia de Protección Mutua of Nuevo Laredo invited the Sociedad de Obreros and the Sociedad Hidalgo to join them in sponsoring the Diez y Seis de Septiembre celebration. The participating mutualistas established an organization with a shared membership, the Junta Patriótica Obrera, which was to direct the celebration and presumably all forthcoming ones.[35]

Filemón L. Garza, the vice-president of the Sociedad Concordia and editor of *El Orden* from Nuevo Laredo, was the first to disclose a rift among the celebration planners. He accused the Junta Patriótica Obrera of seeking to hold the festivities in Laredo and to use the occasion to criticize President Porfirio Díaz. Justo Cárdenas, the editor of *El Correo de Laredo*, used his newspaper to charge that Garza was slandering well-respected persons of different political persuasions. Garza, apparently exasperated with his critics, finally divulged his nationalist sensibilities when he stated that he would never celebrate Mexico's independence in a foreign

---

[34] *Laredo Times*, Aug. 7, 1895; ibid., Aug. 8, 1895; ibid., Feb. 10, 1900; *El Chaparral*, Feb. 25, 1899; *El Defensor del Obrero*, Sept. 30, 1906.

[35] "Las Fiestas Patrias," *El Correo de Laredo*, Aug. 19, 1891; "Preparativos," ibid., Aug. 28, 1891; "Falta de Amor Patrio," Aug. 29, 1891; "Las Fiestas de la Patria," ibid., Aug. 29, 1891; "La Calumnia," ibid., Aug. 30, 1891.

country. The result of the public feud was two separate celebrations, each planned by a Junta Patriótica Obrera.[36] Failing to organize a twin-city celebration, the Laredo mutualistas set out to hold one of the largest public observances that the city had witnessed. The *Laredo Times*, announced that approximately five thousand people, nearly half the population of Laredo, attended the celebration.[37] Tensions and divisions notwithstanding, mutualistas most often cooperated in sponsoring public programs and in waging organizing campaigns. Cooperation between mutualistas at times occurred within the fold of federations of organizations.

The growth of the mutualista tradition is also evident in the work of Masonic societies within their statewide networks. At least two Masonic organizations were established in Laredo during the early 1890s, the Soberana Capilla Rosa Cruz "Manuel Dublán" and the Soberana Logia "Melchor Múzquiz." Three others appeared during the early 1900s, La Orden de Caballeros de Honor No. 14, the Sociedad Mutualista Masónica Benito Juárez, and a lodge named after Ignacio Zaragosa.[38]

Nicasio Idar, a prominent figure in Laredo Masonic circles, played a critical role in building ties with mutualista organizations and in energizing a social movement against discrimination and inequality that included both types of organizations throughout the state. As the editor of *La Crónica*, Idar called on Masonic organizations and mutual aid societies to participate in a statewide meeting at Laredo to discuss issues in the communities and strategies for resolving them. Organizations from throughout the state responded to the 1911 call and met as El Primer Congreso Mexicanista, the first such gathering recorded in Mexican Amer-

---

[36] "Documentos Importantes," *El Correo de Laredo*, Sept. 1, 1891; "Documentos Importantes," ibid., Sept. 2, 1891; "La Guerra de los Pequeños," ibid., Sept. 2, 1891; "Rumor," ibid., Sept. 9, 1891; "No Fue Cierto," ibid., Sept. 10, 1891.

[37] "Junta Patriótica," *El Correo de Laredo*, Sept. 8, 1891; "Ceremonial, Aprobado por la Junta Patriótica de Esta Ciudad para Celebrar el 81 Aniversario de la Independencia de México," ibid., Sept. 13, 1891; "Súplica," ibid., Sept. 16, 1891; "Conciudadanos," ibid., Sept. 17, 1891; "Las Fiestas de la Patria," ibid., Sept. 17, 1891; *Laredo Times*, June 28, 1890.

[38] Hernández, *Mutual Aid for Survival*, 60–67; Zamora, *World of the Mexican Worker*, 78.

ican history. According to a statement issued by the delegates, they hoped to establish "a federation of community organizations that could lead a unified struggle against discrimination and inequality in Texas."[39] The delegates established the Gran Liga de Beneficiencia y Protección, the federation that was to lead the struggle. Although Masonic and mutual aid societies represented at the meeting continued to maintain fraternal relations, the Gran Liga dissolved shortly thereafter for unexplained reasons.[40]

Aside from providing Idar the necessary backing to organize El Congreso Mexicanista, La Orden de Caballeros de Honor actively participated in one of the most impressive networks of Mexican organizations in the Southwest. This Masonic circle included twenty-four lodges in Texas and four in Mexico with an approximate membership of 100 to 250 per lodge. La Orden de Caballeros also promoted unity and mutualism through a separate statewide network affiliated with the Gran Logia Masónica de México. The Laredo lodge had ninety members while the Corpus Christi and Brownsville lodges claimed eighty and three hundred members respectively.[41]

While the mutualista organizations appeared across three decades in the late nineteenth century, their impulse in Laredo peaked during the 1890s. Mexicans succeeded in uniting and forming organizations which strove to alleviate the most basic and pressing needs faced by members of their community. Immigrant and U.S.-born men and women participated in what amounted to an all-inclusive Mexicanist posture. Moreover, mutualistas persisted and proliferated in this decade, and although their achievements were uneven they sought unity according to national, moral, material, and democratic ideals best expressed by the Sociedad Hidalgo para Auxilios Mutuos' motto: *Unión, Paz y Trabajo.*

---

[39] Zamora, *The World of the Mexican Worker,* 61, 81, 97–99.

[40] Cynthia E. Orozco, "The Origins of the League of United Latin American Citizens (LULAC) and the Mexican American Civil Rights Movement in Texas with an Analysis of Women's Political Participation in a Gendered Context" (Ph.D. diss., University of California, Los Angeles, 1992), 164–172.

[41] Hernández, *Mutual Aid for Survival,* 60–67; José E. Limón, "El Primer Congreso Mexicanista de 1911: A Precursor to Contemporary Chicanismo," *Aztlán,* 3 (Spring, 1972), 85–118.

# Part Two:
# The Twentieth Century

Emilio Zamora's essay offers an expanded view of mutual aid societies around the turn of the century. Influenced by the work of English historian Edward P. Thompson, he points out that mutualistas reflected and reinforced a popular ethic of mutuality and a Mexicanist political identity. Conditions of poverty, discrimination, and inequality gave rise to a pronounced collectivist and Mexican identity expressed by the mutual aid societies in many different ways. These organizations in turn mirrored and strengthened values of mutualism and responsible Mexican behavior by promoting important public programs, key services, and internal rules of comportment. Zamora's analysis of Mexican political culture also addresses the role the intellectuals played in "translating" mutualist values and a Mexicanist identity to justify organizing calls in labor and exiled politics.

Rodolfo Rocha addresses one of the most complex events in the early twentieth century, the 1915 armed revolt by Mexicans in South Texas. The large-scale conflict began soon after authorities discovered the Plan de San Diego, which called for armed action against all Anglos. By the time the fighting ended in 1918, an estimated five thousand Mexicans, most of whom were noncombatants, had died at the hands of Texas Rangers, soldiers, and vigilante groups.

While revisionist works by authors such as James Sandos center the discussion on the Plan de San Diego, Rocha stakes out a broader analysis by joining the Mexican Revolution of 1910 with local long-lasting resentments toward the economic marginalization and political exclusion of Mexicans since 1836. For Rocha, then, the revolt must be seen as one in a string of political responses to subordination and as an expanding movement that merged with political interests and agendas of the Mexican Revolution immediately across the border.[1]

María Cristina García addresses the process of adaptation in the urban setting of Houston. The process of adjustment to American life which became widespread beginning in the post-1920 years may have been devoid of the dramatic violence associated with the San Diego Revolt and the Mexican Revolution, but it was no less important in the lives of Mexicans in Texas. Social inequality, grinding poverty, and demeaning acts of discrimination continued. The Americanization movement presented another dilemma: the very institutions that Mexicans approached for help in surviving their difficult conditions sought to divest them of their cultural capital. This, according to García, was evident when Anglo reformers arrived to establish settlement homes in Houston. Settlement homes were institutions established by Anglo women to help immigrants and "ethnics" adapt to American life, and this social work in Houston was one of their earliest contact with Mexicans in Texas.[2]

Focusing on institutional aims rather than on Mexican agency, García examines the manner in which Anglo social reformers at one of these homes, Rusk Settlement House, dealt with Americanization, segregation, and repatriation. Rusk was clearly an agent of Americanization, although it also underwent

---

[1] James A. Sandos has written the most recent work on the San Diego revolt: *Rebellion in the Borderlands; Anarchism and the Plan de San Diego, 1904–1923* (Norman: University of Oklahoma Press, 1992).

[2] Vicki L. Ruiz has produced another study that examines settlement work and Mexicans. Sarah Deutsch, on the other hand, has addressed a related issue—conflictual cultural relations between Anglo women missionaries and Hispana women in New Mexico during the turn of the century. Ruiz, "Dead Ends or Gold Mines" Using Missionary Records in Mexican American Women's History," *Frontiers*, 12 (1991), 33–56; Deutsch, *No Separate Refuge: Culture, Class, and Gender on an Anglo-Hispanic frontier in the American Southwest, 1880–1940* (New York: Oxford University Press, 1987).

some Mexicanization, that is, it received the informal cultural influence that Mexicans brought to bear on Rusk primarily by virtue of their numbers and the institution's general affinity for things Mexican. The exchange, however, was uneven and Americanization continued on its generally unabated course.

García does not differentiate between Mexicans and Mexican Americans or discuss the role that Rusk played in relations between the communities, although Arnoldo De León and Thomas Kreneck point to a process of biculturation early in twentieth-century Houston. Rusk survives to this day as a social service agency and community center; García suggests that the settlement house continues to meet Mexican needs. Her explanation is that the settlement house increased its Mexican representation among the staff and made changes that reflected the community's changing needs.[3]

---

[3] Arnoldo De León, *Ethnicity in the Sunbelt: A History of Mexican Americans in Houston*, Mexican American Studies Monograph Series, No. 7 (Houston: University of Houston Mexican American Studies Program, 1989); Thomas Kreneck, *Del Pueblo: A Pictorial History of Houston's Hispanic Community* (Houston: Houston International University, 1989).

# Mutualist and Mexicanist Expressions of a Political Culture in Texas

EMILIO ZAMORA*

In the Mexican world of politics, little is more obvious than the widespread proliferation of mutual aid societies between the 1880s and the 1920s. It is also apparent that this preferred organizational form coexisted and cooperated with other more specialized organizations, some of which surpassed the mutual aid societies in number and importance during subsequent periods. Less apparent in the historical literature, however, is the role that mutual aid societies played as a staging area for the development of other organizations. My work on Texas reveals that mutual aid societies did more than sponsor the formation of new organizations. They also served as the chief proponents of at least two formative sets of interacting collectivist values in their communities. These popular mutualist and nationalistic values imbued political actions and ideologies with a sense of common experience and

* Emilio Zamora is associate professor at the University of Houston where he teaches courses on U.S. labor, Texas, and Mexican American history. His major publications include: *El Movimiento Obrero Mexicano en el Sur de Texas, 1900–1920*, *Chicano Discourse* (with co-editor, Tatch Mindiola), and *The World of the Mexican Worker in Texas*. This essay is a revision of a chapter from *The World of the Mexican Worker in Texas*. Dr. Zamora is currently working on a book-length study of Mexican workers in Texas during the Second World War.

83

identity, and provided an essential cultural frame of reference for Mexicans in public life.[1]

The Mexican community of Texas registered continuous expressions of proper moral and nationalistic behavior. Despite opposing class and ethnic organizing appeals, calls for unity openly adhered to an ethic of mutuality, or the collective idea that Edward P. Thompson attributes to English working-class culture and its politics. This ethic was often expressed in Mexicanist terms that declared and promoted an all-inclusive, nationalist identity. Mutualist values such as fraternalism, reciprocity, and altruism prescribed human behavior, and established a cultural basis for moralistic and pan-Mexican political action that was to set things right, as Juan Gómez-Quiñones points out.[2]

Voluntary organizations expressed the clearest visions of mutualism and a Mexicanist sense of community in their conscious working-class endeavors. Their fundamental concern was to help each other survive the very difficult conditions under which they lived and worked. *Mutualistas*, however, did not always confine their attention to the immediate and pressing material interests of their largely working-class membership, nor did they simply embrace a narrow self-help outlook. Mutual aid societies also reinforced collectivist values with resolute statements of purpose in support of egalitarian and moral principles, an active

---

[1] Recent general and focused works that treat political history in Texas include: Emilio Zamora, *The World of the Mexican Worker in Texas* (College Station: Texas A&M Unversity Press, 1993); Juan Gómez-Quiñones, *Roots of Chicano Politics, 1600–1940* (Albuquerque: University of New Mexico Press, 1994).

[2] Edward P. Thompson, *The Making of the English Working Class* (New York: Vintage Books, 1966), 418–425. For an excellent discussion on the issue of culture as a basis for Mexican political action, see Juan Gómez-Quiñones, "On Culture," *Revista Chicano-Riqueña*, 5 (Primavera, 1977), 29–47. Spanish-language newspapers and mutual aid societies frequently used the term *Mexicanista* to express their all-inclusive working interest and concern in a Mexicanized community. It signified a unitary sense of community and a form of cultural nationalism. I use the term because it captures the collectivist working-class spirit of the times. See the following for a provocative comparative examination of an important organizational expression of this Mexicanist outlook and the cultural nationalism of the recent Mexican civil rights movement. José Limón, "El Primer Congreso Mexicanista de 1911: A Precursor to Contemporary Chicanismo," *Aztlán*, 5 (Spring and Fall, 1974), 85–117.

civic role, and strict rules that disciplined their members into conscious proponents of the ethic of mutuality and a Mexicanist identity. Intellectuals, in turn, articulated these principles and values into different calls for unity and collective action, including unionism. Consequently, even different and at times opposing groups adhered to the same legitimating set of fundamentally unifying principles and values as the subsequent discussion on ethnic and homeland politics seeks to demonstrate.

An imported artisan tradition associated with guilds and mutual aid societies in Mexico during the late 1800s combined with a similar, yet smaller-scale artisan past along the border, and gave rise to some of the first such organizations in Texas. Industrialization in Mexico contributed to the proliferation of mutual aid societies when it eliminated handicraft trades and forced artisans to seek self-organization. They established these organizations to defend their social status and to protect their economic interests. The formality and ritualism of these organizations as well as the upstanding and self-respecting behavior of its members also must have contributed to organizational life in Texas. Local needs and grievances, however, were the most important and immediate determinants in the establishment of mutualista organizations. The subordinated position and status of Mexicans in the socio-economy created the need to give institutional expression to historical and contemporary grievances. The most pressing need, however, was for mutual support.[3]

Mutual aid societies met the material needs of their members with emergency loans and other forms of financial assistance, job-seeking services, and death and illness insurance. They also offered their members leadership experiences in civic affairs, sponsored other institutions like newspapers and private schools, organized popular community events for entertainment, socializing, and public discourse. Mutualista organizations thus provided their members and communities a sense of belonging and refuge

---

[3] Leticia Barragán, Rina Ortiz, and Amanda Rosales, "El mutualismo en el siglo XIX," *Historia Moderna,* 3 (Oct., 1977), 2–10. For a description of this type of organization as an incipient union structure among railroad workers in Mexico, see Alfredo Navarrete, *Alto a la Contrarrevolución* (México, D.F.: Testimonios de Atlacomulco, 1971), 116–120.

from an often alien and inhospitable environment. The community, in turn, accorded the members and especially the officers the highly respected status of responsible, civic-minded individuals. Mutualistas also served as a major point of organizational unity that spawned local and regional political struggles.[4]

Mutualista leaders promoted a Mexicanist identity and pan-Mexican unity in their communities with organizing appeals that were directed at both immigrant and U.S.-born Mexicans. A researcher assisting in the preparation of a study on Mexican immigration noted this in the late 1920s when he observed that Mexican Nationals usually joined local organizations once they obtained a job and decided to stay for an extended period of time. He was so impressed with the prevailing spirit of cooperation evident among Mexican Nationals and U.S.-born Mexicans that he remarked:

It is rare to find a city with fifty or more Mexicans that does not have a Mexican society. In cities where the Mexican population is large such as in San Antonio, Houston, Dallas, Laredo, etc., Mexican Nationals become members of the numerous Texas Mexican organizations. The Texas Mexicans, in turn, join the Mexican Nationals in their organizations.[5]

The pressing social problems facing the community no doubt compelled Mexicans to seek change and improvements collectively. The need for mutual support, and discontent over the effects of discrimination and inequality alone, however, do not explain the spirit with which they gave themselves to a high-sounding cause of moral redemption. Additional motivations

---

[4] For studies on Mexican communities and organizational life in Texas, see: Julie Leininger Pycior, "La Raza Organizes: Mexican American Life in San Antonio, 1915–1930: As Reflected in Mutualista Activities" (Ph.D. diss., University of Notre Dame, 1979); Arnoldo De León, *Ethnicity in the Sunbelt: A History of Mexican Americans in Houston* (Houston: University of Houston Mexican American Studies, 1989); Zamora, *The World of the Mexican Worker in Texas.*

[5] Report by Luis Recinos, Manuel Gamio Papers, Bancroft Collection (University of California, Berkeley). Recinos was a member of a research team that produced the classic work on immigration: Gamio, *Mexican Immigration to the United States; A Study of Human Migration and Adjustment* (Chicago: University of Chicago Press, 1930). All translations in this essay are by the author.

originated in the indignation that Mexicans felt against a form of racial discrimination that denied them their humanity and sense of self-worth. A conversation between an immigrant named Carlos Ruiz and John Murray, the editor of the San Antonio AFL paper *Pan American Labor Press*, illustrates the bitterness with which some Mexicans responded to racism.[6]

The reported conversation began on the border, probably in El Paso, as Ruiz was undergoing the dehumanizing experience of fumigation. After pointing out that Mexicans did not treat their visitors in such a discourteous manner, he took Murray to a store where he bought him a then popular postcard showing Texas Rangers on horseback with lariats tied to three dead Mexicans reportedly killed during the San Diego revolt. His point was that Anglos did not value the life of a Mexican. Clearly bitter about his reception and the racial violence that occurred in 1915, Ruiz then took Murray to a bookstore in the Mexican community. There, he pointed out with injured pride and moral authority the books that Mexicans read. The library had works by leading writers including Poe, Spencer, Darwin, Kropotkin, and Marx and sold them at affordable prices. Ruiz added,

. . . it is the Mexican in blue overalls, the labor leader, as you call him, that supports these libraries of world-wide knowledge and passes all that he learns to his brothers who may not be able to read. And more, those are the books read not only by Mexicans but by organized labor throughout Latin America.[7]

In obvious reference to the popular belief among Anglo labor that Mexicans were unorganizable, Ruiz ended the conversation with the observation that though Mexico had fewer industrialized cities than the United States, its workers organized at a higher rate.[8]

---

[6] John Murray, "Hands Across the Border," John Murray Papers, Bancroft Collection (University of California, Berkeley).

[7] Ibid.

[8] Ruiz's insistence on demonstrating the true worth and importance of Mexicans as a response to Anglo racism parallels the story of the folk hero Gregorio Cortez. Cortez became a celebrated hero in part because he captured the prideful imagination and sense of indignation among large numbers of

Ruiz's feelings of pride and honor were not restricted to individuals. They found nationalist expression in the public political arena. Organizing appeals, for instance, often made reference to pan-Mexican unity and an abiding sense of nationalist responsibility. One of the earliest calls for a statewide conference, El Congreso Mexicanista, made through the Laredo daily, *La Crónica*, revealed this prevailing Mexicanist sense of unity and cause that guided regional organizing efforts. Prior to the conference, Clemente Idar, one of its major planners, gave his attention to such issues as lynchings, unity, and discrimination in the schools and in the work place. Among his most consistently expressed concerns was the exploitation of Mexican workers, an issue that chafed nationalist sensibilities because, "Texas-Mexicans have produced with the sweat of their brow the bountiful agricultural wealth known throughout the country, and in recompense for this they have been put to work as *peones* on the land of their forefathers."[9]

Idar also affirmed a Mexicanist identity. Mexican Nationals, he noted, suffered exploitation despite the guarantees of the Treaty of Guadalupe Hidalgo, while U.S.-born Mexicans were denied the protection and guarantees of the constitution. He concluded that "We are in the same situation," as he urged his readers to assist the more recent arrivals in adjusting to their new life in Texas. After the conference, he continued to encourage immigrant and U.S.-born alike to join as brothers in the redemptive cause against discrimination. He took special care to assure Mexican Nationals that the U.S.-born would not abandon them:

---

Mexicans when he stood up to defend his honor and his rights, "With his pistol in his hand," and to demonstrate his skill as a horseman during the well-publicized chase. More importantly, the Cortez campaign revealed a regional sense of identity that responded to appeals for unity around the politically charged and symbolically important issues of group honor and pride. "Rasgos biográficos de Pablo Cruz; extinto fundador de 'El Regidor'," *El Regidor*, Aug. 18, 1910, p. 1; "El Guarda de Bravo," ibid., May 26, 1904, p. 11. For a scholarly treatment of Gregorio Cortez and the variants of the ballad that have survived, see Américo Paredes, *With His Pistol in His Hand; A Border Ballad and Its Hero* (Austin: University of Texas Press, 1971).

[9] "El león despierta," *La Crónica* (Laredo), July 13, 1911, p. 6.

We that have been born in this country understand our responsibilities as citizens, but we also feel a profound love for and the most exalted interest in our mother race because we are by destiny her progeny. This nationality and this deep love for the Mexican race runs like blood through our veins.[10]

Clemente's father, Nicasio, welcomed the delegates in terms that paid special tribute to their ongoing community activism as the natural fulfillment of a basic moral imperative: "You are the apostles of goodness, the propagandists of unity, the workers of culture, the soldiers of progress, the defenders of the right and justice of our people."[11]

The delegates that spoke at the conference also imbued their Mexicanist appeals for unity with a sense of moral righteousness and responsibility. The speakers spoke in vehement terms and with an oratorical style on the continuing loss of land, the violated rights of Mexican workers, school discrimination and exclusion, violence against Mexican youth in legal custody, and the need for class and national unification. These were the same issues that Idar enumerated when he made his call for the conference, indicating a general consensus among the delegates and the memberships they represented.[12]

F. E. Rendón, Grand Chancellor of the Mexican Masonic network, paid special tribute to the patriotism, altruism, and "sense of humanity and nobility," that guided the work of El Congreso Mexicanista. They were fulfilling a high and noble purpose in seeking the moral emancipation and material improvement of Mexican people. Masonic organizations, Rendón noted, shared

---

[10] Clemente N. Idar, "El Congreso Mexicanista triunfa: se discute nuestro proyecto," *La Crónica* (Laredo), Apr. 13, 1915, p. 1.

[11] "A los señores delegados al Congreso Mexicanista," *La Crónica* (Laredo), Sept. 14, 1911, p. 2.

[12] Limón, "El Congreso Mexicanista de 1911: A Precursor to Contemporary Chicanismo," 85–117. The assembly heard presentations by unattached individuals, a representative of the City of Laredo, and spokespersons for the following organizations: Sociedad de Obreros, Igualdad y Progreso (Laredo); Sociedad, Hijos de Juarez (Laredo); and La Agrupación Protectora Mexicana (San Antonio). The article by Limón includes some of the speeches delivered at the conference.

the delegates' concerns especially for the immigrant drawn by false promises and subjected to extreme forms of exploitation. Inspired by a sense of ethical purpose, Rendón ended his talk with a call for unity, under "the precious flag of Justice and Reason," and as "one grand family of high repute, before which the machinations and offenses of our enemies will fall."[13]

Youth and women also participated in the conference as official speakers. A young woman Hortencia Moncayo, came before the assembly representing a private school, Escuela "La Purisima," with a call for young people to follow the lead of the true mentors of youth, the civic-minded Mexicans who were participating in the conference. Like Rendón, Moncayo underscored the exploitation of Mexican workers as a key concern among the delegates. She also expressed a sense of indignation juxtaposed with feelings of pride and patriotism:

I wish that everyone who has the blood of Cuauhtemoc running through their veins will unite as one and be respected by any foreigner who wishes to treat them like beasts of burden. Mexicans have always been free and sovereign and have shed their blood for liberty and for the beloved motherland that has given us birth.[14]

Señora Soledad Flores de Peña offered a women's perspective to the goals of unity and improvement. She first commended the delegates for their work as the "honest gladiators of Texas-Mexican rights," who had won the hearts of the people and had encouraged many to join their ranks. Many more were ready to second their initiatives. However, it was necessary to pause and reflect on the responsibilities of everyone concerned. "I, like you," Flores de Peña told the delegates, "think that the best means to achieve it [unity and progress] is to educate women, to instruct her, encourage her at the same time that you respect her."[15]

---

[13] F. E. Rendón, "Conferencia," *Primer Congreso Mexicanista, Discursos Y Conferencias: Por La Raza Y Para La Raza* (Laredo: Tipografía de N. Idar, 1912), 7–8.

[14] Hortencia Moncayo, "Discurso," *Primer Congreso Mexicanista, Discursos Y Conferencias: Por La Raza Y Para La Raza,* 15. Moncayo may have been a teacher at "La Purisima."

[15] Señora Soledad Flores de Peña, "Discurso," *Primer Congreso Mexicanista, Discursos Y Conferencias: Por La Raza Y Para La Raza,* 24–25.

Lisandro Peña, the secretary of La Gran Liga Mexicanista, presented a literary piece that made special note of the conference's historical significance. He recounted the history of the Mexican nation through the unselfish and responsible acts of its known and anonymous national heroes. Peña encouraged the delegates to see that their efforts on behalf of their communities fulfilled the most sublime nationalist responsibility in history:

Remember, they died like all brave men die, with their arms around their rifles and holding their flag high. They died for us, for the children of their tomorrow, so that they could have peace and good fortune everywhere, even in foreign lands.[16]

The high-sounding principles and statements of political resolve heard at El Congreso Mexicanista and in numerous public programs that voluntary organizations sponsored throughout the state suggests an enthusiastic and committed leadership. The impressive number of voluntary organizations that appeared throughout the state further indicates that Mexicans responded favorably to the organizing appeals. What was the ethical content of these appeals and how did the organizations manifest and reinforce the unifying ethic of mutuality in their communities and among their members? To answer this important question it is necessary to examine the internal workings of such organizations.

Mutual aid societies gave concrete and conscious manifestation to the ethic of mutuality through their highly responsible and civic-minded activities. They first practiced their commitment to the ethic of mutuality by extending important services to the membership. Moreover, mutualista members cemented this commitment by adhering to strict rules disciplining them into "exemplars of true moral values." These statements of purpose and rules appear in nine surviving constitutions and by-laws, which are representative sources of information because founding members normally made few modifications to copies that originated in Mexico and circulated among organizations in Texas. The eight organizations that generated these documents

---

[16] Lisandro Peña, "Heroes Anónimos," *Primer Congreso Mexicanista, Discursos Y Conferencias: Por La Raza Y Para La Raza,* 13.

represented five South Texas towns and cities: San Antonio, Alice, Brownsville, San Benito, and Laredo.[17]

Members adopted a number of specific objectives to promote mutualism within and outside the organization. All the organizations established an insurance fund which made disability payments to ill members for up to thirty days and paid funeral costs in case of death. They also contributed to a widow's fund that provided assistance to the family of the deceased member. Other sources of mutual and community assistance included informal job-seeking services for their members, charity funds to help needy families in the community, and savings funds which extended emergency loans to members. In some cases, the organizations established libraries, newspapers, and private schools for children and adults in the community. In all cases, they sponsored celebrations during Mexico's national holidays and the organizations' anniversaries.

The material benefits that the insurance coverage, emergency loans, and job placement assistance brought to the members were obvious. Most of them were poor and often without a stable source of employment. The schools, libraries, and newspapers were important contributions to the educational advancement of the membership and the community. These activities also contributed to the moral regeneration of the members and the community they served. The insurance and savings funds reinforced a measure of trust among members who contributed

---

[17] This section is based on the following documents: Sociedad Benevolencia Mexicana, *Constitución y Leyes*, 1875 (San Antonio: G. F. Sigmond y Cía., 1889); Sociedad de Obreros, Igualdad y Progreso, *Reglamento General*, 1890 (Laredo: Gate City Printing Office, 1891); Sociedad Mutualista Hidalgo y Juárez, *Reglamento*, 1900 (Alice: Tipografía de "El Genio," 1900); Gran Liga Mexicanista de Beneficiencia y Protección, *Constitución and Reglamento* (Laredo: Tipografía de N. Idar, 1912); Sociedad Union de Jornaleros, *Reglamento General*, 1915 (Laredo: Imprenta de "XYZ," 1915); Sociedad Mutualista, Hijos de Juárez, *Reglamento General*, 1891 (Laredo: n.p., 1916 and 1924); Sociedad de Conductores y Obreros Unidos, Fe y Adelanto, *Reglamento General*, 1918 (Laredo: n.p., 1923); Sociedad Mutualista Protectora Benito Juárez, Reglamento General, 1920 (Brownsville: Preciado Publishing Co., 1926). The year following the titles are the dates when the organizations were founded. The last organization was from San Benito, although its constitution was printed in Brownsville.

their meager resources with the expectation that their money would be handled honestly and that they would receive their due benefits. The regular and timely payment of the required monthly fees and contributions also fostered frugality and a sense of responsibility.

The charity funds, schools, newspapers, and public celebrations broadened the organizations' sphere of influence as examples of disinterested and morally rejuvenating public service. In Laredo, La Sociedad Union de Jornaleros saw in the patriotic celebrations an opportunity to demonstrate their adherence to a Mexicanist identity. The organization agreed that it needed to sponsor the celebration of "national holidays with the necessary solemnity to insure that our members and our children do not lose the precepts of our nationality." The Sociedad Hijos de Juárez added that its members should seek to promote through the press or their own newspaper, "ideas in support of the moral and material development of the social masses." In San Benito, mutualistas made one of the most impressive gestures of community service when they decided to admit into their school children from families who could not afford to pay the required fees.

The strict internal rules that mutual aid societies adopted to define the responsibilities and proper "moral comportment" of their members contributed the most to the practice of the ethic of mutuality. First of all, persons who applied for admissions had to be of sound moral character. The organization confirmed this by requiring recommendations from at least one member who acted as a sponsor and a committee that formally reviewed his local reputation as a responsible family person and law-abiding citizen. The membership was required to vote unanimously in favor of positive recommendations by the sponsor and the committee. Otherwise, the applicant was rejected.

Rules also prohibited behavior that, according to La Sociedad Hidalgo y Juárez from Alice, was "unbecoming to honest men." Vagrancy, giving oneself to vices, irresponsible family behavior, slander, and defamation against the organization and their brethren were cause for depriving members of their rights, and in some cases for suspending them from the organization.

Members were discouraged from informally accusing others of these failings. Instead, organizations instituted a formal grievance process that allowed the membership to render a judgment on the basis of a recommendation by a jury of between five and ten members who heard opposing arguments.

Mutual aid societies also observed strict rules during discussions and debates in order to avoid unnecessary conflicts and to foster a sense of propriety and mutual respect. They placed time limits on the arguments or presentations that each member made before the body. They also prohibited the use of offensive language and suspended anyone who left a meeting in the middle of a dispute or who threatened to quit the organization because of a heated discussion. Moreover, they avoided conflicts by appointing a committee to first review a sensitive issue before the membership was given an opportunity to discuss the matter.

These efforts to control the nature of the internal discussions reflected a concern for maintaining fraternal relations among the members and for projecting an image of sobriety and mutual consideration. It did not necessarily mean, however, that they shunned controversial issues. For instance, although most of them declared a ban on discussions of a religious or political nature, they all endorsed the idea of promoting political unity, an endeavor often fraught with controversial and acrimonious debate. Members also participated in contentious political activities such as political campaigns, and exiled politics in their communities. Their reluctance to treat controversial issues signified an attempt to control possible excesses with a basic understanding, i.e., unity was to be maintained on the basis of mutual respect and proper regard for the views of others.

Mutualistas also maintained friendly relations with sister organizations. Members in good standing of sister organizations who visited or moved into the area were always welcomed and sometimes seated in a position of honor with the executive committee. Mutualista organizations encouraged members who moved to other areas to join sister organizations. They usually gave departing members letters of recommendation and other documents to facilitate their admission.

Mutual aid societies also spoke about extending their spirit of mutualism beyond the confines of their organization. La Sociedad Benito Juárez from Laredo, for instance, proposed to "Help in all ways possible in the development of other societies by establishing relations of reciprocity within and outside the country." La Sociedad Mutualista Protectora, Benito Juárez from San Benito declared that it sought "progress and unity among the entire Mexican working class in this country, as well as of the U.S.-born." The Alice mutual aid society named Hidalgo y Juárez explained that "philanthropy and humanitarian sentiments" would guide their efforts to build unity among "all social classes."

The internal discipline of the mutualistas and their attendant reputation as responsible and civic-minded institutions gave importance and ideal meaning to the ethic of mutuality as a source of unity, identity, and civic pride. This ethic, however, generally remained tied to mutual aid societies until intellectuals defined and translated key cultural values into specific political objectives or strategies.

One of the best sources for examining the manner in which intellectuals conducted these translations is in the formal presentations they made during public meetings sponsored by mutual aid societies. In some important instances, they utilized moralistic and nationalistic precepts in support of workers' unity. Intellectuals demonstrated that collectivist values could be used to justify such strategies as unionism, as well as efforts of a purely mutualist character. Like the presenters at El Congreso Mexicanista, they often spoke about the need for moral rejuvenation and civic participation. Many of them, however, sought to promote the values of mutualism, fraternalism, and reciprocity within larger political struggles that sought to effectuate change in both Mexico and the United States. One of the most sought-after speakers in Laredo contributing to this discourse on culture and politics was Sara Estela Ramirez.[18]

---

[18] My remarks on Ramirez are based on the following works: Emilio Zamora, "Sara Estela Ramirez: Una Rosa Roja en el Movimiento," in *Mexican Women in the United States: Struggles Past and Present*, ed. Adelaida del Castillo and Magdalena Mora (Los Angeles: UCLA Chicano Studies Research Center Publications, 1980);

Ramirez, a teacher, poet, journalist, and early supporter of the exiled Partido Liberal Mexicano (PLM), came to Laredo around 1895 from Saltillo, Coahuila, where she attended a teachers' school, Ateneo Fuentes. Like many other Mexicana teachers who arrived in South Texas at the turn of the century, she may have been recruited by one of the many mutual aid societies and groups of parents that established private schools, or *escuelitas*, in response to the experience of exclusion and segregation in the public schools. As a teacher, she joined numerous other young, usually single, women who, by virtue of their roles as educators, assumed highly respected roles as intellectuals and community leaders. During the twelve years she lived in Laredo, Ramirez was especially notable for her literary activity in local Spanish-language newspapers, including poems and articles in two of her own, *La Corregidora* and *La Aurora*, and for her political association with the PLM.[19]

Ramirez's writings and speeches clearly place her within the liberal political tradition that produced some of the more radical critiques of the economy, society, and the state in Mexico prior to the revolution. As one of the earliest supporters of the anti-Diaz PLM movement, Ramirez exhibited a positivist style of thought and political nationalism that was popular in Mexico at the time. Underlying her critiques was a view of change as inevitable in its evolutionary thrust towards a more egalitarian society in a Mexico properly governed by just laws and guided by morally responsible behavior among the country's citizenry and leadership. Ramirez

---

Inez Hernández Tovar, "Sara Estela Ramirez: The Early Twentieth-Century Texas Mexican Poet," (Ph.D. diss., University of Houston, 1984); Mathilde Rodríguez Cabo, *La Mujer y La Revolucion* (México, D.F.: Frente Socialista de Abogados, 1937), 20–22; Lucina G. Villarreal, "Mujeres de la Revolución," *El Popular* Apr. 29, May 1, 4, 6, and 7, 1939; Teodoro Hernández, "Las Tinajas de Ulua," *El Universal Gráfico* Aug. 23, 1943, p. 162. The last three publications place Ramirez among the leading female historical figures of the early 1900s. According to Rodríguez Cabo, Ramirez "was a defender of women and fought for their spiritual and economic liberation, and established some mutual aid organizations for women."

[19] The PLM was an exiled anti-Diaz organization credited with organizing in Texas pre-1910 uprisings that erupted along the Mexican side of the border. Historians recognize some of its leaders, especially Ricardo Flores Magón, as intellectual precursors of the Mexican Revolution of 1910. The PLM established its

added an impressive ethical outlook that condemned exploitation and oppression and that justified cooperative ideals as the
foundation for struggle. She gave a full exposition of her views in
a talk during the twenty-fourth anniversary celebration of La
Sociedad de Obreros, Igualdad y Progreso.[20]

Ramirez proposed the ideals of altruism and mutualism practiced by La Sociedad as moral guideposts for solidarity among
workers seeking to build effective working-class unity throughout
the world. She gave rhetorical force and ethical meaning to this
view with a thematic allusion to the individual's relation to nature
within a framework of determinism and free will. Ramirez's talk
was in three parts. First, she complimented the organization for
waging a "noble struggle" against such evil forces as egoism and
avarice within its ranks. The organization's membership was
bound together by a "law of humanity, by a sense of spiritually
innate altruism." She used both altruism and mutualism synony-
mously to mean a sense of fraternal respect, and spiritual and
material assistance, values that were within the reach of everyone
by the very nature of being humans. This, according to Ramirez,
was made evident by the exemplary behavior of the members of
La Sociedad. In the second part of her talk, she recounted the
converse state of affairs among workers in general. They were
alienated, divided, disorganized, and subject to failure as workers

first exiled headquarters at Ramirez's home in 1904. The following provide exam-
inations of the PLM and its relationship with the Mexican community in Texas:
Juan Gómez-Quiñones, *Sembradores, Ricardo Flores Magón y El Partido Liberal
Mexicano; A Eulogy and Critique*, Monograph No. 5 (Los Angeles: UCLA Chicano
Studies Research Center, 1973); Zamora, *The World of the Mexican Worker*. For an
examination of these private schools and the role that young immigrant Mexi-
canas played, see Emilio Zamora, "Las Escuelitas: A Texas-Mexican Search For
Educational Excellence," *Los Tejanos: Children of Two Cultures*, Proceedings of the
South Texas Head Start Bilingual-Bicultural Conference (Edinburg: South Texas
Regional Training Office, 1978), 13–25.

[20] A copy of her presentation appears in, Zamora, "Sara Estela Ramirez; Una
Rosa Roja en el Movimiento," 168. The PLM paper described La Corregidora as
"one of the few newspapers that can be truly called liberal; its mature ideas teach
at the same time that they strengthen convictions, and the healthy patriotism that
informs its articles brings growing enthusiasm and love for the motherland which
suffers so much under the yoke of despotic leaders." "La Corregidora," *Regen-
eración*, Oct. 7, 1901, p. 9.

in struggle. They lacked both a spiritual sense of fraternity, reciprocity, and the knowledge that "their arms maintain the wealth and growth of industry." Sometimes even unions lacked a sense of common interest and purpose. Ramirez concluded by exhorting Mexican workers in the audience to unite and to draw from within, "something grand, something divine, that will make us sociable, that will ennoble us as human beings."

Ramirez reasoned that nature equipped humans with the spiritual capacity to practice fraternity. Humans, however, had created conditions that bound them to violate this universal law. Often, these violations were conscious products of the free will. A return to the natural order meant an acceptance of the dictates of nature. Only in total harmony among themselves could workers be complete human beings. As moral statements, their logic legitimized communitarian values as cornerstones in a workers' struggle and justified its continuance until an inevitable reconstructed end was achieved.

The writings of José María Mora, a socialist orator and labor leader from Laredo, also demonstrate support for the ethic of mutuality as the basis for local and international workers' struggles. We know little about Mora. He was actively involved in mutualista and unionist activities and may have been a member of Federal Labor Union No. 11,953, an American Federation of Labor (AFL) union of Mexican railroad workers from Laredo that waged impressive organizing and strike campaigns between 1905 and 1907. He also published extensively in local newspapers on the need for political unity of Mexicans as workers. Mora delivered a speech before El Congreso Mexicanista as a member and official delegate of La Sociedad. In 1918, he once again achieved local prominence when he was elected president of a typographical union affiliated with the AFL.[21]

---

[21] The following commentary draws from three of his articles from *El Defensor del Obrero* (Laredo) and the speech he presented at El Congreso Mexicanista. These works are representative of his writings. José María Mora, "Un comentario," ibid., Nov. 25, 1906, pp. 173–175; "La ley debe ser igual para todos los hombres," ibid., Jan. 20, 1907, pp. 225–227; and "Discurso pronunciado por su autor, el Sr. J. M. Mora, delegado por La Sociedad de Obreros, Igualdad y Progreso," In *Primer Congreso Mexicanista, Discursos y Conferencias, Por La Raza y Para La Raza*, 16–18.

Like Ramirez, Mora propagated political ideas with an explicit moral thrust that he associated with the work of mutual aid societies. He also used nature to justify equality, fraternity, and reciprocity and to describe the objective conflict between workers and the bourgeoisie. Mora also urged the moral revitalization of workers' consciousness within mutual aid societies and labor unions. Moreover, he argued that it was especially important for Mexican workers to establish a natural order of equality and fraternity.

Mora believed that nature embodied reason in its most pure form and applied this reason without regard to alleged differences among humans and plants. It was as if nature prescribed moral behavior, treating everyone equally: "That is why we say that nature manifests EQUALITY; thus, in this sense we are all equal."[22] However, social forces and the political machinations of the bourgeoisie undermined this equality. The bourgeoisie justified the class structure and its privileged position in society through alliances with the state and its military apparatus and by claiming a special redeeming relationship with God. More importantly, the bourgeoisie reinforced its position with repressive actions against organized workers. This was the case with the textile workers in Orizaba, Mexico, and the railway workers in Laredo, Texas.[23] Mora suggested that the privileged classes were morally corrupt and beyond hope of true redemption. Thus, it fell on the actual producers in society, the workers, to redirect the course of humanity towards equality and fraternity.

Mora believed that divisions among workers were man-made and thus unnatural. The deliberate political actions of the bourgeoisie and its defenders often maintained these divisions. It was necessary for workers to understand that they had common material interests. They also had a moral obligation to practice equality and fraternity. Once in harmony among themselves, within the

---

[22] Mora, "La ley debe ser igual para todos," 225.

[23] Mora was making reference to the famous textile strike in Mexico that precipitated the 1910 Mexican revolution and to the defeat of Federal Labor Union No. 11,953. For a treatment of the early phase of the labor movement in Mexico, see Moisés González Navarro, *El Porfiriato, La Vida Social* Vol. 4, in *La Historia Moderna de México,* ed. Daniel Cosío Villegas (México, D.F.: Editorial Hermes, 1957). For information on the Laredo railroad strike involving the Federal Labor

organizations that practiced the basic laws of humanity, workers were further obligated to extend principles of cooperation and support beyond their organizational confines. This meant that workers should treat other poor people with equal respect. Mora reasoned:

If we are happy when we unite as brothers, inspired by a principle of mutual protection, with common rights, without causing each other harm, without offending or even mildly hurting our fellow workers, we will be happier when everyone refrains from abusing the weak and defenseless.[24]

Unity was sequential and directional. It began with workers in struggle. It involved mobilization and sought moral salvation. In Texas, it fell on Mexican workers to fulfill the historical imperative of effective working-class unity.

Mora's call for working-class unity and struggle at El Congreso Mexicanista suggested popular support for the ethic of mutuality as an essential organizing element among Mexican workers. He reminded the delegates that,

The issue that we are concerned with at this moment directs us to work for the unification of the Mexican worker and that united as one complete family we will be guided by the principle of fraternity.[25]

Fraternity, according to Mora, was an inherent predisposition among humans who often denied it by contributing to the oppression of others. This was the reason why in the mutual aid and fraternal societies, "it is said 'one for all and all for one,' and the avaricious ones say everything for us and damn the people."[26]

Feelings of indignation and concern over the effects of discrimination, inequality, and violence gave special importance to the working-class ethic of mutuality as a source of Mexicanist unity and identity. In the face of divisions and difficult living and working conditions, Mexicans looked inwardly and reinforced an outlook that not only gave them a sense of importance, but a

---

Union, see Zamora, *The World of the Mexican Worker,* 110–132.

[24] Mora, "El Sr. J. M. Mora," 17.

[25] Ibid., 16.

[26] Ibid., 17.

meaningful recourse to address their myriad problems. Mutual aid societies reflected the popular ethic of mutuality and reinforced it when they assumed the political responsibility of promoting its values of fraternalism, reciprocity, and altruism through self-discipline, internal services of mutual support, and civic involvement.

The leadership gave added meaning to collectivist and egalitarian ideals with a language of Mexicanist struggle and righteous cause. The members offered concrete examples of the proper moral behavior expected of truly responsible Mexicans in their communities. Intellectuals, in turn, provided refined philosophical formulations that translated moral precepts into specific political strategies and goals. The allusions to a God-like Nature by intellectuals like Ramirez and Mora suggests an added frame of reference, a Christian belief system that was popular among the largely Catholic Mexican population. I have restricted my focus, however, to the ethic of mutuality as defined by the English historian Thompson in his study of the English working class. Additional work in the area of culture and politics no doubt will discover other sources of collective identity and their function in the world of Mexican politics.

Although other political groups like the PLM may have operated on the basis of well-developed and focused political programes of action, Ramirez and Mora demonstrated that workers' struggles drew inspiration, meaning, and direction from the deep well of mutualism. Mutualist values may have originated in a working-class culture, but they acquired a Mexi-canist political meaning in a world that was often defined in racial and nationalist terms. The result was the elaboration of a moralistic and nationalistic political culture that served as a basis for promoting labor organization and workers' rights.

# The Tejano Revolt of 1915

RODOLFO ROCHA*

The Mexican Revolution of 1910 brought change for Mexico and hope for Mexican Americans. When the fighting ceased, a new Mexican elite had replaced the *Científico* ruling class and the country began a process of reconstruction that promised a better life for its citizens. Mexican Americans living in the South Texas region of the Rio Grande Valley, on the other hand, were briefly encouraged to hope for better days when local Mexicano revolutionists, influenced by the ideology and armed action of the revolution, sought to redress the suffering they had experienced for generations. The Tejano revolt of 1915, which was concentrated in the Valley as part of a larger South Texas armed movement known as the San Diego revolt, did not produce the dramatic results evident in Mexico. It nevertheless underscored the notion that discrimination, inequality, and deep-seated dissatisfaction in South Texas could also generate support for a social movement that promised fundamental changes.[1]

* Rodolfo Rocha is a former chair of the Department of History currently serving as dean of the College of Arts and Humanities at the University of Texas-Pan American in Edinburg, Texas. He has taught U.S., Texas, and Mexican American history courses and has published numerous articles and chapters on Mexican Americans in Texas history. He is completing a book-length study on the Mexican Revolution along the Texas border.

[1] I use the terms Mexican and Tejano interchangeably when referring to Mexican-origin people. When the discussion warrants it and the data at hand allows it, I underscore the nativity of persons with the use of Mexican Nationals

On January 15, 1915, a Mexican seeking support for a revolutionary movement in Texas approached Dr. Andrés Villarreal, an exile who supported anti-Carrancista elements in McAllen, Texas. Villarreal went to Deodoro Guerra, a local businessman and political figure, who then informed Hidalgo County authorities of the plot. Basilio Ramos was subsequently arrested for attempting to solicit recruits in the United States. When officers searched Ramos, they discovered in his possession the San Diego Plan, a detailed call to arms that sought to foment a revolution against the United States with the intention of carving out independent republics for Mexicans, Native Americans, and African Americans in the Southwest. The arrest of Ramos made the entire episode moot. A Federal judge dismissed an indictment for sedition, describing the whole incident as ludicrous.[2]

Such a dismissal suggested that Mexicans in Texas did not have a just cause for rebellion and that they were intellectually incapable of formulating such a sophisticated call to arms. The subsequent armed actions by Tejano guerrilla groups led local authorities to posit a more logical yet equally dismissive view. They continued to deny the homegrown nature of the rebellion,

---

and Mexican Americans. The terms Rio Grande Valley and Valley refer to the approximately five-mile-wide strip of land alongside the border extending from Brownsville to Mission. South Texas refers to the region south of a line that begins at Del Rio and extends northeast with the Nueces River to Corpus Christi. For articles on the Plan de San Diego, consult the following: William M. Hager, "The Plan of San Diego, Unrest of the Texas Border in 1915," *Arizona and the West*, 5 (Winter, 1963), 327–336; Allen Gerlach, "Conditions Along the Border-1915, the Plan de San Diego," *New Mexico Historical Review*, 43 (July, 1968), 192–212; Juan Gómez-Quiñones, "Plan de San Diego Reviewed," *Aztlán: Chicano Journal of the Social Sciences and the Arts*, 1 (Spring, 1970), 124–132; James A. Sandos, "The Plan of San Diego, War and Diplomacy on the Texas Border, 1915–1916," *Arizona and the West*, 14 (Spring, 1972), 5–24; Charles H. Harris III and Louis R. Sadler, "The Plan of San Diego and the Mexican-United States War Crisis of 1916: A Reexamination," *Hispanic American Historical Review*, 58 (Aug., 1978), 381–408. Also consult a recent book-length study on the subject: James A. Sandos, *Rebellion in the Borderlands: Anarchism and the Plan of San Diego, 1904–1923* (Norman: University of Oklahoma Press, 1992).

[2] Sandos, "War and Diplomacy on the Texas Border," 9; Hager, "Unrest on the Texas Border," 328–329; Ciro R. de la Garza-Treviño, *El Plan de San Diego* (Ciudad Victoria: Universidad Autónoma de Tamaulipas, 1970), 33–34.

preferring instead to believe that revolutionists from Mexico had instigated the whole affair. Although some of the dissidents originated in Mexico and joined others from South Texas in response to the San Diego Plan's call, there is good reason to believe that the initial fighting concentrated in the Rio Grande Valley owed its origins primarily to local conditions rather than to political formulations by a political elite from Texas or Mexico.

Unlike the San Diego Plan which called for a revolution from Texas to California, the Tejano Revolt primarily challenged conditions in the Valley and the immediate South Texas region. Moreover, it did not trigger the massive uprising outside the Valley that people expected. Trouble along the border, however, did not cease completely in 1915. Fighting continued in 1916 with armed raids occurring in the Big Bend, Laredo, San Ygnacio, and San Benito. Nevertheless, most of the 1916 raids were not a part of the 1915 revolutionary movement in Texas. They were a product of the explosive situation created by Francisco Villa's incursion into Columbus, New Mexico, the American punitive expedition force in Mexico, and the clashes between American and Mexican forces at Parral and Carrizal.[3]

The intense fighting associated with the Tejano Revolt resulted from a relatively unique set of social relations that characterized the Rio Grande Valley. As the historical sociologist David Montejano has pointed out, this South Texas area had the highest concentration of Mexicans and had elaborated an inflexible and racially defined social structure in its unique path of agricultural development. The border strip from Starr County to Laredo and a short distance beyond claimed a ranching industry and a more prominent and stable Mexican landowning class, two key factors that explain its less conflict-ridden relations and the relative absence of insurrectionist politics. The border corridor extending from the Eagle Pass-Del Rio area to the Big Bend country was also devoted to ranching. Equally important, this area was sparsely populated and the presence of the famed Mexican revolutionary, Francisco Villa, across the border limited

---

[3] Michael Tate, "Pershing's Punitive Expedition: Pursuer of Bandits or Presidential Panacea?" *Americas*, 32 (July, 1975), 61.

raiding and seditious activity that was not within his control. A large military force in El Paso also deterred such activity.[4]

Extreme poverty, discrimination, and inequality, as well as the seemingly few prospects for change, most probably stimulated the guerrilla raids in the Valley. The depressive conditions on Mexico's side of the border aggravated matters as the growing immigrant flow responded to the incessant demand for low-wage labor and reinforced the Mexican's bottom position in the socio-economy. Mexicans in northern Mexico, for instance, experienced sporadic shortages of food in the first half of 1915 and increased significantly the numbers of immigrants coming to South Texas. Military officials in Mission were cognizant of this and feared unrest among the disaffected because of a "lack of food and work" along both sides of the border. By the first week of June, hundreds of refugees had arrived in the Valley, leading authorities to issue added warnings. Texas Ranger captain J. J. Sanders, for instance, claimed that many of them were crossing to steal cattle or horses and becoming the lawless element that was joining the revolt. Public concern led Brownsville city fathers to meet in mid-June to find a solution to the high rate of unemployment among the refugees in the city. They were nevertheless unable to avoid a crisis. In August, the Brownsville daily *El Porvenir* received a letter signed by "the people" which threatened to kill certain wealthy people in the city unless they hired the poor.[5]

---

[4] David Montejano, *Anglos and Mexicans in the Making of Texas: 1836–1986* (Austin: University of Texas Press, 1987), 117–128; Virgil Lott, "The Rio Grande Valley," Unpublished manuscript, Rio Grande Valley Historical Collection (Learning Resource Center, University of Texas-Pan American, Edinburg, Tex.), 83; Eric Tanner, "The Texas Border and the Mexican Revolution" (Master's thesis, Texas Tech University, 1970), 48; J. B. Wilkinson, *Laredo and the Rio Grande Frontier* (Austin: Jenkins Publishing Co., 1975), 402. Additional histories that treat Mexicans in Texas include: Arnoldo De León, *Mexican Americans in Texas; A Brief History* (Arlington Heights, Ill.: Harlan Davidson, 1993); Emilio Zamora, *The World of the Mexican Worker in Texas* (College Station: Texas A&M University Press, 1993); Juan Gómez-Quiñones, *Roots of Chicano Politics, 1600–1940* (Albuquerque: University of New Mexico Press, 1994).

[5] J. H. Johnson to Secretary of State, Feb. 20, 22, Aug. 12, 1915, microfilm, U.S. Dept. of State, Records Relating to the Internal Affairs of Mexico, 1910–1929

Although many Mexicanos earned more money in Texas than in Mexico and could claim an improved condition, they increasingly expressed dissatisfaction. Some resented the general climate of discrimination and inequality that at times involved physical abuse and mistreatment in the farms. This is not to suggest, however, that all Anglo employers abused their workers; many were fair with their laborers. The early Anglo arrivals were especially noted for the friendly relations they developed with Mexicans in the ranching industry. Anglo newcomers who followed the initial waves quickly learned, however, that Mexicans could be exploited to offset the high cost of undeveloped farm land and expenses associated with clearing the brush and constructing irrigation systems. The resulting exploitative situation included more distant relationships and racially defined ideas that justified the maintenance of a low-wage labor force. The larger society reflected the developing relations in the farms with residential segregation, discrimination in public establishments, and destitute Mexican communities.[6]

Violence also characterized the border region and exacerbated relations between Mexicans and Anglos. The Valley had long been the home of a lawless element involved in smuggling, cattle and horse theft, and murder. Local authorities either lacked the means to enforce the law or engaged in the depredations themselves. To make matters worse, increasing numbers of Texas Rangers were assigned to the area and applied a violent and racial brand of law and order that wrought a virtual reign of terror on the Mexican population. Texas Rangers quickly earned the

---

(National Archives, Washington, D.C.; cited hereafter as IAM); Frederick Funston to Secretary of State, Feb. 22, 1915, ibid.; *Brownsville Herald*, Apr. 19, 1915, p. 1, June 14, 1915, p. 4; *San Antonio Express*, June 9, 1915, p. 3. See the following, for views on Valley conditions: Frank C. Pierce, *Texas' Last Frontier; A Brief History of the Lower Rio Grande Valley* (Menasha, Wis.: George Banta Publishing Co., 1917), 32–33; Lott, "The Rio Grande Valley," 7–10; "On the Mexican Border," *New Republic*, 4 (Oct. 9, 1915), 256.

[6] George Marvin, "The Quick and the Dead on the Border," *World's Work*, 33 (Jan., 1917), 299; Montejano, *Anglos and Mexicans in the Making of Texas, 1836–1986*, 167–169, 222–228; Zamora, *The World of the Mexican Worker in Texas*, 30–54.

reputation of practicing *la ley fuga* (shooting suspects allegedly trying to escape) when they detained Mexicans on suspicions of smuggling. Many Mexicans, some of whom were probably innocent of any crime, died by lynching or other forms of summary field executions at the hands of the Rangers. Some who escaped or feared capture along with their aggrieved relatives and friends would join the seditionists or at least refuse to support efforts to quell the revolt.[7]

Although the revolt occurred primarily in the Valley, it also produced fighting as far away as the Laredo area. The Mexican Americans and Mexican Nationals who participated in the uprising directed their anger against wealthy and influential Anglos as well as against Mexicans who joined the opposition and lent support to the Rangers and military force stationed in the Valley. The raids on stores, ranch properties, railroads, and individual homes began during the early part of 1915. Although they became more frequent and violent by May, few considered them a serious threat, preferring to view them as the work of individual malcontents and common criminals. By November, however, the increased and well-organized armed activity involving numerous bands of between ten and one hundred men could no longer be discounted so easily.

The uprising clearly drew inspiration from the Mexican Revolution. In some instances, calls to arms in Mexico pointed to the United States as a common enemy and thus entertained the idea of opposition on all fronts. Military officials and state and local authorities searching Tejano homes in the outlying ranches, for instance, discovered circulars that appealed to the local population to "rise in favor of the revolutionary leader Venustiano Carranza and of independence because at the rate we are going

---

[7] Testimony of R. B. Creager, Nov. 8, 1915, p. 380, Proceedings of the Joint Committee of the Senate and House in the Investigation of the Texas State Ranger Force, 1919 (Texas State Archives, Texas State Library, Austin; cited hereafter as TSA)); Sen. Morris Sheppard to Secretary of State, Nov. 8, 1915 (IAM); "Jesse Perez Memoirs," pp. 56–57 (Center for American History, University of Texas at Austin; cited hereafter as CAH); H. L. Ransom to Henry Hutchings, Oct. 11, 1915, Adjutant General Papers (cited hereafter as AGP) (TSA). George B. Hufford to Henry Hutchings, Jan. 23, 1915, ibid.

here we soon will be living as slaves of the Americans." Inspiration notwithstanding, discrimination and inequality encouraged Mexicans to join with the rebels. This explains why numerous observers noted widespread support from the local citizenry. Long-standing grievances associated with the war between Mexico and the United States and the subsequent period of intense conflict and land loss also encouraged local support. Some Tejanos had witnessed their parents or grandparents lose their lands and hoped to one day regain them by joining with the raiders. They reportedly sought to "take all the land back that you Gringos stole from us."[8]

Although it is difficult to determine the nativity of the participants of the revolt, it is clear that many of the seditionists were U.S.-born or longtime Texas residents and that in some cases they had established reputations as rough-and-ready individuals. Some had lived in Texas for extended periods but had gone to Mexico as fugitives from the law. A former Brownsville policeman named Carlos García, for example, apparently commanded one of the raiding bands operating out of Mexico in 1913 after a conviction for assault. Procopio Elizondo, an officer in Gen. Emiliano Nafarrate's Tampico Army Corps, also joined the revolt after a 1902 conviction for the murder of Texas Ranger W. E. Roebuck. Alberto Cabrera, another major figure in the revolt, had been indicted in Starr County for the murder of federal judge Stanley B. Welch in 1906. The two most important leaders of the revolt, Luis de la Rosa and Aniceto Pizaña also experienced difficulties

---

[8] San Antonio *Express*, Sept. 8, 1915, p. 1; Testimony of Lon C. Hill, U.S. Cong., Senate Committee on Foreign Relations, Investigation of Mexican Affairs, Sen. Doc. 285, 66th Cong., 2nd Sess., 1919, pp. 1262–1263 (Hearings cited hereafter as IMA); Cayetano González-Perez to Venustiano Carranza, Aug. 9, 1915, Archivo de Venustiano Carranza (Centro de Estudios de Historia de Mexico, Mexico City, Mexico); Charles C. Cumberland, "Border Raids in the Lower Rio Grande Valley—1915," *Southwestern Historical Quarterly*, 57 (Jan., 1954), 286; Clifford B. Casey, "Soldiers, Ranchers and Miners in the Big Bend," *U.S. Department of Interior, National Park Service, Office of Archeology and Historical Preservation, Division of History* (Washington, D.C.: U.S. Government Printing Office, Sept., 1916); Pierce, *Texas' Last Frontier*, 90; Gómez-Quiñones, "Plan de San Diego Reviewed," 127; Charles Spears to U.S. Attorney General, Aug. 6, 1915 (IAM); *Brownsville Herald*, Aug. 10, 1915, p. 1.

with the law in Cameron County. De la Rosa had been arrested by Texas Rangers for allegedly stealing cattle. Pizaña frequently ran into trouble with Rangers and on July 21, 1915, was arrested for carrying a pistol in Brownsville.[9]

Victims of abuse also crossed the border or had relatives in Mexico who harbored resentments. Some were even bent on avenging the death of a cousin, uncle, brother or friend. In some cases, relatives or friends of persons who died under questionable circumstances in Texas had influential relatives and friends in places like Matamoros. Adolfo Muñoz, for instance, who was lynched in July, had a brother living in Matamoros who was a city policeman. Moreover, many of the troops stationed in the Matamoros-Reynosa area were local residents and had relatives in Texas. This explains why in some instances local authorities and military personnel in the Mexican border region provided sanctuary to the seditionists and even joined in their periodic forays into Texas.[10]

The seditionists struck at symbols of Anglo dominance in the form of prominent individuals known for their anti-Mexican behavior or important development markers such as ranches and railroads. They attacked the property of prominent Valleyites such as Sam Robertson and James B. McAllen and on one of these occasions killed the president of the "law and order" league, A. L. Austin. The raiders destroyed irrigation pumping stations along the Rio Grande and the rail line between San Benito and Brownsville, symbols of Anglo exploitation of the land and the working class. One of the most dramatic actions was the attack on the King Ranch station at Norias in 1915. Although the attack was repulsed, it underscored the revolt's aversion to concentrated wealth and power in lands once owned by Mexicans.

---

[9] J. J. Sanders to Henry Hutchings, Apr. 4, 1916, W. P. Webb Collection (CAH); De la Garza-Treviño, *El Plan de San Diego*, 37–45; *Brownsville Herald*, Aug. 12, 31, 1915; *San Antonio Express*, Sept. 3, 1915, p. 1, Oct. 20, 1915, p. 1.

[10] [Military] Weekly Report, June 26, 1915, Records Relating to the Political Relations Between the United States and Mexico, 1910–1929, National Archives Microfilm, Microcopy No. 3134 (NA), (cited hereafter as PR); Funston to Adjutant General, Oct. 21, 1915 (IAM); *Brownsville Herald*, Aug. 25, 1915, p. 1, Nov. 19, 1915, p. 1.

Local and state authorities initially found it inconceivable that the raids could be part of a well-organized revolutionary plot. When the raiding intensified during the latter part of the summer and the beginning of fall, the connection became more believable especially since a number of raiders taken prisoner confessed to fighting for the same ideas expressed in the Plan. The rank and file dissidents may not have read or even comprehended the Plan's ideological formulations. They did, however, understand the abuses experienced by Mexicans and were willing to make the ultimate sacrifice for change that the Plan advanced. Some of the leaders of the revolt, on the other hand, most probably were aware of the San Diego Plan. However, historians have been unable to discover a conclusive connection. This strongly suggests that the initial phase of the revolt occurred independent of the San Diego Plan.

Equally suggestive were the personal reasons and localized circumstances that led some key leaders to wage a relatively spontaneous armed revolt. Pizaña, for instance, became the leader of the raiders in response to a violent personal affront and a unique set of circumstances rather than as a response to a call to arms by the San Diego Plan. He had lived at the Tulitos ranch in the vicinity of San Benito for fifteen years and took up arms when one of his Anglo neighbors threatened him with the help of an armed group of men. During the August shootout at Pizaña's ranch, his twelve-year-old son Guadalupe was wounded and eventually lost a leg. Aniceto escaped unharmed but became very embittered. His anger grew when he recognized that his family's experience reflected a general pattern of violence against Mexicans. He concluded that the solution was to drive Anglos out of the Valley. By September he had identified a sufficient number of like-minded Mexicans in the area to initiate the Tejano revolt.[11]

---

[11] Testimony of Lon C. Hill, pp. 1255, 1263–1265 (IMA); Testimony of José T. Canales, *Investigation of the Texas Ranger Force,* 859; Ciro R. de la Garza-Treviño, *Tamaulipas: Apuntes Históricos* (Ciudad Victoria: Universidad Autónoma de Tamaulipas, 1956), 122–1225; Pierce, *Texas' Last Frontier,* 90; *San Antonio Express,* Aug. 4, 1915, p. 1. Mrs. Pizaña has lived in exile at Matamoros since August 1915. She stated that the shootout began at dawn and lasted for two hours. Mrs. Pizaña also claimed that Aniceto had always been a law-abiding person and that the

Carranza has received most of the blame for the disorders along the border primarily because of the support that Nafarrate, his regional military commander, gave the revolt. Carranza, however, exercised a very tenuous control over his field commanders. Most commanders operated as a law unto themselves. Their armies operated as guerrilla forces, expert in hit-and-run tactics, assassinations, and brigandry. Moreover, once the forces of Francisco Villa had been driven out of the border, many idle Carrancista soldiers became restless and joined the raiders. Some may have participated in the revolt to avenge a personal wrong or to support the political aims of the seditionists, while others joined the raiders for loot since the Carranza's Constitutionalist government did not pay its soldiers adequately.[12]

Carranza's failure to restrain his officers led many people to believe that he approved of the raiding. Carranza retained Nafarrate even after his own Consul at Brownsville called for his removal. He is reported to have provided material support to Pizaña and de la Rosa during 1915. Nafarrate also provided free passage to seditionists who recruited men in the northern Mexican region. Ramos, for instance, had in his possession a pass signed by Nafarrate that guaranteed him movement across Constitutionalist lines.[13]

Carranza's failure to stop publication of anti-American and

---

"americanos" wanted to drive them off their land. Interview with Mrs. Aniceto Pizaña, June 14, 1980.

[12] Edwin Lieuwen, *Mexican Militarism; The Political Rise and Fall of the Revolutionary Army, 1910–1940* (Albuquerque: University of New Mexico Press, 1968), 23; Wilkinson, *Laredo and the Rio Grande Frontier*, 402; Sandos, "War and Diplomacy on the Texas Border," 5–24. Previously cited historians such as Hager, Sandos, Harris, Sadler, and Cumberland argue that Carranza was responsible for some of the forays and may have encouraged the fighting by failing to reign in some of his military leaders along the border. Most Anglos in the Valley also believed that Carranza was responsible for the revolt.

[13] Testimony of J. A. Garza, *Investigation of the Texas State Ranger Force*, 1078; R. Ciro Garza-Treviño, *Historia de Tamaulipas; Anales y Efemerides* (Ciudad Victoria, Tamaulipas: Universidad Autónoma de Tamaulipas, 1954), 230; Randolph Roberts to Secretary of State, Oct. 3, 1915 (IAM); Secretary of War to Secretary of State, Sept. 26, Nov. 11, Dec. 4, 1915, *Papers Relating to the Foreign Relations of the United States* (Washington, D.C.: U.S. Government Printing Office, 1924), 1, 4.

especially pro-sedition propaganda in the region also led to his being charged with complicity in the movement. Favorable and at times exaggerated newspaper coverage was especially noticeable. For example, late in August newspapers in Matamoros, Tampico, Monterrey, Veracruz, and Mexico City described the Tejano Revolt as a success and stated that five thousand revolutionists had captured several Texas towns, among them Brownsville, and concluded that American forces defending the border had been forced to withdraw. It is doubtful that newspapers could have carried such stories without the approval of the Constitutionalist government.[14]

Carranza may have allowed the raids to continue in his attempt to obtain U.S. recognition for his government. This is a suggestive proposition because Carranza took actions against the seditionists' use of Mexico as a safe haven once recognition became imminent in October. He replaced Nafarrate with Gen. Eugenio Lopez who introduced into the region nearly one hundred Tehauntepec Indian soldiers who had the reputation of being good brush fighters. Lopez and his replacement denied free movement to the seditionist leaders and began to maneuver militarily against guerrilla groups on the Mexican side of the border. One of the earliest actions that General Lopez took against the seditionists occurred on October 30, 1915, when his troops killed fifteen raiders in a battle near Matamoros. Carranza employed a separate and secret strategy to undermine the revolt. He offered Pizaña and De la Rosa $50,000 each to end the revolt. Carranza also rewarded De la Rosa with a regular commission of unknown rank in the Mexican Army and granted Pizaña some land at El Encino, near Ciudad Victoria.[15]

The revolt could not have survived without the encouragement or assistance of Constitutionalist officials along the river front. Some Carrancista subordinates endorsed the plan and the

---

[14] Harris and Sadler, "War Crisis of 1916," 386–388; A. Garrett to Secretary of State, Aug. 26, 27, 28, 1915 (IAM); *Brownsville Herald*, Aug. 28, 1915, p. 1, Nov. 11, 1915, p. 1, Dec. 4, 1915, p. 1.

[15] Cumberland, "Border Raids in the Lower Rio Grande Valley—1915," 298; Harris and Sadler, "War Crisis of 1916," 405; Sandos "War and Diplomacy on the Texas Border," 18–19; *Brownsville Herald*, Oct. 4, 1915, p. 1; *El Paso Morning Times*, Aug. 14, 1915, p. 1, Oct. 5, 1915, p. 1; *El Sol de Tampico*, Mar. 3, 1957, p. 1.

revolt, but "official" endorsement from the Constitutionalist government is doubtful. The leaders of the revolt, on the other hand, probably understood that Carranza would abandon his seemingly indifferent view of them once he obtained recognition. At any rate, the revolutionists continued with their campaign. Although hobbled by the loss of their sanctuary, they managed to wage two of their most daring raids after the official recognition of Carranza: the assault on the railroad line between Brownsville and San Benito and the Ojo de Agua incident.[16]

Opposition to the raids increased and often led to violent excesses against Tejanos in the Valley. This reaction victimized innocents and added numbers to the ranks of the dissidents. The revolt created a state of general hysteria among residents in South Texas who feared an invasion from Mexico and a possible war of racial retribution on a large scale. Among the most dramatic reactions was the formation of vigilante groups that roamed the Valley in search of raiders. Other Valley residents joined home rifle clubs or volunteered as special deputy sheriffs. Public fear that bred these reactions also provided authorities the latitude to wage campaigns intended to suppress the revolt as well as to discourage peaceful Mexicanos from entertaining seditious ideas.[17]

City and county officials met on several occasions to develop a plan to deal with the raiders. Most of them felt unprepared to handle the situation. They did, however, agree that it was necessary to inflict summary punishment on any bandit or supporter who was captured. They also felt it necessary to regain control over law enforcement. San Benito mayor J. H. Lyons, for example, ordered every male twenty-one to sixty years old to register

---

[16] Randolph Roberts to Secretary of State, Oct. 3, 1919 (IAM); William Edwards, "U.S.-Mexico Relations, 1913–1916; Revolution, Oil and Intervention" (Ph.D. diss., Louisiana State University, 1971), 363–364.

[17] Moises Gonzales-Navarro, "Xenofobia y Xenofilia en la Revolución Mexicana," *Historia Mexicana*, 18 (Apr.–June, 1969), 579; Testimony of Lon C. Hill, 1254 (IMA); Wesley Hall Looney, "The Texas Rangers in a Turbulent Era" (Master's thesis, Texas Tech University, 1971), 15; Lott, "Rio Grande Valley," 22; J. F. Houston to Gov. James Ferguson, Sept. 6, 1915, AGP; *Brownsville Herald*, Aug. 3, 1915, p. 1, Oct. 23, 1915, p. 1.

with city officials and to stand by for police duty. He also ordered all citizens in the city to register their arms. After the train-derailing outside San Benito in October, local officials also supported the two hundred Valleyites who met in Brownsville and made the appeal for increased federal and state assistance. Although the raids had subsided by then, merchants and citizens in Brownsville also asked city fathers to rigidly enforce vagrancy laws. Moreover, most Valley communities organized law-and-order leagues to protect their property.[18]

Gov. James Ferguson responded to the constant clamoring for help with an appeal of his own to the federal government. When the federal government denied his request, Ferguson asked the state legislature for ten thousand dollars to increase the Ranger force. By August 1915, Ferguson had increased the Ranger force in the Valley to fifty. Reflecting the state of hysteria in the Valley, the new Rangers promised to clear the border of any Mexican suspected of association with the revolt. The governor also offered a thousand dollar reward for the capture of Pizaña and De la Rosa, dead or alive. The reward, posted in October, was too late and too little since the raids had all but ended.[19]

In order to contain the violence, law officers used various means to restrict the mobility of the Tejano population. First, most city governments enforced a vagrancy law that prohibited Mexicanos from moving freely throughout the area unless they carried an official pass provided by their employers or local authorities. They also closely monitored and even prohibited traditional gatherings such as dances and holiday celebrations. In mid-September, for instance, Sheriff Vann of Cameron County issued an order that made public Mexican dances unlawful. State officials also used a health department order in June that allowed

---

[18] *San Antonio Express,* Aug. 6, 1915, p. 1; *Brownsville Herald,* Sept. 8 , 1915, p. 1, Sept. 9, 1915, p. 1, Oct. 20, 1915, p. 1, Oct. 23, 1915, p. 1; Stephen M. Vassberg, "The Mexican Bandit Activities in the Sebastian, Cameron County Texas Vicinity of 1915" (Unpublished graduate paper, Dept. of History, Prof. Gilberto R. Cruz, Pan American University, Edinburg, Texas, 1977), 8.

[19] Claude A. Adams to Henry Hutchings, Sept. 6, 1915, AGP; *Brownsville Herald,* Mar. 6, 1915, p. 1, Mar. 24, 1915, p. 1, June 10, 1915, p. 1, Sept. 6, 1915, p. 1, Oct. 28, 1915, p. 1.

local officials to forbid Mexican males capable of bearing arms from immigrating into Texas unless they had proof of legitimate business.[20]

Local law enforcement officials, soldiers, and vigilante committees often searched Tejano homes ostensibly on well-founded suspicions although the intent was also to undermine support for the revolt. Soldiers typically stood guard outside the home while the others conducted their investigation with threats, beatings, and even death. A gun in the possession of a Tejano often resulted in certain death on the grounds that the suspect was most probably a raider. These erstwhile defenders of order carried a list of persons suspected of aiding the raiders. Anyone could place a Mexican on the list without justification. Numerous unsuspecting Mexicans thus disappeared. Some most certainly were killed, while others left their properties in search of more safe surroundings in the larger towns or across the border.[21]

According to some early estimates, twenty-five Anglos and at least 176 Tejanos were killed between August and October. Sixty-four died in August, sixty in September, and fifty-two in October. Most of the fatalities involved noncombatants who had the misfortune of meeting up with armed Mexican seditionists or over-zealous Anglo authorities and citizens. Some of the Mexicans, however, suffered highly suspicious deaths at the hands of authorities and vigilantes while others were removed from jails by "unknown parties" and lynched. Violence was so pervasive that military officials at times had to intercede to protect prisoners from the wrath of Rangers and vigilante groups.

Killing Mexicans became such a common occurrence that many of the dead went unreported. This is one of the reasons why historians have amended the low estimates by contemporaries and calculated that between three hundred and five thousand Mexicans lost their lives in the turmoil by 1916. In an effort

---

[20] *Brownsville Herald,* Oct. 28, 1915, p. 1, Oct. 29, 1915, p. 1, Oct. 30, 1915, p. 1.

[21] Testimony of R. B. Craeger, *Investigation of Texas State Ranger Force,* 577–578; *Brownsville Herald,* Aug. 16, 1915, p. 1, Sept. 13, 1915, p. 1, Sept. 14, 1915, p. 1.

to suppress the raids, American officials and citizens turned to lawless action and killed hundreds, perhaps thousands, of Tejanos. Some were shot trying to escape or resisting arrest; others were simply lynched. Many were innocent of any complicity with the raiders, but as Mexicans were suspected of being bandits or a least sympathizers. Frequently, when a Tejano was deemed a raider, not only was he killed, but his brothers, and brothers-in-law also were assumed to be guilty and arrested or killed. Even his cousins were carefully watched.[22]

President Woodrow Wilson and Gen. Frederick Funston, the military commander of the South Texas region stretching from El Paso to Brownsville and inland to San Antonio, initially thought that the revolt was a local affair with resident Tejanos committing acts of brigandry. Accordingly, they believed that state officials and not the federal government had the major responsibility of resolving the problem. Wilson was also reluctant to increase U.S.'s military presence on the border for fear of impairing the already fragile relations with President Carranza. Wilson and Funston committed troops to the border only after military patrols came under direct fire from the raiders and they became convinced that a general uprising was close at hand.[23]

General Funston had the difficult, if not impossible, task of bringing a sense of order to a highly volatile and seemingly uncontrollable situation. One of his major concerns was that the conflict along the border would escalate into an unmanageable international problem. This meant that he had to minimally assure border residents that their safety was secure. Additionally, the violent excesses of local and state authorities often required that the military provide protection to prisoners and innocent bystanders. The U.S. military force in South Texas included four

---

[22] *San Antonio Express*, Aug. 15, 1915, p. 1; *Brownsville Herald*, Nov. 27, 1915, p. 6; Walter Prescott Webb, *The Texas Rangers; A Century of Frontier Defense* (2nd ed.; Austin: University of Texas Press, 1965), 478; Ford Green, "The Infamous Plan of San Diego," *Old West*, 12 (Winter, 1975), 8–19; Lott, "Rio Grande Valley," 85–87; Testimony of R. B. Craeger, *Investigation of Texas State Ranger Force*, 355.

[23] Wilkinson, *Laredo*, 406; Edwards, "U.S.-Mexico Relations," 389; *San Antonio Express*, Aug. 8, 1915, p. 1.

thousand troops in September, a small number considering Funston's responsibilities. Two months later the troop strength reached a figure of about twenty thousand. Convinced that the seditionists were using the Mexican side of the border as a staging area for the raids, Funston immediately ordered patrols along the river front to intercept them. Local and state officers from that point on assumed the responsibility of policing the interior.[24]

Approximately fifty percent of the Tejano population left the Valley to escape the violence and terror. They left their jobs and abandoned their homes, taking with them only those household goods that would fit in conveyances such as carts or wagons. Others sold their homes for almost nothing. The exodus began in mid-August and reached a mid-September peak of twenty-five hundred. The migration continued despite assurances by military local officials that the army would provide protection. By early November over seven thousand Mexicanos had crossed at Brownsville and Hidalgo. Immigration officials noted that thousands more crossed at other points beyond their official watch.[25]

The brutal treatment of Mexican border residents by local and state authorities, especially the Texas Rangers, contributed to the out-migration. This was well known in the Mexican communities along the border as well as among military officials. At the time of the fighting, numerous local officials disregarded the military's opinions regarding the Ranger excesses and maintained that refugees simply wanted to end their self-imposed exile in Texas. In late August, Carranza had issued a general amnesty to all exiles, guaranteeing their safety if they returned. Some officials, like Brownsville mayor Albert Browne were more concerned

---

[24] Lott, "Rio Grande Valley," 87; George Marvin, "Invasion or Intervention," *World's Work*, 32 (May, 1916), 59; Harris and Sadler, "War Crisis of 1916," 389; Sandos, "War and Diplomacy on the Texas Border," 13–14; Testimony of William G. B. Morrison, *Investigation of Texas State Ranger Force*, 24; Looney, "Texas Rangers," 19; Cumberland, "Border Raids," 305; *Brownsville Herald*, Sept. 6, 1915, p. 1.

[25] *Brownsville Herald*, Sept. 11, 1915, p. 1, Sept. 15, 1915, p. 1; Clarence C. Clendenen, *Blood on the Border; The United States Army and the Mexican Irregulars* (London: Macmillan Co., 1969), 187; Testimony of John Kleiber, p. 1279 (IMA); Testimony of Lon C. Hill and James B. Wells, *Investigation of Texas State Ranger Force*, 691, 1159; Weekly Reports, Sept. 4, Oct. 16, 1915, PR.

over a depleting labor supply than claims of unjust violence. He tried to convince them that their fears were unfounded, but his advice went unheeded.[26]

Some Anglo families also exited the Valley. Many of the rural residents, however, moved their families to the bigger border towns where they felt safer. Others moved in with neighbors, determined to battle anyone who threatened to steal their stock or threaten their lives. The seventy-three raids that occurred in 1915, however, proved less dangerous to Anglo life and property than expected. Although Anglo deaths drew the most attention from the press and authorities, the raiders probably killed less than thirty of them and brought the economy of the Valley to a standstill for only one year. They disturbed life but did not bring any significant amount of destruction to Anglo-American ranches, railroads, bridges, and irrigation pumps.[27]

General discontent and aggrieved feelings built up over generations to produce the revolt. Although it may be tempting to see it as the organized response to the call to arms by the Plan de San Diego, the lack of evidence to support such an association suggests otherwise. Long-standing grievances associated with persistent poverty, social discrimination, labor exploitation, physical abuse, and violence, coupled with the nagging memory of land loss, encouraged Mexicanos to join the revolt or to sympathize with the persons who took up arms. Once the revolt began, some capitalized on the opportunity to avenge or to make personal gains by looting while others joined in response to the violent reaction that ensued. Carranza was probably the most visible opportunist when he used the occasion to gain recognition for his government. Support for the revolt, however, came primarily from Mexicanos who saw in the revolt the means by which to challenge their exploitation and domination.

---

[26] Weekly Report, Oct. 30, 1915, PR; Testimony of Louis Brulay and James B. Wells, *Investigation of Texas State Ranger Force*, 536, 687; *Brownsville Herald*, Sept. 7, 1915, p. 1, Sept. 16, 1915, p. 4.

[27] J. J. Sanders to Henry Hutchings, July 22, 1915, AGP; Charles Askins, *Texans, Guns, and History* (New York: Frederick A. Praeger, 1963), 210; *Brownsville Herald*, Aug. 23, 1915, p. 1, Sept. 13, 1915, p. 1.

# Agents of Americanization:

## *Rusk Settlement and the Houston Mexicano Community, 1907–1950*

MARÍA CRISTINA GARCÍA*

The Settlement House movement emerged in the late 1880s, a manifestation of the larger social, political, and cultural movement in U.S. society known as Progressivism. Stanton Coit and Charles B. Stover founded the first settlement house, the Neighborhood Guild, in New York City. By 1910 there were over four hundred settlement houses in the country. Among the more famous were Chicago's Hull House, Boston's South End House, and New York's Henry Street Settlement. In Texas, settlement houses appeared in Austin, San Antonio, Houston, El Paso, Fort Worth, and Corpus Christi.[1]

Although some settlement houses were affiliated with churches or religious denominations, most were secular institutions. The founders were more concerned with assisting the temporal rather

---

* Maria Cristina Garcia is associate professor of history and Latino studies at Cornell University. She is the author of *Havana USA: Cuban Exiles and Cuban Americans in South Florida, 1959–1994*. Dr. Garcia is currently working on a book on Central American immigration.

[1] Correspondence between the directors of the various Texas settlements reveals a network of effective relations within a national settlement movement. For examples of this correspondence, see Papers of Franklin I. Harbach,

than the spiritual needs of the urban population. Alarmed by the new urban, industrialized America, especially the growing gap between rich and poor, reformers, or so-called "progressives," sought to bring education, "culture," and hope to the slums. Most settlement workers were young and idealistic, and came from sheltered, middle-class families, their values shaped by Calvinist morality and the Social Gospel movement. Many graduated from U.S. colleges and universities where they studied the novel area of the social sciences. The settlement house provided a site for fieldwork and became the training ground for a new class of professional social worker.[2]

Women were particularly drawn to settlement work. The majority of the staff and volunteers were typically women. This was the case in Houston. With few careers open to women throughout the United States, the settlements provided an outlet for their skills and talents, as well as their moral outrage regarding pressing social problems. Many were the first of their generation to attend a university, although they were as limited in their career options as their less educated sisters. Well-known settlement workers included Jane Addams, Ellen Gates Starr, Lillian Wald, and Vida Scudder.[3]

Settlement workers across the United States lived among the poor, in the very neighborhoods and slums where their centers

---

Houston Metropolitan Research Collection (Houston Public Library), (cited hereafter as HMRC). Scholars have been negligent in studying settlement work among Mexicans. An important exception is a study that focuses on El Paso: Vicki L. Ruiz, "Dead Ends or Gold Mines?: Using Missionary Records in Mexican American Women's History," *Frontiers,* 12 (1991), 33–56.

[2] Robert M. Crunden, *Ministers of Reform: The Progressives' Achievement in American Civilization,* 1889–1920 (New York: Basic Books, 1982), 16–25, 64–89; Allen F. Davis, *American Heroine: The Life and Legend of Jane Addams* (New York: Oxford University Press, 1973), 24–66, 73–74; *Houston Settlement Association Yearbook* (1909), 10–11.

[3] Scholars have written extensively on Jane Addams. See, for example, Allen F. Davis, *American Heroine* (New York: Oxford University Press, 1973). Addams's autobiography gives a detailed account of Hull House in Chicago which she founded with the assistance of Ellen Gates Starr. Jane Addams, *Twenty Years at Hull House* (New York: Macmillan, 1910). For biographies of Starr and Scudder, see Elizabeth H. Carrel, "Reflections in a Mirror: The Progressive Women and the Settlement Experience" (Ph.D. diss., University of Texas at Austin, 1981).

were situated. Immigrants from eastern and southern Europe comprised the majority of the urban poor in the Northeast and Midwest, living in overcrowded and poorly ventilated tenements like those captured for posterity by photographers Jacob Riis and Lewis Hine. Settlements in Texas and the Southwest also served European immigrants, but after 1910 they catered to poor Mexican immigrants and African Americans who were migrating to the cities.

Settlements provided charitable assistance in the form of hot meals, free baths, medical care, and small loans. Their principal mission, however, was to serve as outposts of education and culture. Reformers sought to introduce immigrants to American customs and values—to melt the "unmeltable ethnics" that White Anglo-Saxon Protestants feared. To fulfill this goal, most settlement houses offered classes in English and American history as well as in practical subjects such as housekeeping, cooking, and household management. Contact with the poor and the foreignborn, on the other hand, influenced settlement workers to become champions of progressive legislation regarding child labor, eight-hour working days, and the right to unionize.[4]

Settlement houses in Texas were patterned after this model of activity. One of the first to emerge was the Rusk Settlement House in Houston, which was founded in 1907 by Sybil Campbell, a teacher at Rusk Elementary School in the Second Ward. Campbell became interested in social work upon finding an abandoned child on her school steps one cold, rainy morning. The child's mother had gone to work and had no one to take care of her. Campbell learned that dozens of children regularly roamed the area without any supervision because their parents worked full time and could not afford child-care. Recognizing a need in the community, she enlisted the assistance of a local women's club and rented a small cottage where they established a free day nursery and kindergarten.[5]

In February 1907, Campbell and a group of women who had

---

[4] *Houston Settlement Association Yearbook* (1909), 14; ibid. (1910), 39.

[5] Ibid. (1909), 12; Corrine S. Tsanoff, *Neighborhood Doorways* (Houston: Neighborhood Centers Association of Houston-Harris County, 1958), 1–3.

joined in her crusade established the Houston Settlement Association to coordinate local settlement activities and link their efforts to the national movement. The association would eventually become an umbrella organization overseeing many different settlements in the poorer wards of the city. They moved to a larger building on Runnels Street in the Second Ward, and by the end of 1907 sponsored cooking classes, sewing classes, recreational activities for children and teenagers, and a social club for young women. They also maintained the nursery and kindergarten, and provided clothing and food to the indigent. Overwhelmed by inexperience, they hired a small staff in 1909, among them James P. Kranz, a professional social worker from Minnesota who became the director of the association.[6]

That same year, they moved into a larger facility, the old Settegast home on the corner of Gable and Maple streets near Rusk school in the Second Ward. The building became known as Rusk Settlement. They remodeled the building to house a library, reading room, game room, and social parlors, as well as a dispensary and medical clinic. Under an arrangement with the city, the settlement used without charge the Rusk school playground, auditorium, gymnasium, and showers after school hours. Rusk Settlement became a full-serving social center in the neighborhood. Children used it for classes and recreation in the day, and adults in the late afternoons and evenings. It served the needs of residents living within a four-square-mile area, bordered by Buffalo Bayou, Preston Avenue, Harrisburg Road, and the northern city limit. From 1910 to 1920, the settlement served an estimated twenty-five hundred people. In 1929, it served almost twenty-nine thousand.[7]

During the first years of operation, the Houston Settlement Association paid the salaries of three full-time settlement workers at Rusk, including Krantz, and paid the salaries of four to eight

---

[6] *Houston Settlement Association Yearbook* (1909), 13; Tsanoff, *Neighborhood Doorways*, 2–5.

[7] *Houston Settlement Association Yearbook* (1909), 13–14; ibid. (1910), 6. In 1929, the Rusk Settlement budget was $6,929.10. By comparison, Bethlehem House, which targeted the African American community, had a budget of $3,933.47 and served some 5,000 people. Tsanoff, *Neighborhood Doorways*, 19–20.

nurses who comprised the "Visiting Nurses Department." The latter traveled from door to door, offering medical assistance and
informing residents of services available to them at the settlement.
By 1934, the Visiting Nurses Department had assisted close to
eighteen thousand patients and had made 39,134 home visits.
The association also enlisted the aid of doctors who volunteered
their services during weekly visits to Rusk's medical clinic. As the
programs at Rusk expanded, the number of paid workers increased. Funding was limited, however, and this forced the Settlement Association to rely increasingly on volunteers. During the
first few years of operation, funding came primarily from dues
paid by several dozen association members. By 1920, the association relied on grants from the city, the Community Chest, and
donations from local churches, clubs, and private individuals.[8]

The Settlement Association and Rusk Settlement were a response to major social and economic changes. Among them were
a growing and expanding local economy that dramatically
increased the size of a highly diversified work force. Employment
opportunities in the railroads, petroleum industry, and ship
channel attracted thousands, both U.S. and foreign-born. In
1910, the population of the Second Ward was predominantly
Jewish (three-fifths of the population) and African American
(one-fifth); the rest were German, Irish, and Mexican. Rusk initially catered to the European immigrants of the area. After 1920,
however, the neighborhood became predominantly *Mexicano*.
Poor Mexican families had been migrating from other parts of
Texas and revolution-torn Mexico in search of economic opportunities. Approximately two thousand Mexicans lived in Houston

---

[8] The Houston Settlement Association was instrumental in founding
Houston's Social Service Bureau in 1916. It was established as a coordinating
agency overlooking the operations of all the city's social welfare institutions. In
that year, the Visiting Nurses Department became an independent unit of the
Houston Social Service Bureau. Also, the association became the "Settlement
Department" of the Social Service Bureau. In 1932, however, the settlement committee voted to become an independent agency once again, under the Community Chest. Tsanoff, *Neighborhood Doorways*, 7–9, 21–24. A sample financial report is
available in: Houston Social Service Bureau, "What is the Houston Social Service
Bureau?," 1919 Annual Report, pp. 24–33, Box 1, Records of the Houston Social
Service Bureau, HMRC.

in 1910; by 1930 their numbers had increased to fifteen thousand. In 1940 the Mexican community boasted twenty thousand residents, despite outmigrations occasioned by repatriation efforts and the Great Depression.[9]

The Mexican community was primarily working class, a small segment of the population was middle class. The new arrivals settled close to their place of employment, around the central business district, railroad yards, or ship channel. This prompted a "white flight" into the suburbs that was facilitated by technological advances such as the street car. Thus, the residential areas surrounding the central business district became increasingly segregated. Once the Second Ward became El Segundo Barrio, Rusk adapted its programs to meet the needs of the Mexicano residents.[10]

The Settlement Association founded other settlements after Rusk, including Brackenridge Neighborhood House on Whitty Street (1916), and Bethlehem Neighborhood House off Buffalo Drive (1917), and Douglas Settlement on McGowan Avenue (1934). The last two targeted the African-American community. Bethlehem and Douglas settlements functioned in much the same fashion as Rusk. They operated a day nursery and kindergarten; after-school recreational activities for children and teenagers; and classes for adults. Bethlehem settlement also trained African-American women for work in domestic service, and trained young girls for future employment as maids through their "Little Housekeepers" club.[11]

The facilities at Bethlehem and Douglas, however, were vastly inferior to Rusk's. Although all the settlements were deeply in need of renovation, conditions at Douglas and Bethlehem were

---

[9] Arnoldo De Leon examines the growth and transformation of Houston's Mexican American community in *Ethnicity in the Sunbelt*. Other sources include: Francisco A. Rosales and Barry Kaplan (eds.), *Houston: A Twentieth Century Urban Frontier* (Port Washington: Associated Faculty Press, 1983); and Arturo F. Rosales, "Mexicans in Houston: The Struggle to Survive, 1908–1975," *Houston Review*, 3 (Summer, 1981), 224–248.

[10] De Leon, *Ethnicity in the Sunbelt*, 11–14.

[11] *Social Survey*, 1 (May, 1918), 2, Records of the Houston Social Service Bureau, Box 1, Folder 4, HMRC.

particularly hazardous. Association members readily admitted that these buildings were fire traps. Mules belonging to the Board of Education roamed the children's playground at Douglas for years until a fence was installed. Bethlehem had no playground until the 1930s when the city provided the necessary funds. Bethlehem was also situated next door to the city dump. Despite petitions from the association, the city dump was not removed until 1938 when the city paved it to make way for the new Jefferson Davis Hospital. Bethlehem settlement was ultimately demolished in September 1940 when the Housing Authority appropriated the site for a housing project. A new settlement for African Americans was not established until the late 1940s despite the fact that more people attended activities at Bethlehem than at the all-white Brackenridge Settlement.[12]

Many of the staff members and volunteers at Rusk Settlement lived among the people they served while others lived within walking distance and thus witnessed on a firsthand basis the poverty and crime in the Second Ward. These conditions worsened as the older and more affluent residents moved into the suburbs. Moreover, city government increasingly neglected the wards around the central business district. The large fashionable homes became dilapidated boarding houses or apartments. As a result many homes in the Second Ward lacked running water, proper ventilation, inside toilets, baths, and electricity. In one of the worst cases, settlement workers found that one "sanitary closet" and one water hydrant served the needs of eight families. *Jacales* of tin, sheet iron, and barrel stays emerged along Buffalo Bayou. Houses of prostitution and beer saloons sprang up in several neighborhoods. Streets were full of potholes and garbage, and sidewalks were virtually non-existent. Some streets were so

---

[12] The Settlement Association blamed the delay on the city. The Community Chest, which provided much of the settlement's funding, encouraged the curtailing of all new activities during the war. That the city chose to regard the relocation of Bethlehem as a "new activity" suggests that assisting the African-American community was not a top priority. A new settlement for African Americans, Hester House, in the Fifth Ward, was not established until the late 1940s. Tsanoff, *Neighborhood Doorways*, 9–12; 29–30; *Social Survey*, 1 (Apr., 1918), 5, Records of the Houston Social Service Bureau, Box, Folder 4, HMRC.

narrow that cars and wagons could scarcely pass.[13]

The Rusk School playground was so muddy that officials dumped loads of shell on the ground. This led to injuries among the children who were barefoot or had worn-out shoes. Across the settlement were railroads and freight depots with all their hazards to the children's well-being. Nearby was the slum district known as *El Alacrán* because of the numerous scorpions from the nearby bayou. Also in the vicinity was "Schrimpf Alley," a notorious side street known for the extreme poverty of its residents and the high crime rates. Settlement workers did not blame the Mexican residents for the conditions they encountered; rather, they blamed the problem on an insensitive city government. As one worker noted: "Those who enter our gates will live as we permit them to live."[14]

Rusk workers tried to understand the community they served. They combed the entire four-square-mile area, interviewing residents, filling out surveys, and gathering statistical data for their new Bureau of Information. They collected data on the number of local businesses, schools, churches, and beer saloons; street, utility, and sewer conditions; number of households and children; types of available recreation and amusement; employment opportunities and jobs held by residents; and rate of unemployment. They surveyed the community annually, published the data, and shared it with the mayor's office, local charities, and welfare agencies.[15]

---

[13] Tsanoff, *Neighborhood Doorways*, 1–2, 14–18; *Social Service* (1914), 12, Records of the Houston Social Service Bureau, Box 1, Folder 1, HMRC.

[14] "What is the Houston Social Service Bureau?," 15; "Thirty Years of Houston Social Work; An Interview with Bertha Wolf," *Houston Review*, 4 (Winter, 1981), 89–104; De Leon, *Ethnicity in the Sunbelt*, 27; Tsanoff, *Neighborhood Doorways*, 17.

[15] Rusk acted as the catalyst for the creation of Houston's first school of social work, the Texas School of Civics and Philanthropy. Founded in 1916, its students frequently served as volunteers in local settlement work. Beginning in the 1940s, Rusk, in cooperation with the local branch of the Social Security Agency, also began training Central and South American social workers. Houston Social Service Foundation, "Announcements, 1916–1917," *Texas School of Civics and Philanthropy*, 1 (Oct., 1916), 1–11, Records of the Houston Social Service Bureau, Box 1 Folder 6, HMRC; *Annual Report of United Charities* (1912), 1–36, Records of the Houston Social Service Bureau, Box 1, Folder 1, HMRC.

Rusk served as a mediator and cultural interpreter between the Mexicano community and the larger society particularly in the area of social services. Settlement workers sought to access resources to serve the Mexican community at the same time that they pursued a cultural goal, to introduce the Mexican immigrant to the political process as it functioned in Texas. Local government ignored the predominantly Mexican area of the city, so the settlement workers, together with the more influential members of the Mexicano community, pressured officials to release funds for needed projects involving new sewers, traffic signals, or paved streets. Most of the time, however, their petitions were unsuccessful and Rusk workers were forced to take matters into their own hands. For instance, when the city refused to provide needed sanitation, despite the rising disease rates in the ward, Rusk organized local residents into clean-up crews to collect the accumulated garbage.[16]

In 1936, when the city government refused to install a traffic light despite claims by settlement workers that a nearby intersection was extraordinarily dangerous to children, the settlement acquired "evidence" to support their petition. In true progressive fashion, Rusk workers counted the number of cars that passed each hour for a full day. They reported an hourly rate of between eight hundred to one thousand, and pointed out that children dodged approximately twelve to thirteen cars per minute. Despite their detailed study the city failed to act. City officials claimed a lack of funds, and promised only to paint a notice warning drivers to slow down and watch for children. In the end, settlement workers had to provide children with poles that they extended into the intersection to help slow the traffic.[17]

The political commitment of the settlement workers varied. While they spoke out against conditions in the poorer wards of the city, and lobbied the city for more funding, they were not

---

[16] As early as 1914 the settlement house reported alarmingly high rates of typhoid, tuberculosis, smallpox, trachoma, and impetigo. Several cases of typhoid were reported on just one street where houses were constructed near dirty cesspools. *Social Service* (1914), 12, Records of the Houston Social Service Bureau, Box 1, Folder 1, HMRC.

[17] Tsanoff, *Neighborhood Doorways*, 17–18.

always willing to take a stand on political issues that impacted the Mexicano community. Some argued for child labor restrictions and better working conditions, while others defended temperance and prohibition, believing that without alcohol, most social ills would disappear. Few spoke out against segregation, however. They were highly cautious, refusing to jeopardize their funding by taking a stand against a popular albeit racist convention. In 1933, for instance, the Settlement Association shut down the new Magnolia Park Settlement for Mexicans after an angry mob protested its presence in the predominantly Anglo neighborhood.[18]

While the association claimed it closed Magnolia Park to protect their "Mexican neighbors" from further insult and violence, it was clear that they were bowing to pressure from the white community. Later that year, the association's attempt to create a settlement adjacent to Hawthorne School, this time in a predominantly Mexicano neighborhood, also failed. The school principal insisted on separate activities for the Anglo and Mexican children. When settlement workers agreed they found themselves unable to attract support among the Mexicano residents.[19]

Rusk workers never publicly advocated segregation. However, it is probable that they supported it in private. Some of the promotional literature of the association suggested that at least some of the workers regarded the Mexicans as culturally inferior. They celebrated the Mexicans' courage, diligence, and good humor, but were quick to point out the limitations their culture placed upon them. Mexicans were portrayed as a quaint people, victimized by their heritage. Association members seemed almost astonished when they turned out in large numbers to attend their educational programs.[20]

---

[18] The Magnolia Park Settlement (later renamed Neighborhood House) was founded in 1933. It was situated on the corner of 75th and Canal Streets until the city inspector closed the center as a health hazard in 1938. A new cottage was founded on the 5500 block of Canal Street, "just at the edge of the Mexican district," but in a predominantly white residential area, thus provoking the conflict. Tsanoff, *Neighborhood Doorways*, 27–29.

[19] Ibid., 26.

[20] One observation by a nursery-schoool teacher at Rusk illustrates this point.

During and after World War I, settlement workers sought to "Americanize" Mexicanos. The campaign intensified when the association discovered that of the 967 "foreigners" who applied for citizenship between 1902 and 1919, only eighteen were Mexican. Settlement workers blamed these low numbers on the proximity of Mexico and the immigrants' hopes of returning to their homeland, but they also blamed the U.S.-born, "who more often than not shows [the Mexicano] that they are unwelcome." The settlement concluded they could best help the immigrants by teaching them to "be Americans."[21]

These were the war years, when a person's loyalty and patriotism could be called into question, and the fear of subversion and bolshevism permeated the media, City Hall, and congressional hearings. Such suspicions and fears were often directed at Mexicans in Texas as a result of rumors of German intrigue as well as social banditry and revolutionary activities along the border.[22]

Settlement workers capitalized on the patriotic fervor of the times to reinforce their "americanizing" and service mission by pointing out that extending social services to the immigrant population engendered patriotic citizens. As one of them noted:

We must keep everybody in good health as far as possible, and that means well fed and well-clothed, sheltered and cared for. The reward is a robust, contented, united and efficient people, fit to carry on the war, or compete honorably with all rivals in times of peace.[23]

---

When commenting on her Mexican students she said, "We try to make good first-graders out of our young pupils. They are under considerable handicap because in their homes they speak Spanish mainly . . . The children are intelligent and responsive . . . [they] are very musical and have a fine sense of rhythm . . . They have names like Concepción, Guadalupe, and Juan; but they are good Americans all." Elwood Street, "Little Journeys to the Homes of Great War-time Services," Text of interview aired by KPRC, Apr. 15, 1944, Papers of Franklin I. Harbach, Box 1, Folder 2, HMRC.

[21] "What is the Houston Social Service Bureau?," 16.

[22] See the following for discussions on the experiences of Mexicans during the war period: David Montejano, *Anglos and Mexicans in the Making of Texas, 1836–1986* (Austin: University of Texas Press, 1987); Emilio Zamora, *The World of the Mexican Worker in Texas* (College Station: Texas A&M University Press, 1993).

[23] *Social Survey*, 1 (May, 1918), 4, Records of the Houston Social Service Bureau, Box 1, Folder 4, HMRC.

With such sound logic, city funding increased in the postwar years.

The most obvious way to Americanize the Mexicanos was to teach them English especially since numerous Second Ward residents who had been born and raised in Houston did not yet speak the language. English classes became the settlement's priority. Night classes for adult males met three times a week for six months each year to study grammar and practice conversational skills. Between fifty and one hundred students usually attended these classes. An overjoyed settlement worker underscored the significance of the impressive attendance: "When you consider that of the Mexicans enrolled, 53 were grown men who had spent the day in the railroad shops or yards, or in other forms of hard manual labor, you can better understand the eagerness and earnestness which these people are manifesting in their study of our language." When the classes stopped for the summer months the adult students met at least once a week to practice what they had learned over the course of the year. These practice sessions were also well attended.[24]

Women had their own separate English classes in the afternoons which focused on basic vocabulary related to their day-to-day lives as homemakers. They learned the names of food, clothing, and furniture, how to ask questions in stores, and how to converse with their children's teachers. Settlement workers obviously sought to socialize Mexican women into roles as wives and mothers. This did not mean that the settlement was inattentive to women working outside the home. They realized that economic necessity required many women to work, and sought to accommodate them with English classes and recreational activities in the evenings. Settlement workers clearly understood that an Americanization program would be successful if it targeted women, the principal transmitters of cultural values in the community.[25]

---

[24] *The Community: A Review of Philanthropic Thought and Effort* (Houston: Houston Social Service Foundation, May, 1919), 4.

[25] "What is the Houston Social Service Bureau?," 16. For a discussion of women's roles in the Americanization campaigns, see: George Sanchez, "'Go After the Women': Americanization and the Mexican Immigrant Woman, 1915–1929," Working Paper Series No. 6 (Stanford: Stanford Center for Chicano Research, 1984).

The Americanization classes evolved into citizenship courses that involved instruction on history and government, and the daily routine of reciting the Pledge of Allegiance. To entice more students, Rusk Settlement added a social hour with singing as well as guitar and mandolin playing after the evening classes. During the 1920s, as more local churches provided volunteers, Bible classes were also instituted.[26]

Children were the easiest to Americanize. Although still segregated, the public schools were already socializing the students. The settlement house simply extended the Americanization efforts into the after-school hours. This involved the establishment of local chapters of the Boy Scouts, Girl Scouts, Camp Fire Girls, and assorted other clubs such as the Bluebirds, the Rusky Roses, and the Roseland Steppers. Recognizing the importance of recreation in instilling patriotic ideals, they also sponsored Halloween and Christmas parties, Easter egg hunts, parties and dances, musical concerts, camp fire sing-alongs, hikes, and various sports activities. Ironically, many of these Americanizing activities were segregated, prohibiting Mexican children from having important socializing contact with their Anglo-American peers.

The Great Depression dampened the spirits of the Americanization campaign as the settlement workers directed their attention to relief efforts. From 1930 to 1932, Rusk Settlement served as a repatriation center, a gathering place for Mexicanos awaiting transportation to Mexico. Although the city proposed the plan, the more established Mexican Americans and the Mexican Consulate financed and coordinated repatriation efforts. An estimated two thousand people were repatriated to Mexico in the early Depression years. In 1933, when the Mexican community was unable to continue underwriting the campaign, the Settlement Association and the city's unemployment-relief organizations negotiated the transportation of more than a hundred destitute families.[27]

---

[26] *Social Survey*, 1 (May, 1918), 1.

[27] Representatives from various Mexican American organizations formed the "Comité Pro-Repatriación" which sponsored fund-raising activities for the necessary funds. These efforts revealed a growing rift within the Mexicano community,

Settlement workers did not consider repatriation to be inconsistent with their social service and Americanizing goals because they believed that this was a viable solution to increasingly distressing conditions. Few other alternatives existed. The City of Houston refused to provide work relief for indigent Mexicans, and non-citizens were barred from New Deal projects. Mexicanos turned to Rusk Settlement, *mutualista* organizations, and other community institutions for assistance. The numbers, however, were more than these benefactors could handle. In previous years, the settlement had acted as an unofficial referral service for jobs in construction and domestic service, but now few employers were hiring. Throughout the 1930s, the settlement sponsored Mexican fiestas and other fund-raising activities to supplement city moneys. They also secured donations of food and milk from local businesses, but this was not enough to ease the hunger or ameliorate the condition of poverty. Settlement workers often served children their only meal of the day, typically a slice of bread and molasses in the mid-afternoon. They saw repatriation, therefore, as a means of easing the pressure on the community.[28]

Settlement workers also held that the decision to emigrate was voluntary, no family or individual was to be returned to Mexico "who did not volunteer to go." Settlement records do not indicate if any type of coercion was used to convince individuals and families to "volunteer." Repatriation nevertheless had dire consequences. It uprooted individuals and families that had established long residence and citizenship in the United States. Many of them found life in Mexico financially difficult while the young and acculturated had problems adjusting to their new surroundings. Predictably, an undetermined number returned to the Second Ward after the Depression.[29]

During the 1940s, Rusk Settlement tried to involve local residents in homefront activities by encouraging them to support Red

---

between the native and the foreign-born. The Mexican consulate also arranged the transportation of hundreds of families across the border. De Leon, *Ethnicity in the Sunbelt*, 47–48; Tsanoff, *Neighborhood Doorways*, 25–26.

[28] Tsanoff, *Neighborhood Doorways*, 26.

[29] Ibid., 26.

Cross activities, purchase war stamps, observe rationing, plant "victory gardens," and cooperate with the Federal Canning Project. Settlement workers also provided important services to men and women working in wartime industries. For instance, they increased the nursery-school hours and expanded their athletic program. If the Mexicans were proving their loyalty to the United States by assisting the war effort—overseas and at home—the least the settlement could do was to accommodate them.[30]

Ironically, while Rusk Settlement promoted Americanization, it also functioned as a center of *Mexicanización.* The Rusk library contained books and periodicals in Spanish donated by the Mexican consul. Local residents could also attend concerts, lectures, and plays in Spanish at the Rusk school auditorium. Various Mexican clubs, organizations, and mutualistas held their meetings at the settlement and promoted a sense of *Mexicanidad* with activities such as the celebration of patriotic Mexican holidays. A local chapter of *La Cruz Azul* (Blue Cross), sponsored by the Mexican government, supplemented the charitable assistance the settlement provided to local residents.[31]

Notwithstanding the settlement's efforts, most first-generation immigrants from Mexico—like their counterparts from countless other countries—resisted acculturation. Many who arrived during and after the Mexican Revolution, particularly members of the middle class, considered themselves exiles rather than immigrants, and they hoped to eventually return to their homeland once conditions settled. If poorer Mexicanos attended English and civics classes, it was not because they were patriotic but because they sought the practical benefits that such classes offered them; fluency in English improved their chances of success. In the meantime, they benefited from a network that offered them vital support and information, as well as a familiar sense of cultural

---

[30] Tsanoff, *Neighborhood Doorways,* 62–63. Mexicans frequently encountered discrimination in war-time industries, and were relegated laboring jobs if they were hired at all. Local residents, including members of LULAC Council 60, worked with the Fair Employment Practice Committee to correct these inequalities. De Leon, *Ethnicity in the Sunbelt,* 91.

[31] *The Social Service Bureau* (1921), 24, Records of the Houston Social Service Bureau, Box 1, Folder 1, HMRC.

identity and belonging in an often hostile environment. This network included Spanish-language newspapers, restaurants, theaters, grocery stores, tailor shops, civic and social clubs, political organizations, churches, and private schools. Mexicanos clearly sought to assimilate economically while maintaining cultural boundaries to survive as a community.[32]

Rusk Settlement ultimately failed in its mission to "Americanize" Second Ward residents. The goal of Americanization—integration—was impossible to realize. All around them were reminders that society allowed only limited participation in the form of segregated schools and restaurants, unequal wages, and low-skilled jobs. The city's reluctance to provide basic services and improvements isolated them further. Moreover, Mexicans were not even represented in the settlement staff. While a few such as Félix Tijerina, Mary Reyna, and Dr. John J. Ruiz served on an advisory board, Mexican Americans did not join the staff until the 1950s. Americanization, therefore, was less a promise of equal opportunity than an attempt to ease Anglo anxieties over the threatening "alien" in their midst. The promotional literature of the Settlement Association, which emphasized the Mexicans' eagerness to learn English, probably did ease some of the collective anxiety. However, census figures and news reports were a constant reminder to the Anglo community that Mexicans were migrating to their city in increasingly larger numbers. There would always be new people who needed Americanization.

The Mexicano community did, of course, assimilate culturally. The Americanization campaign as well as pressures from the public schools, the entertainment media, and some Mexican organizations such as LULAC contributed to this change. Mexicanos, however, were not passive individuals who simply received pressure intended to mold them into Americans. Like other immigrants, they consciously and deliberately acculturated in order to survive and even exploit their new surroundings. This involved learning English, institutional protocols, and strategies of negotiating in a

---

[32] Milton Gordon discusses the models of assimilation elaborated in sociological literature on the basis of the Euro-American immigrant experience. *Assimilation in American Life* (New York: Oxford University Press, 1964).

racially charged political environment. Mexicanos also lived in a Mexican world that was of their own making. They thus also maintained a distinctive Mexican community partly characterized by a Spanish language, patriotic holiday celebrations, and an abiding emotional attachment to Mexico. This ethnic world stood as a reminder that the pressures to resist Americanization were formidable.

The Houston Settlement Association also failed as a truly progressive voice in the community. While Rusk Settlement strove to represent the ideals of the larger settlement movement and of the Progressive era, Houston was not Chicago or New York and strategies that presumably worked in the urban Northeast did not work in Texas. While Rusk strove to represent the ideals of the larger settlement movement and of the Progressive era, it could never effectively counter the racism of the larger Texas society that prevented Mexicanos from becoming full participants. Rusk Settlement, however, must be appreciated within its proper context. Like all such settlements, it was primarily an attempt to assist immigrant communities in adjusting to their new homes. Settlement workers spoke in grandiose terms about changing the hostile environment and the culture of the immigrants. Their accomplishments were less dramatic, although they provided important services that often made the immigrants' adjustment process bearable and sometimes meaningful.

# Part Three:
# Biography and Literature

Yolanda Romero makes an important contribution to the neglected area of Mexican women biographies. She sketches the life of Trini Gáamez, a labor and community activist from Hereford, a rural community in the Texas Panhandle region. Her work on behalf of Texas Rural Legal Aid, the Texas Farm Workers' Union, and the Southwest Voter Registration and Education Project brings to mind other women who labored bravely in the Mexican social movement of the twentieth century but still await the attention of historians.[1]

Romero's work is also community history primarily because her town and region serve as the immediate context for Gámez's story. She makes an important contribution here as well, especially since historians have neglected Mexican communities from the Panhandle region. In examining this context, Romero focuses on racial domination and political repression in the lives of Panhandle residents in part to explain the obstacles that Gámez had to overcome in her personal as well as in her public life.

Félix Almaráz discusses the writings of Carlos E. Castañeda, the first Mexican American to achieve great success as a professional historian in Texas. Born in Tamaulipas, Mexico, and raised

---

[1] Aside from the papers presented at the conference, the following studies include biographical accounts of Mexican American women from Texas: Emilio Zamora and Roberto Calderón, "Manuela Solís Sager and Emma Tenayuca; A Tribute," In *Chicana Voices: Intersections of Class, Race, and Gender*, Proceedings of

on the Matamoros/Brownsville border, Castañeda was a prolific borderlander as well as an important civil rights leader in the Mexican community of the 1930s, 1940s, and 1950s. Almaráz who is himself an accomplished borderlands historian has become Castañeda's biographer with countless articles on his life and scholarly work. Here, he assesses Castañeda's career as a historian, focusing on how his critics treated him.

One of Almaráz's concerns is to defend Castañeda from his detractors. He points out that much of the criticism leveled against Castañeda was unfair and suggests that his critics may have been irked by Castañeda's occasional idiosyncratic behavior, that is, his public display of honors from the Catholic Church. This is a provocative suggestion that points to anti-Catholic and possibly anti-Mexican prejudice operating in Castañeda's life. Almaráz encourages this thought further by noting that despite his scholarly successes, the University of Texas at Austin did not appoint Castañeda to a faculty position until he had rendered government service at the home front during World War II. Almaráz also levels a suggestive critique against Chicano scholars, particularly Gilberto M. Hinojosa and Mario T. García, when he points out that Castañeda was more productive than any of his current counterparts. If Castañeda is a "giant among Hispanic scholars," has the National Association for Chicano and Chicana studies been derelict in its failure to honor him posthumously as one of its most distinguished representatives? Is it because Castañeda failed to "champion the human dignity of Indian cultures" as Almaráz surmised?

Ramón Saldívar, a literary theorist, analyzes the work of Américo Paredes, long recognized for his *With His Pistol in His Hand.* Here, Saldívar studies a novel Paredes wrote in the late 1930s and published in the 1990s, circumstances that allow our contributor to comment on the author's broadly relevant commentary. The novel, *George Washington Gómez,* is set in the context

---

the National Association for Chicano Studies (eds.), Teresa Córdova, et al. (Austin: Center for Mexican American Studies, University of Texas at Austin, 1986); Irene Ledesma, "Unlikely Strikers: Mexican American Women in Strike Activity in Texas, 1919–1974" (Ph.D. diss., Ohio State University, 1992); Martha Cotera, "Of Del Rio," Paper presented at the Texas State Historical Association Conference, Austin, Texas, 1995.

of the San Diego Revolt, addressed previously in this collection by Rodolfo Rocha.

Utilizing a cultural studies approach, Saldívar points to what he calls the "borderlands of culture" which Washington Gómez's family faced in the form of cultural and social change in the South Texas border region. Like García's Houston residents, these border Mexicans faced Americanization, which Paredes partly addresses in the process of naming. The naming of a child is laden with questions of politics, culture, and identity, he suggests; this is the "Mexican and American" dilemma which many members of La Raza have confronted. Names, and thus identity, fall within what Saldívar calls "a particular discursive history." Paredes's subject, George Washington Gómez, and possibly Paredes himself, struggle to define themselves and their place in a bifurcated society—Mexican and American.

# Trini Gámez, The Texas Farm Workers, and Mexican American Community Empowerment:

*Toil and Trouble on the Texas South Plains*

Yolanda Romero*

The majority of the Mexican-origin population of the South Plains region came from Mexico and South Texas as migrant agricultural laborers between 1900 and 1930. Entire families traveled together, following the same route season after season. Relatives joined the migrating families and shared in the expenses as the need for additional labor increased. With time, increasing numbers decided to settle permanently, giving rise to a growing number of U.S.-born Mexicans in the region. Some established businesses to provide services for the expanding Mexican population. When these initial migration waves populated the Texas Panhandle, *barrios* in towns such as Hereford began to develop. Although Anglos often continued to perceive the new settlers as transients, these barrios became well-established communities.[1]

---

* Yolanda Romero received her Ph.D. from Texas Tech University and teaches U.S. and Mexican American history at North Lake College in Irving. She is the first Mexican American woman to receive a Ph.D. in history from a Texas institution. Dr. Romero is currently preparing her dissertation for publication and also conducting a study of Tejanos in the Vietnam war.

[1] Trini Gámez, interview, July 28, 1989, Southwest Collection (Texas Tech

Permanency did not translate into social integration for the Mexican residents of Hereford. Like other area communities of predominantly Mexican agricultural laborers, Mexicans from Hereford faced continuing social discrimination in the work place, schools, and businesses. This reinforced their bottom position in the socio-economy. With the advent of the Chicano civil rights movement of the 1960s, however, Mexicans began to challenge their minority condition, resulting in important events and changes that were momentous by local standards and reflective of wider social and political trends. Homegrown activists emerging during this period provide a vantage point from which to recover and assess these local developments. One such activist was Trinidad (Trini) Gámez.[2]

Trini had barely turned eighteen when she eloped with Refugio in 1946 and ventured into Hereford in search of work. They joined a migrant labor force that was already playing a vital role in the development of the ranching and farming economy in the area. The size of this mobile work force varied depending on the time of year. The San Jose labor camp, a nearby government-sponsored migrant housing facility, for instance, processed around thirty thousand persons during the cotton picking seasons of the 1950s. The labor camp guaranteed Anglo ranchers and farmers a large and ready supply of exploitable workers. Although employers throughout Texas generally embraced popular anti-Mexican prejudices, they welcomed migrant workers as highly regulated, low-wage labor. Other Anglos who may not have benefited directly from such an arrangement were apt to practice segregation against migrant families settling in Hereford.[3]

Trini's family commuted from San Antonio, and in 1948 they

---

University, Lubbock, Tex.). This and other interviews cited throughout were conducted by the author. Copies of all taped interviews have been deposited in the Southwest Collection. The Texas Panhandle is located in the Northwest Texas portion of the Great Plains. The Panhandle community of Hereford is in southeast Deaf Smith County.

[2] Unless otherwise noted, Trini's biographical information is based on the Gámez, interview, July 28, 1989.

[3] See the following recent studies for examinations of Mexican labor exploitation and social segregation in Texas: David Montejano, *Anglos and Mexicans in the*

decided to settle in a segregated Hereford neighborhood. They continued working long hours for low pay as cotton pickers in the area and on the migrant trail. Adding insult to injury, Anglos in town did not welcome them. Trini remembers signs in restaurant windows and on rental property that announced "no Mexicans allowed" and "whites only." As demoralizing as these problems were, some residents like Trini became indignant enough to assume a civil rights leadership position in Hereford. Her story illustrates both an individual's determined sense of justice and a community's capacity for survival and assertiveness.

Trini was born in a rural community in Karnes County, Texas, on May 1, 1929. Two important experiences associated with Mexico stand out in her family's history. Her great grandfather, Juan Antonio Alvarez, had fought at the famous 1862 battle of Puebla, Mexico, against invading French forces. Next to this somewhat lustrous piece of memory was the story of Trini's parents coming to Texas from Guanajuato where her mother's affluent family lost everything during the Mexican Revolution of 1910. Trini's personal treasured remembrance, on the other hand, was her widowed grandmother, Guadalupe Alvarez Sanchez. She accompanied the family to Texas and became the most important influence in Trini's life.

Grandmother Sanchez brought and shared something more valuable than material wealth—her knowledge and wisdom. Although not a well-educated woman, she promoted the value of education in her family and taught Trini and her siblings to read and write before they reached school age. She rounded off their education by teaching them to play the violin and the mandolin. As important as this educational experience was, Trini maintains that her grandmother's most enduring lesson was the need to remain confident and even proud, qualities that she used to define and give meaning to her life in northwest Texas.

Trini dropped out of the tenth grade when she married, and began working as a migrant farm worker. She spoke English well,

*Making of Texas, 1836–1986* (Austin: University of Texas Press, 1987); Emilio Zamora, *The World of the Mexican Worker in Texas* (College Station: Texas A&M University Press, 1993).

however, and was outspoken. She invariably became a spokesper-
son and an interpreter for the Mexican people in Hereford. Trini
recalled her initiation as an activist immediately upon arriving at
Hereford. She encountered a Mexican farm worker who had
been paid with an unsigned check. Trini took the worker's com-
plaint to a friendly Anglo lawyer who helped her obtain the employer's signature.

In 1955, seven years after the birth of her first child, Trini
and her husband left the migrant work force and continued
working in the cotton fields around Hereford. Like Trini, most
Mexican women worked on farms. Chores often varied on the
migrant trail depending on the woman's life cycle. A typical day
for married women or female heads of household began at four
in the morning with tortilla-making for breakfast and lunch-pack-
ing for the laboring family. They often had to use their ingenuity
to cook meals because of inadequate facilities. Sometimes they
had to build fires or use single kerosene burners. After a day of
work in the fields, a trip to the grocery store was necessary to pre-
pare supper. Without refrigerators, women used coolers to store
food. They rarely bought meat, cooked dinner late at night, and
cleaned the kitchen or fireplace before going to bed. Women
also washed and sewed late at night or on days when there was no
work.[4]

Children also worked in the fields to supplement the family
income. Although their ages varied, parents typically expected
girls to work by the time they were twelve. Unless an older woman
stayed home to care for the children, all of them went to the
fields. Moreover, migrant families often expected boys and girls
who knew English to represent them in their dealings with the
growers.

Trini elected to remain at home as her family grew and her
child-rearing responsibilities increased. This did not deter her
from participating in public life. In fact, she became motivated to
participate in school activities to insure that her children received
a good education. Trini joined the Parent Teacher Association

---

[4] Gámez, interview, July 28, 1989; Catarina García Ovalle, interview, July 28, 1988; Connie Ynostrosa Veanueva, interview, June 17, 1990.

(PTA) when her children reached school age. She eventually became PTA vice-president and a volunteer room mother. As such, Trini was an exception in her community. She was the first Mexican woman to participate in such school activities. Other mothers did not because they were unable to speak English or feared a racist reception from school officials. Also, Trini lamented, many husbands refused to allow their wives to attend PTA meetings.[5]

Trini continued to participate in public school activities and made sure that all nine of her children graduated and received some college training. One of the conclusions she drew from this experience was that the school environment was somewhat different from the larger community. She claims, for instance, that Anglo mothers and teachers did not discriminate against her while she worked as a volunteer. Partly because of this, Trini was attracted to an educational career. In 1968 Trini began work as a bilingual aide making one hundred dollars a month. Soon thereafter, Trini realized more than ever the "seriousness of the Mexican American situation."

Trini's newfound awareness occurred within the context of the Mexican American civil rights movement that developed during the 1960s and 1970s. The decade of the 1960s was especially important to her political development as she observed Mexican Americans throughout the United States as well as in the Panhandle area increase their involvement in politics and labor organizing. In 1960, for example, Mexican Americans in Hereford organized "Viva Kennedy" Clubs in support of John Kennedy's presidential bid and encouraged further political participation in the region. Well-established groups such as the League of United Latin American Citizens (LULAC) and the American G.I. Forum also began to make forays into previously unorganized areas such as the Panhandle and inspired further self-organization.[6]

---

[5] Gámez, interview, July 28, 1989; Cecilia Gámez Garza, interview, Aug. 8, 1989.

[6] For histories that address the recent Mexican American experience, see: Arnoldo De León, *Mexican Americans in Texas; A Brief History* (Arlington Heights, Ill.: Harlan Davidson, 1993); Juan Gómez–Quiñones, *Chicano Politics: Reality and Promise, 1940–1990* (Albuquerque: University of New Mexico Press, 1990); Montejano, *Anglos and Mexicans in the Making of Texas.*

The AFL-CIO also made important contributions by conducting publicized investigations of discrimination against Mexican workers. The 1967 strike by the Amarillo AFL-CIO Packinghouse Workers, Local 1202, was especially important in drawing attention to the issues of discrimination and organizing among Mexican workers. The strikers included two hundred Mexican Americans and fifteen African Americans. The strike took on a racial tone in part because employers hired only Anglos as supervisors and foremen. Management's recalcitrance during negotiations also suggested anti-minority views. The strike failed when the company replaced the strikers with scab workers from Dallas and Juárez, Mexico. Despite the defeat, the unionists made an important contribution in energizing a broadly defined social movement in the Mexican American community of the Panhandle.[7]

Other Mexican American organizations such as the Brown Berets, Raza Unida Party, and Catholic Church groups joined the political community of the Panhandle. These groups surfaced in 1971 as the Chicano Movement intensified political activity and expanded into previously isolated areas. Although there were important ideological differences among such groups, their combined efforts increased the political participation of Mexican Americans and accentuated a popular sense of self-determination.[8]

Trini developed politically and intellectually in the midst of these profound political changes in her community. Through her job as a bilingual aide, Trini received the opportunity to go to school. At the age of forty she obtained a high school equivalency degree and entered South Plains Junior College. She graduated in 1974 with an Associates degree and began working towards a teaching degree at West Texas State, an undertaking Trini did

---

[7] Lubbock *Avalanche Journal,* June 6, 1966, Mar. 15, 1967; Henry Muñoz to H. S. Hank Brown, Oct. 16, 1967, Texas AFL-CIO, Mexican American Affairs Records, 1953–1971, Special Collections (University of Texas at Arlington, Arlington, Tex.).

[8] Lubbock *Avalanche Journal,* June 6, 1966. See the following, for histories of these and other Mexican American groups: Carl Allsup, *The American G.I. Forum; Origins and Evolution* (Austin: University of Texas Press, 1982); Jay P. Dolan and Gilberto M. Hinojosa, *Mexican Americans and the Catholic Church, 1900–1965* (Notre Dame: University of Notre Dame Press, 1994); Ignacio M. García, *United We Win;*

not complete. All along, she continued to work as an aide and to participate in local politics. She decided to run for political office soon after obtaining her Associates degree. Although Trini received only seventy-four votes on her first try for a position on the school board, she ran again on several other occasions. She may not have succeeded in getting elected, but her campaigns gave her important organizing experience and established her presence as an important political voice in her community.

Trini decided to expand her political involvement in 1975 when she attended a Texas State Teachers Association (TSTA) meeting and was inspired to become a union organizer. Upon returning to Hereford she, along with a TSTA assistant from Austin, decided to call an organizing meeting among teachers and aides. Her bold action, however, drew opposition. The school superintendent attended the meeting and argued against the union. This intimidated the teachers and aides to the point that no one would speak out. After this failed effort, Trini decided to quit and look for a better-paying job. After short stints at a restaurant and the Community Action Student Health Program, Trini joined Texas Rural Legal Aid (TRLA) in December 1978. Her work as a TRLA paralegal brought her full circle to her working origins when she was assigned to work with migrant workers in their self-organizing efforts.

Prior to her work with the local TRLA, however, Trini began yet another important political activity that contributed to her development. This involved voter education and registration work in association with the Southwest Voter Registration Education Project (SVREP). The San Antonio-based SVREP was instrumental in bringing local groups from throughout the

---

The Rise and Fall of La Raza Unida Party (Tucson: Mexican American Studies and Research Center, University of Arizona Press, 1989); Cynthia E. Orozco, "The Origins of the League of United Latin American Citizens (LULAC) and the Mexican American Civil Rights Movement in Texas with an Analysis of Women's Political Participation in a Gendered Context, 1910–1929" (Ph.D. diss., University of Texas at Austin, 1993); Guadalupe San Miguel, "Let All of Them Take Heed: Mexican Americans and the Campaign for Educational Equality in Texas, 1910–1981 (Austin: University of Texas Press, 1987); David Sanchez, Expedition through Aztlán (La Puente Calif.: Perspectiva Press, 1978).

Southwest to improve Mexican American political participation. The SVREP also made possible the election of Mexican American candidates to public offices in places such as Hereford by making successful redistricting challenges.[9]

Political activists like Trini drew immediate benefit from SVREP activities. For instance, she had the opportunity to meet and discuss important political issues with state legislators such as Froy Salinas and other activists like Bidal Aguero, owner and editor of Lubbock's *El Editor*. These SVREP-sponsored meetings encouraged Trini to embrace the strategy of registering Mexican American voters and encouraging others to run for political office. Trini and other participants also came to understand how the practice of gerrymandering Hereford residents denied Mexican Americans equal representation in local offices.

This was especially evident in the manner in which one precinct line had been drawn to split in half the neighborhood that grew out of the San Jose labor camp. Most of the Mexican American population lived in the camp; assigning voters in the community to two different precincts meant that its combined voting strength was diluted and Mexican American candidates were effectively denied a chance to get elected. In 1977, three of Trini's relatives filed suit against the county to redraw its precinct lines and to eliminate at-large elections for the city commission and school board. The suit eventually forced Hereford to redraw its precinct lines in a more equitable manner, making it possible for Mexican Americans to finally get elected.[10]

Trini saw the arrival of the TRLA as an opportunity to pursue another strategy that could bring immediate benefits to the most impoverished of the Hereford Mexican American population. She was especially motivated to assist in providing legal services to farm workers because of a gnawing concern that in her youth she

---

[9] Louis Dubose, "Hispanic Power in the Panhandle," *Texas Observer*, Jan. 15, 1988, pp. 11–15. The following works address the work of the SVREP in Texas: David V. Cruz, "Takeover in Texas," *Nuestro*, 2 (July, 1978), 11–12; Gómez-Quiñones, *Chicano Politics; Reality and Promise, 1940–1990*, pp. 110–111, 164–167; Montejano, *Anglos and Mexicans in the Making of Texas*, 290–292, 296–297.

[10] Louis Dubose, "Hispanic Power in the Panhandle," Lubbock *Avalanche Journal*, Apr. 15, 1992.

had aided Anglo farmers control farm workers. In 1951, for instance, a powerful farmer paid his workers' poll tax so they would vote for his candidate. Trini was his interpreter.[11]

Her association with the TRLA gave Trini an opportunity to join in another important legal challenge. In this instance, Cecilia Gámez Garza, Trini's daughter, and several other Mexican American residents sued Deaf Smith County for discriminatory hiring practices. The TRLA case involved sixty-four Mexican Americans who proved they had been unfairly denied county employment. In 1985 Judge Mary Lou Robinson of the Federal District Court in Amarillo ordered the Deaf Smith County personnel department to revise its hiring practices. The county also agreed to set up the "Deaf Smith Class Settlement Fund" of $60,000.00 for the plaintiffs, $8,500 to go to Cecilia, and $56,500 to Texas Rural Legal Aid. Cecilia maintains that she never would have sued without Trini's encouragement and support.[12]

Trini was also instrumental in assisting organizing efforts among farm workers in the Hereford area beginning in the late 1970s. The United Farm Workers Organizing Committee (UFWOC) had previously sent organizers to Texas. They confined their work to South Texas until the Texas leadership broke with the UFWOC, established the independent Texas Farm Workers Union (TFWU), and assigned an organizer, Jesús Moya, to the Hereford area. Moya set up the TFWU organizing headquarters outside Hereford, in an addition alongside the Catholic church in the San Jose labor camp. The union headquarters occupied one small room; it contained a desk, two folding tables, chairs, a water cooler, and a telephone. Trini was assigned by the TRLA to assist the TFWU's organizing campaigns in Hereford, Dimmitt, Plainview, Hale Center, and other small communities in the area. This was eventful. No other labor organization had waged such a systematic organizing effort among Mexican farm workers in the

---

[11] Rolando Ríos, interview, July 10, 1985; S. T. Rendón, interview, July 11, 1985; Lisa Rámos, interview, July 26, 1985; Gilbert Herrera, interview, July 10, 1985; *El Editor* (Lubbock), Oct. 12, 1977; *Lubbock Avalanche Journal*, July 17, 1985, Dec. 14, 1986.

[12] *Hereford Brand*, Jan. 27, 1985; Gámez Garza, interview, Aug. 8, 1989; Gámez, interview, July 28, 1989.

area, and the TRLA had designated her a key intermediary.[13]

TRLA lawyers and Trini provided legal advice to the union and non-union workers while on the picket lines as well as during non-strike periods. They discussed work contracts with the workers and advised them concerning accommodations, wages, transportation, and health care. They informed them of their right to file lawsuits against minimum-wage violations and other infractions. Trini also joined TRLA lawyers in assuring the workers that the agency was always available to assist them should other needs arise.[14]

In 1980 the TFWU paralyzed Howard-Gault growers at Hereford with a strike that lasted the entire six-week onion-picking season, and then moved on to the La Mantia packing sheds at Dimmitt in Castro County. At a time when the minimum wage was $3.10, Howard-Gault and La Mantia workers earned the equivalent of $1.85 an hour. Workers demanded the minimum wage as well as drinking water and toilets. During the strikes two farmers in Castro County sprayed picketers with anhydrous ammonia gas and another farmer exposed himself to female farm workers. Trini and Moya were almost arrested when they jumped a six-foot cyclone fence that surrounded one of the labor camps to hand out flyers to workers. The American G.I. Forum, the Meat Cutters Union, LULAC, and churches in the Panhandle as well as in Houston, Austin, and San Antonio aided the strikers. Sadly, the strikes resulted in a suit by an association of growers, packers, and shippers alleging picketing infractions by the TFWU and the TRLA. The federal court found on behalf of the plaintiffs.[15]

Despite this defeat, TFWU organizing activities encouraged other workers to challenge conditions in the farms with the assistance of the TRLA. In 1983, for instance, a group of young female workers from Hereford solicited the help of the TRLA in a

---

[13] Gámez, interview, July 28, 1989; Montejano, *Anglos and Mexicans in the Making of Texas*, 284–285.

[14] Gámez, interview, July 28, 1989.

[15] Jesús Moya, interview, July 25, 1989; *Howard Gault Co. v. Texas Rural Legal Aid* (1985), U.S. District Court, N.D. Texas, Amarillo Division; Rod Davis, "The Onion Revolt," *Texas Observer*, Nov. 20, 1987, pp. 2–8; Jan A. Grandolfo, "Migrant Housing Comes to Hereford," *Texas Observer*, Nov. 20, 1987, pp. 14–15.

dispute involving a packing-shed supervisor, Roberto Ruiz. The women complained that Ruiz had demanded that older women pick as well as pack the cucumbers being processed in the packing shed. The older women refused to follow Ruiz's instructions on the grounds that their contracts did not call for picking fruits and vegetables. Their daughters, in turn, decided to approach the TRLA for advice.[16]

Trini once again played an important role as an intermediary between the TRLA and Mexican American agricultural workers. She and a TRLA lawyer met with the women and agreed to lend their support. With this assurance, the women decided to protest Ruiz's refusal to negotiate. They protested with a public campaign that involved pickets and the distribution of flyers, leaflets, and posters. When Ruiz still refused to negotiate, the TRLA filed suit. In so doing, the strikers were setting another example of Mexican American defiance against inequality in Hereford. Approximately two hundred workers participated in the strike, most of them women. They were especially impressive with their elated expressions of solidarity which included much singing and a friendly spirit on the picket line and during meetings. The public support they garnered, as well as a favorable court decision, added to the cause for celebration. Trini captured the newfound pride evident among the workers: "al fin el trabajador habia tenido el valor de salir al frente y defender sus derechos." Workers finally had the courage to step forward and defend their rights.[17]

Trini also witnessed an emergent reaction to the Mexican American's assertiveness. This involved opposition against the TRLA for the support that it gave Mexican Americans in the Hereford area. Congressman Larry Combest, for example, asked for an investigation of the agency and reduced appropriations maintaining that the TRLA had instigated racial tension and violence and had undermined the "once bright future" of Hereford's economy. Congressman Phil Gramm joined in the appropriations assault while Wes Fisher, the mayor of Hereford and

---

[16] Gámez, interview, July 28, 1989; Gámez Garza, interview, Aug. 8, 1989.

[17] Gámez, interview, July 28, 1989.

owner of packing sheds, chimed in with the charge that "TRLA had pitted Mexicans against Anglos." Sheriff Travis McPherson of Deaf Smith County added that TRLA lawyers "were involved in communism," and "supplying these people with the information and they're telling them all about the Federal laws and everything."[18]

Support outside Hereford, however, galvanized in support of the TRLA. In 1986 when Combest introduced an amendment to eliminate an appropriation for three million dollars, TRLA supporters rose to the agency's defense. Mexican American state legislators such as Al Luna from Houston and Paul Moreno from El Paso expressed concern that the critics were castigating the TRLA for doing its job well. Moreno and Luna also warned that an attack on the TRLA would offend the Mexican American voter. Other statewide leaders such as Beatrice Cortes, representing Archbishop Patricio Flores of San Antonio, joined Moreno and Luna in defending the TRLA. Congressman Henry B. Gonzales added observations to the debate on the basis of two visits to Hereford. He stated that TRLA lawyers were heroes, adding, "God bless the Legal Services and the lawyers who have been willing to work at reduced fees and everything else in behalf of this cause." Partly as a result of this response, the U.S. Congress decided to continue TRLA appropriations.[19]

Despite Congressmen Gonzales's attempt to draw attention to the local nature of the farm workers' struggle in places such as Hereford, the focus on the TRLA overshadowed the important role that Mexican American workers and local activists like Trini played in the Mexican American civil rights movement. Still, Trini's life story provides a window through which to appreciate

[18] Geoffrey Rips, "The Possibility of Democracy," *Texas Observer*, Jan. 24, 1986, pp. 2–4; Dubose, "Hispanic Power in the Panhandle"; Louis Dubose, "Gramm Strikes Out," *Texas Observer*, Nov. 20, 1987, pp. 2–3; *Hereford Brand*, Mar. 6, Dec. 20, 1985; Odessa *American*, Dec. 24, 1985.

[19] Rips, "Political Intelligence," *Texas Observer*, Aug. 15, 1986, p. 16; Rips, "The Possibility of Democracy," *Texas Observer*, Jan. 24, 1986, pp. 2–4; Letter, Bidal Aguero to Congressman Kent Hance, Jan. 22, 1980, Bidal Aguero Papers, Southwest Collection (Texas Tech University, Lubbock, Tex.); *Amarillo Daily News*, Dec. 10, 26, 1985; Dallas *Times Herald*, Dec. 17, 1985; *Lubbock Avalanche Journal*, Feb. 21, 27, 1985, Mar. 10, July 18, 1986.

the resistive spirit of this movement, its victories and its defeats. Trini's firsthand experience in recent important historical events also provides a singular source of information that can assist us in reconstructing much of the unwritten record in Mexican American history. Lastly, Trini exemplifies the experience of inequality and the persevering and civic-minded nature of the Mexican American activist. She is sixty-four years old and continues to travel by herself in search of farm worker families in need of legal advice. She encourages the good fight for equal rights and intends to continue her work with Texas farm workers for as long as she is physically able.

# Carlos E. Castañeda:

## *The Historian and the Critics*

FÉLIX D. ALMARÁZ JR.*

For nearly three decades, from the 1930s to the 1960s, the name of Carlos Eduardo Castañeda stood prominently for his sound scholarship and inspirational teaching. Even now, no Mexican American historian has come close to duplicating or exceeding his record of twelve books and more than seventy-five articles. Likewise, no U.S. scholar of Mexican descent has received as many honors and distinctions. In recognition of his monumental seven-volume series, *Our Catholic Heritage in Texas, 1519–1936*, the Vatican honored him with the highly coveted knighthood in the Equestrian Order of the Holy Sepulchre of Jerusalem. Also, the Academy of American Franciscan History granted him the Junipero Serra Award of the Americas. At the peak of his career, the Government of Spain bestowed knighthood upon Castañeda in the Order of Isabel the Catholic. Among other accolades, Don Carlos garnered recognition from the Texas Philosophical Society, the Hispanic Society of America, La Academia de Historia de Guatemala, and El Centro de Estudios de Argentina. Compiling such an admirable record of achievement carried with it a burden

* Félix Almaráz is professor of history at the University of Texas at San Antonio. He is the former president of the Texas State Historical Association. His latest books are *Knight Without Armor: Carlos Eduardo Castañeda, 1896–1958* and (with José Cisneros) *Faces of the Borderlands*.

of joy and sorrow. Castañeda's evolving scholarship naturally attracted its share of praise and detraction, the content of which formed an variegated pattern of values and perspectives.[1]

Castañeda's life spanned six decades, from 1896 to 1958. Born in Camargo, Tamaulipas, Mexico, orphaned at the age of twelve, reared and educated by elder sisters in Matamoros and Brownsville, Castañeda enrolled at the University of Texas at Austin to study engineering. He completed most of his course work in three years. However, without the benefit of a scholarship the prospects of earning the degree appeared bleak. Through the intercession of a Paulist priest and chaplain of the Newman Club, Father J. Elliot Ross, Castañeda met the Texas historian, Eugene C. Barker, with whom he immediately nurtured a mentor-disciple relationship. To support himself through school and to assist his sisters in Brownsville, Castañeda, although he had not earned a degree, sought employment as a civil engineer. Field work in Hillsboro, Texas, and Tampico, Mexico, however, convinced Carlos that he was not meant to be an engineer. Changing goals, he resumed his close association with Barker, then emerging as one of Texas's premier historians, to fulfill all requirements for a degree in history and Spanish.[2]

With B.A. and M.A. degrees earned in 1921 and 1923, Carlos, now married and with a family, turned to teaching Spanish as an intermediate profession. He began his teaching career at Beaumont High School, continued at Brackenridge High School in San Antonio, and later at the prestigious College of William and Mary in southeastern Virginia. Just prior to his self-imposed exile in the Old Dominion, Castañeda researched and published his initial contributions to history, two essays on Franciscan evan-

---

[1] Félix D. Almaráz Jr., "Carlos Eduardo Castañeda, Mexican-Historian: The Formative Years, 1896–1927," in Norris Hundley Jr. (comp.), *The Chicano: Essays* (Santa Barbara: American Bibliographical Center/Clio Books, 1975), 57. In 1815, Ferdinand VII created the Order of Isabel la Católica to recognize the merits of "sons of Spain who have contributed to the prosperity and goodwill of the Americas." "Priest Earns Spanish Honor," *Santa Fe New Mexican*, June 17, 1992, Fray Angélico Chávez File (Archives of the Archdiocese of Santa Fe, Santa Fe, New Mexico).

[2] Almaráz, "Carlos Eduardo Castañeda, Mexican-American Historian: The Formative Years, 1896–1927," 57.

gelization in Texas and the borderlands. During his short stint as associate professor of Spanish, Castañeda also organized and directed two summer school institutes in Mexico City. Meanwhile, with Barker's encouragement, he translated nineteenth-century documents on Mexican Texas, two of which appeared in the *Southwestern Historical Quarterly:* "Statistical Report on Texas by Juan N. Almonte" and "A Trip to Texas in 1828." He prepared five other translated documents for publication in a hardback anthology, *The Mexican Side of the Texan Revolution.*[3]

In 1927, Castañeda assumed the curatorship of the Genaro García Collection at the University of Texas in Austin, a body of rare and specialized materials in Mexican history that gradually evolved into the Latin American Library. At this time Carlos affirmed his commitment to the school of Borderlands history pioneered by Herbert Eugene Bolton by studying under the tutelage of Professor Charles Wilson Hackett at the Austin campus. Through his friendship with Professor Barker, Carlos also established a highly valued association with the Texas Historical Commission of the Knights of Columbus. This contact resulted in a longtime friendship with its chairman, Rev. Dr. Paul J. Foik, C.S.C., of St. Edward's University. Coincidentally, the Texas Historical Commission had resolved to observe the 1936 centennial of Texas independence from Mexico with a comprehensive study of the Catholic Church's contributions to the history of the state. The working relationship that easily developed between Carlos and personnel of the Texas Historical Commission culminated in an invitation for him to write one of the seven volumes projected for the series.[4]

---

[3] Carlos E. Castañeda, "The Early Missionary Movement in Texas," *The Missionga*, 35 (Dec., 1921), 360–361; "Father Antonio Margil de Jesús," *The Missionga*, 37 (June, 1924), 163–164; (July, 1924), 197–199; *The Flat Hat* [campus newspaper, College of William and Mary], Oct. 3, Nov. 7, 1924, May 23, Sept. 25, 1925 (Archives of the College of William and Mary, Earl Gregg Swern Library, Williamsburg, Va.); C. E. Castañeda (trans.), "Statistical Report on Texas by Juan N. Almonte," *Southwestern Historical Quarterly*, 28 (Jan., 1925), 177–222; C. E. Castañeda, "A Trip to Texas in 1828: José María Sanchez," *Southwestern Historial Quarterly*, 29 (Apr., 1926), 249–288; Carlos E. Castañeda (trans.), *The Mexican Side of the Texan Revolution* (Dallas: P. L. Turner Co., 1928).

[4] Félix D. Almaráz Jr., "Carlos E. Castañeda's Rendezvous with a Library: The

Castañeda's search for original and seldom consulted documents took him to Mexico City in 1930, where he met the renowned Bolton and France V. Scholes of New Mexico. While working with these senior scholars, he discovered the long-lost history of Texas by Fray Juan Agustín de Morfi, Franciscan chaplain, chronicler, and traveling companion of El Caballero Teodoro de Croix, Commandant General of the Interior Provinces, during their inspection of communities in the northern borderlands in 1778–1779. The discovery and translation of this rare and valuable history, and its subsequent publication by the Quivira Society of Los Angeles, catapulted Castañeda into the ranks of borderlands and Latin American historians. Translating, editing, and interpreting Fray Morfi's *Historia* fulfilled the last requirement for the doctorate which he received in 1932 from the University of Texas.[5]

Economic hardship during the Great Depression forced Castañeda to leave temporarily the librarian's job at the University of Texas in order to assume the superintendency of the San Felipe Public Schools in Del Rio, a segregated instructional system for Mexican Americans. During his second self-imposed exile, Carlos and his family endured difficult times along the border. Notwithstanding these setbacks, in addition to school administration, Castañeda eagerly researched and wrote the second volume of *Our Catholic Heritage in Texas*. Characteristic of his meticulous research that focused on landmark events in the early history of the Lone Star State, he provided a descriptive subtitle, *The Mission Era, The Winning of Texas, 1693–1731*. Impressed with the quality of Carlos's scholarship, Father Foik rallied the Texas Historical Commission behind a recommendation to invite him to write the first volume, initially assigned to a prominent scholar who had failed to produce an acceptable manuscript. Carlos finished his

Latin American Collection, 1920–1927—The First Phase," *Journal of Library History*, 16 (Spring, 1981), 315–328; Félix D. Almaráz Jr., "Exploring the Paper Trail of Carlos Eduardo Castañeda," Carl Hertzog Lecture Series, No. 6 (El Paso: Texas Western Press, University of Texas at El Paso, 1994), 8.

[5] Félix D. Almaráz Jr., "The Making of a Boltonian: Carlos E. Castañeda of Texas—The Early Years," *Red River Valley Historical Review*, 1 (Winter, 1974), 329–350.

next assignment with a manuscript subtitled *The Mission Era, The Finding of Texas: 1519–1693*. Completed in time for the Texas Centennial celebration, Foik and the Knights of Columbus contracted Von Boeckmann-Jones Company of Austin to publish the first two volumes of the series. Coinciding with the foregoing events, Castañeda petitioned the Justice Department for United States citizenship.[6]

Castañeda's encounter with the critics began during his sojourn in Virginia when he directed two summer school trips to Mexico in 1925 and 1926. Concerned that alarming reports in the American press about civil unrest south of the border might affect enrollment for the summer institute, Carlos wrote an interpretive essay on deteriorating church-state relations in Mexico during the presidency of Plutarco Elias Calles. In the essay, with a provocative title "Is Mexico Turning Bolshevik?" he described and assessed the church-state controversy strictly in terms of political issues and not, as most American journalists portrayed conditions in their dispatches to editors, as a destruction of religious doctrine by an insensitive secular government emulating a Soviet model. Keenly aware of his status as permanent immigrant who had not applied for naturalized citizenship, yet cautiously unwilling to castigate the Mexican government's anti-clerical policies of President Calles, Castañeda deftly side-stepped the controversy by focusing on the historical evolution "of a long-standing conflict." Conceding that atrocities had been perpetrated by partisans on both sides of the struggle, he viewed the volatile problems in Mexico as a natural adjustment in church-state relations:

It is only fair to look at the situation impartially. If the Government has acted somewhat harshly, if it has gone to extremes, as it undoubtedly has,

---

[6] Félix D. Almaráz Jr., "Carlos E. Castañeda and Our Catholic Heritage: The Initial Volumes (1933–1943)," *Social Science Journal,* 13 (Apr., 1976), 27–37; Declaration of Intention, Number 79182, July 27, 1933; Petition for Naturalization, Number 95279, July 17, 1933; Application for a New Naturalization Paper, Number 17-B-202, Dec. 12, 1935; Duplicate Declaration of Intention, Number 845, Jan. 8, 1936; Certificate of Citizenship Number 3852566, Petition Number 756, June 8, 1936; Immigration and Naturalization Service, United States Department of Justice, Washington, D.C.

we must remember that the pendulum has to swing according to the law of gravitation, going from one extreme to the other, but after oscillating for a definite period of time it must finally come to the midpoint of perfect equilibrium. . . . Let us not be embittered by our present experience. Mexico is and will continue to be one of the staunchest supporters of the Church. The work of the early missionaries is too firmly imbedded to be undone in a day. The Church has nothing to fear; it can well afford to give an example of moderation and of true Christian resignation by trying to comply with the law, and thus carry on its work, which has been so rich in its fruits in spite of the opposition it has encountered.[7]

This commentary on current events in Mexico placed Castañeda in an awkward position with Catholic critics. Responding to Carlos's essay, a conservative professor of literature at Notre Dame University, Charles Phillips, vehemently attacked some of the contents: "Mr. Castañeda's argument takes no account of his many self-contradictions; such, for example, as his granting the actuality of the persecution and his calling it at the same time an 'apparent' persecution. It can't be both! But, at any rate, my summing up will be accepted, I am sure, as fair." The confrontation with Phillips revealed a dilemma that plagued Castañeda on two levels. At the uppermost level the clash of ideas represented an initiative on Carlos's part to convince college officials at William and Mary that, because of his intimate knowledge of the culture of the host country, he was capable of looking after the welfare of summer school students and faculty in Mexico. At a deeper level, based on prior research experience in cataloging the old Spanish records in the Bexar County Courthouse in Texas, Carlos perceived himself as an emerging borderlands scholar whose future success depended on accessibility to archival sources in Mexico and the goodwill of curators in charge of depositories.[8]

Striving to attain lofty scholarly goals, Carlos prophetically summarized the price that he would pay for being a borderlands

---

[7] C. E. Castañeda, "Is Mexico Turning Bolshevik?" *Catholic World*, 113 (June, 1926), 372.

[8] Charles Phillips, "The Trouble with Mexico: A Reply to the Foregoing Article," *Catholic World*, 113 (June, 1926), 372; Carlos Eduardo Castañeda, "A Report on the Spanish Archives of San Antonio" (M.A. thesis, University of Texas at Austin, 1923).

historian, balancing in the process the responsibility of family life and the demands of the academy: "The tax of this double contribution becomes . . . a strain. Perhaps future generations will some day sing the glories of the unknown scholar who through long years of painful, nerve-wrecking effort gradually add[s] in a humble way to Human knowledge and poorly raise[s] a family.[9]

Actually, Carlos earned a reputation as a librarian before he gained recognition as a historian. In that transitional development, he sharpened his objectivity and literary expression by reviewing the works of other scholars. For example, in evaluating two contributions of Frederick C. Chabot, *San Antonio and Its Beginning* and *The Alamo, Altar of Texas Liberty,* Castañeda, gently but firmly took the author to task:

Both books are well presented, with artistic and interesting illustrations and the notes on these are the best part of the work. It is to be regretted that the author has failed to give specific references to his sources, particularly in the sections dealing with the establishment of the first mission on the present site of San Antonio in 1716. The second book is a little better documented, but the practice of giving quotations in the footnotes without indicating the source makes many of them worthless. It is to be hoped that the author will continue to improve in his work and that he will give in future publications the sources of his information to add weight to his own statements and enable others who are interested to verify the facts and build upon his findings.[10]

Castañeda's experience in preparing *The Mexican Side of the Texan Revolution* and translations by Almonte and Sanchez preconditioned him to assay critically a work by Samuel Harman Lowrie, *Culture Conflict in Texas, 1821–1836.* Pointing out that Lowrie had approached the subject from the angle of sociology, Castañeda, weaved a fine web to snare the writer in his own words:

When the author leaves the beaten path of the historian he falls into serious error. Speaking of the reasons for misunderstanding [cultural

---

[9] Castañeda to H. W. Childs, May 31, 1927, Castañeda Papers (Nettie Lee Benson Latin American Collection, University of Texas at Austin).

[10] C. E. Castañeda, review of *San Antonio and Its Beginnings, 1691–1731* and *The Alamo, Altar of Texas,* by Frederick C. Chabot, *Southwestern Historical Quarterly,* 35 (Jan., 1932), 483.

patterns], he says "The servant Mexicans generally learned little about the Americans because of their low position and the language barrier." But from 1821 to 1836 there were no Mexican servants in the American settlements, nor were Mexican farmhands employed at that time. Equally speculative is his attempted explanation of the reasons for the attitude of the Mexicans toward slavery which are to be found in the cultural background of the leaders of the Mexican government.[11]

Never possessing the annihilative instinct that some other scholars may have valued, Castañeda left Lowrie dangling: "As a whole it is an interesting attempt to interpret, sociologically, the movement that resulted in the Texas Revolution, but the conclusions are not based in sufficient evidence to be convincing." That review demonstrated Carlos's general tendency to temper critical evaluation with gentle persuasion.[12]

When Castañeda's books appeared in print, reviews ranged from favorable to moderately reserved. Charles A. Bacarisse, for instance, assessed *The Mexican Side of the Texan Revolution* in the following words:

By temperament, true bilingual ability, and formal training, Castañeda was one of the few great translators in the Southwest. He took care to present accurately the thought of the Spanish original, but made no attempt to render a literal translation or adhere to the peculiarities of style. This gave his work a readability often lacking in translations.[13]

Maynard Gieger, a renowned Franciscan scholar at Santa Barbara Mission in California, offered a cogent assessment of Castañeda's initial contributions, spanning the years 1519 to 1731, in *Our Catholic Heritage:*

The narrative of his early history is not only consecutive, but well-balanced. The development of the great chain of missions is placed in its international setting while the Church-State relations are amply unfolded. The work gives evidence of the author's understanding of the purposes and activities of the friars in their mission fields, joined with a correct use

---

[11] C. E. Castañeda, review of *Culture Conflict in Texas, 1821–1836,* by Samuel Harman Lowrie, *Hispanic American Historical Review,* 13 (Nov., 1933), 483.

[12] Ibid.

[13] Charles A. Bacarisse, "Dedication to Carlos Eduardo Castañeda," *Arizona and the West,* 3 (Spring, 1961), 2.

of ecclesiastical terminology. The style is clear, unadorned, and objective, as is befitting a work of such proportions and industry.[14]

Critic Paul A. F. Walter lauded Carlos's integration of historical events in Spanish Texas with contemporary development in New Mexico. Commenting on the third volume of *Our Catholic Heritage* series, he observed:

Castañeda . . . has given us in this exhaustive and scholarly study of the Texas missions and incidental expeditions from 1731 to 1761, a comprehensive picture of ethnological, historical and cultural value. It does not merely supplement Dr. H. E. Bolton's "Texas in the Middle Eighteenth Century" but throws new light upon the history of the lower Rio Grande Valley where Spanish settlements were actually established on the northern bank . . . by 1753. Much additional information has been gathered from many sources not available heretofore, especially with regard to the history of the stretch of country from the present Presidio to El Paso. It had not even been suspected that several missions were actually established, in the vicinity of the Presidio in 1715, one year before the Ramón expedition of 1716 that resulted in the permanent occupation of East Texas. . . . As in New Mexico there were bickerings between ecclesiastical and military authorities. In more than one instance the story unfolded, dovetails into New Mexico history.[15]

George Peter Hammond, New Mexico administrator and distinguished Boltonian scholar, praised the broad scope of Don Carlos's research initiative:

Castañeda, with the aid of the Texas Knights of Columbus Historical Commission and other agencies, has been able to collect new sources of information that were not available in earlier times and has been able to present a fuller account of Texas in the middle period of the eighteenth century than was possible previously.[16]

---

[14] Maynard Geiger, review of *Our Catholic Heritage in Texas, 1519–1936, The Mission Era, The Finding of Texas, 1519–1693* and *The Mission Era, The Winning of Texas, 1693–1731*, by Carlos E. Castañeda, *Hispanic American Historical Review*, 18 (Feb., 1938), 88–89.

[15] Paul A. F. Walter, review of *Our Catholic Heritage in Texas, 1519–1936, The Mission Era, The Missions at Work, 1731–1761*, by Carlos E. Castañeda, *New Mexico Historical Review*, 13 (July, 1938), 331–332.

[16] George P. Hammond, review of *Our Catholic Heritage, in Texas, 1519–1926; The Mission Era, The Missions at Work, 1731–1761*, by Carlos E. Castañeda, *Pacific*

About Castañeda's talent as a writer, Hammond noted:

The author writes with enthusiasm and tireless zeal. His style is almost conversational and gives evidence of the fact that he has digested his sources well. He has presented an informative and readable narrative, and any student who wishes further information on the period will find a wealth of contemporary source materials in the bibliography.[17]

Another Boltonian, Arthur S. Aiton of Michigan, assessed the first three tomes for the *American Historical Review*. Knowledgeable in the literature of sixteenth-century colonial Mexico, Aiton appreciated the broad range of Carlos's ambitious undertaking. He explained:

In these volumes Dr. Castañeda has combined his skills as a librarian, bibliographer, and historian in an admirable manner. The need for a full-scale history of Texas, here supplied, has existed for some time in view of the great output of articles, documents, and monographs by scholars of reputation in the past thirty years. The bibliographies, citations, and footnotes reveal a patient sifting of this material and the use of a considerable body of new documents from the archives of Spain and Mexico. This is a work which, despite a somewhat misleading title, transcends the limits of purely ecclesiastical history and gives the reader an authentic synthesis of Texan history in all its varied aspects.[18]

Working diligently in the library during daylight hours and on his manuscripts at night and on weekends, Castañeda finished volumes four and five before World War II. Among the critics, Lansing B. Bloom of New Mexico questioned Carlos's interpretation of the secularization of some Texas missions. Failing to appreciate that the priorities of the mission system in Hispanic Texas differed substantially from other borderlands provinces, such as New Mexico or California, he chastised Castañeda for concluding that secularization had occurred earlier. He wrote:

It is unique, in fact, to be told (p. 344) that the missions in Texas "had

_Historical Review_, 8 (Mar., 1939), 124.

[17] Ibid.

[18] Arthur S. Aiton, review of *Our Catholic Heritage in Texas, 1519–1936; The Missiona Era, The Finding of Texas, 1519–1693; The Mission Era, Winning of Texas, 1693–1731; The Mission Era, The Missions at Work, 1731–1761*, by Carlos Castañeda, *American Historical Review*, 44 (July, 1939), 919.

done their work and had accomplished their purpose. They were ready to pass on." This was not true historically in New Mexico, in Pimeria [Sonora and Arizona], nor in California; was it true in Texas? The author's interpretation of this stage of "the mission era" strikes me as somewhat polemical; if we accept at face value the above statement, all the missions in Texas were ready to become self supporting parishes and the missionaries would move on to evangelize other Texan tribes— whereas the voluminous records here given us show that this period was, on the whole, one of decadence rather than of fruition. In fact as the author himself points out (p. 262), even the four [sic] missions in San Antonio and the two in San Juan Bautista were not regarded in 1772 as ready for secularization.[19]

Leaping to judgment, Bloom, a, meticulous scholar, harshly castigated Carlos for these flaws. He alleged a Catholic bias and accused Castañeda of overlooking an earlier source which the critic considered indispensable. Specifically, he noted:

Throughout the work we were curious at the complete lack of any references by the author to the work of one of his colleagues. Based in large part on the same sources used by Dr. Castañeda in his volumes, Dr. Walter P. Webb in . . . *The Great Plains* (1931) devoted a chapter to "The Spanish Approach to the Great Plains." It is a very illuminating analysis, especially of Texas history, for the reader who wants to recover his historical balance and perspective after reading Castañeda. Because of the abundant use of historical sources, we are apt to forget that the controlling theme of Dr. Castañeda and his sponsors is "Our Catholic Heritage."[20]

Castañeda refrained from responding to Bloom's scathing attack. Privately, however, he took comfort in knowing that the New Mexico scholar stood on shaky ground. First, San Antonio's jurisdiction extended over five Franciscan missions, not four as Bloom stated in his review. Second, the two missions located at "San Juan Bautista" operated within the province of Coahuila, not Texas. With respect to Walter Prescott Webb's celebrated hypothesis expounded in *The Great Plains*, Bloom failed to discern

---

[19] Lansing B. Bloom, review of *Our Catholic Heritage in Texas, 1519–1936, The Mission Era, The Passing of the Missions, 1762–1782*, by Carlos E. Castañeda, *New Mexico Historical Review*, 15 (Jan., 1940), 82–83.

[20] Ibid.

that the elder author's scholarship rested exclusively on English-language sources or translations of original documents and not on archival materials found in either Mexico or Spain. Finally, the title of the series led Bloom to conclude that religious doctrine, not the canons of historiography, governed Castañeda's writing.[21]

Still another Boltonian, Peter Matsen Dunne, a Jesuit scholar in California, evaluated Castañeda's contribution against the backdrop of Franciscan evangelization in the borderlands frontier of Coahuila and Texas. From a detached vantage point, Dunne generally commended the wide range of productivity, but he signaled out a few stylistic flaws for which the author, after dedicating more than a decade to the project, had developed an apparent editorial blindness:

A real criticism ought to be made concerning one phrase of the author's usually graphic style. In spots when speaking of [Franciscan] friars the style inclines toward the over-sympathetic or unctuous. We meet too often the "good padre," "good bishop," "burning zeal," "devoted missionary," while twice in one paragraph we have "zealous old missionary." This might argue for some readers an uncritical partiality. Simply the last name for a missionary would at times be more desirable; it would add to the vigor and the variety of the narrative. . . . The slow eye of the reviewer caught only one misprint. There may be others.[22]

Even so, Dunne acknowledged the magnitude of Castañeda's enterprise: "But the last shall be first. These volumes do him honor, for those who have courted the muse of history realize that to him, chiefly, has fallen the immense task of research and composition."[23]

---

[21] See Félix D. Almaráz Jr., *The San Antonio Missions and Their System of Land Tenure* (Austin: University of Texas Press, 1989), 1–7; ibid., *Crossroad of Empire: The Church and State on the Rio Grande Frontier of Coahuila and Texas, 1700–1821* (San Antonio: Center for Archaeological Research, University of Texas at San Antonio, 1979), 6–15; 40–47; Walter Prescott Webb, *The Great Plains* (New York: Grosset & Dunlap, 1931), 138–139.

[22] Peter M. Dunne, review of *Our Catholic Heritage in Texas, 1519–1936, The Mission Era, The Passing of the Missions, 1762–1782,* by Carlos E. Castañeda, *Hispanic American Historical Review,* 20 (Feb., 1940), 116.

[23] Ibid.

In Chicago, another Jesuit critic, Jerome V. Jacobsen, examined Castañeda's fifth volume, published on the eve of American involvement in World War II, with an evenhanded approach. Obviously cognizant of earlier assessments in scholarly journals, Jacobsen alluded to other historians' nit-picking bents:

Dr. Castañeda has performed a notable service of organization of materials. Moreover, he has presented scholars with nearly thirty pages of bibliography of manuscript source materials. He has made judicious use of the materials already printed and of the monograph materials. Some other reviewer may find fault with an occasional interpretation or emphasis, but this reviewer thinks the book [is] a very good book.[24]

In Texas, Eugene C. Barker, with a combination of pride and objectivity that only a senior scholar could extend toward a protege, admired the contents of the fifth volume and the historiographical skills of the author:

Professor Castañeda emerges from the romantic, semi-legendary centuries of Spanish possession which he has done so much to clarify and leaves himself a hundred years of prosaic organization of the church and of its expansion under modern conditions. The founders of this monument to the church chose wisely in selecting him to write the story. His sound historical judgment, his intimate knowledge of the manuscript sources which he himself has done so much to collect for the libraries of the University of Texas and St. Edward's University, and his facility in the Spanish and English languages make his personal equipment unique.[25]

Given the enormous historical sweep of *Our Catholic Heritage,* much of it blazing through pristine territory, it became impossible for Castañeda to sequester himself from error. As a practicing scholar, to be sure, he endeavored to compose his manuscripts as accurately as his talents and source materials allowed. Geography, however, constantly posed a challenge to Carlos, occasionally resulting in misnomers or inexact locations for creeks, rivers, and

---

[24] Jerome V. Jacobsen, review of *Our Catholic Heritage in Texas, 1519–1936, The Mission Era, The End of the Spanish Regime,* by Carlos E. Castañeda, *Mid-America,* 25 (Oct., 1943), 304.

[25] Eugene C. Barker, review of *Our Catholic Heritage in Texas, 1519–1936; Transition Period, The Fight for Freedom, 1810–1836,* by Carlos E. Castañeda, *Southwestern Historical Quarterly,* 55 (July, 1951), 136–137.

streams. For instance, in writing the narrative of Viceroy Luis de Velasco's missionary policy in the Panuco region, roughly north of Tampico and inland from the coast, he mistakenly relied on an earlier work experience in the Mexican oil fields to identify the location. In 1938, Lansing Bloom, conducting research in the Archivo General de Indias in Sevilla, discovered "a letter from Viceroy Velasco to a missionary in Tampico (on the Panuco River)" encouraging the cleric to obtain "information about tribes" reportedly inhabiting the terrain "between the Rio de las Palmas and the Rio Bravo" which the temporal leader inter-changeably called "the Rio Grande." Ecstatic with his discovery, Bloom later revealed in the pages of the *New Mexico Historical Review:* "I told Castañeda I thought he was wrong in identifying these two rivers in his *Catholic Heritage,* now I can prove it."[26]

The success of the first five volumes of *Our Catholic Heritage* enhanced Castañeda's reputation as a historian among profes-sionals. At the Austin campus, however, his career progressed slowly, hindered partly by full-time appointment in the Latin American Collection and part-time status as a faculty member in the history department. Periodically, Charles Wilson Hackett cre-ated temporary vacancies by assuming administrative duties or taking sabbatical leaves of absence, whereupon the history department invited Carlos to teach one or two courses in the Latin American field. One summer before the war, he avidly enjoyed the hospitality of historians at the University of New Mexico, combining teaching duties with a family vacation. Loyalty to the Austin campus consistently guided him back to the Latin American Collection and an office cubicle in the library tower. The outbreak of World War II, however, quickly aroused his patriotic impulses. Too old for frontline combat duty, but physi-cally able to contribute to the war effort, Castañeda obtained a leave of absence from the university library and accepted a gov-ernment post with President Roosevelt's Fair Employment Practice Committee (FEPC). While his scholarly productivity declined, Carlos travelled across the Southwest courageously

---

[26] Lansing B. Bloom, "Notes from Seville," *New Mexico Historical Review,* 14 (Jan., 1939), 120.

investigating complaints of discrimination filed by Mexican American workers in war-related industries. When the war ended, Castañeda returned to Austin where the prestige of the FEPC experience led the administration to reward him with a promotion to senior faculty rank and full-time employment in the history department.[27]

In the spring of 1946, Castañeda reactivated several research projects that he had suspended during the war, one of which was the sixth volume of *Our Catholic Heritage*. Eugene C. Barker, a renowned authority on the Anglo-American period of Texas history, extolled the scholarly virtues of the latest contribution.

In this volume of his monumental work Professor Castañeda reached the Anglo-American period of Texas history, and one need only compare his volume with Henderson Yoakum's excellent pioneer work—published, roughly, a hundred years ago—to realize the progress that historians have made in exploring original sources and following details of this dramatic period. Professor Castañeda had the advantage of painstaking monographs on almost every aspect of the dramatic story, which was the so-called filibustering era, the preliminary colonization project during Spanish rule, the Austin enterprise, the Mexican colonization policies, the conflict of Anglo-American settlers with Mexican authority resulting in the Texas Revolution and final independence of Texas. To some of these topics he has made considerable contributions; in all of them he has explored original manuscript sources, checked the accuracy of previous monographs, corrected inevitable minor slips, added details, and woven the whole story into a continuous, well-articulated narrative.[28]

---

[27] Tom Bowman Brewer, "A History of the Department of History of the University of Texas, 1883–1951" (M.A. thesis, University of Texas at Austin, 1957), 117; Clete Daniel, *Chicano Workers and the Politics of Fairness: The FEPC in the Southwest, 1941–1945* (Austin: University of Texas Press, 1991), 146, 166–175. In the summer of 1941, responding to pressures from African-American workers who harbored grievances against employers, President Franklin D. Roosevelt created the FEPC by executive order. Initially the agency focused attention on the complaints of black workers who represented the "largest and most conspicuously wronged constituency." Shortly after the attack on Pearl Harbor, the FEPC extended its scope of investigation to include Hispanics and other minorities. Daniel, *Chicano Workers and the Politics of Fairness*, xii.

[28] Eugene C. Barker, review of *Our Catholic Heritage in Texas, 1519–1936, The Mission Era, The End of the Spanish Regime*, by Carlos E. Castañeda, *Southwestern Historical Quarterly*, 55 (July, 1951), 136–137.

In tandem with his scholarship and university teaching, Don Carlos picked up momentum on the public-speaking circuit. Usually the issues he spoke on pertained to inequality of opportunity for the advancement of American citizens of Spanish or Mexican ancestry.[29] A combination of such activities characterized the last decade of his life. As in earlier years, Carlos offset what he lacked in material comfort with awards and honors which, not surprisingly, lured additional detractors. Charles W. Ramsdell Jr., a successful writer of tour-guide books, unleashed a cataract of vitriolic opinions of Castañeda whom he linked with Bolton and Barker:

Bolton was a windy-minded promoter who barely took time to locate all the old Spanish landmarks in the wrong places before he hastened to California, where he belonged. The recently canonized Barker was not only incredibly narrow but, I think, dishonest. His protege, Castañeda, was much worse, a very raffish Knight of the Holy Sepulcher; . . . his elucubrations [elucidations?] on Spanish Texas have great gaps in them, and are elsewhere wickedly misleading. The whole Spanish period badly needs a decent job.[30]

To an extent much of the antagonism toward Castañeda's scholarship stemmed from the publicity that followed his major accolades: Knight of the Holy Sepulchre, Serra Award of the Americas, and Knight of the Order of Isabel the Catholic. Certainly, his frequent appearances at public ceremonies attired in elegant regalia as a member of the Equestrian Order of the Holy Sepulchre of Jerusalem enhanced such impressions. Philip J. Sheridan, a graduate student, recalled that Castañeda's Roman Catholic faith was not a simple issue: "He said, yo soy Católico con espada, a Catholic with a sword." Another graduate student, Valdemar Rodríguez, corroborated Sheridan's testimony. Castañeda, said Rodríguez, "was a defender of the Church in every instance. . . . in all of his lectures he defended the Church, as we

---

[29] Carlos E. Castañeda, "Statement on Discrimination Against Mexican Americans in Employment," May 9, 1947, in *Are We Good Neighbors,* ed. Alonso S. Perales (San Antonio: Artes Gráficas, 1948), 59–63.

[30] Charles Ramsdell to Walter Prescott Webb, Sept. 27, 1958, Walter Prescott Webb Papers (Jenkins Garrett Collection, University of Texas at Arlington).

say in Spanish, a capa y espada [with cape and sword)."[31]

These public declarations, combined with the tributes that cascaded upon the volumes of *Our Catholic Heritage* reinforced the general impression that the author was exclusively a Texas church historian. For years Castañeda struggled unsuccessfully to dispel this notion. Joe B. Frantz rendered a balanced assessment of his friend Carlos:

He used to say in his later years that he wished he had poured all that energy and attention that went into Our Catholic Heritage into something of much wider import. With his insights and his knowledge, his energy particularly (fabulous energy) that he could have been one of the really great historians of, you know, intercontinental, international, fame instead of one primarily remembered for being a Church and Texas historian. I don't know, but [there is] no question that Catholic Heritage was a large dose, largely conceived, a whooping amount of work and twenty years out of his life. Perhaps he could have gone in some other direction; but that's what he is primarily noted for. Maybe it is more valuable in the long run. But that was a regret that he had from time to time.[32]

Castañeda's personal desires to the contrary, the litany of praise for *Our Catholic Heritage* increased with the publication of the fifth and sixth volumes. A decade after the end of the Second World War, the manuscript of the concluding volume emerged. Owing to Castañeda's serious health problems, the last volume, subtitled *The Church in Texas Since Independence, 1836–1950*, lacked the fervor and zeal of the earlier work. Notwithstanding the shortcomings of the seventh volume, scholars generally associated the author's name with high standards.[33]

---

[31] Philip J. Sheridan, interview by Félix D. Almaráz Jr., Jan. 26, 1973 (1st quotation), tape recording, San Antonio, Texas [emphasis in original interview]; Valdemar Rodríguez, interview by Félix D. Almaráz Jr., Jan. 24, 1973 (2nd quotation), tape recording, San Antonio, Texas.

[32] Joe B. Frantz, interview by O. Wayne Poorman, May 23, 1972, tape recording, Austin, Texas.

[33] Minutes of the 35th Regular Meeting of the Texas Knights of Columbus Historical Commission, Fort Worth, Texas, May 11, 1953; Castañeda to Monsignor William H. Oberste, Apr. 1, 1958, Knights of Columbus Correspondence File, Catholic Archives of Texas, Chancery of Austin.

In the final decades of the twentieth century, some scholars trained in quantitative methods have taken issue with specific omissions that Castañeda could not fill with documents available to him, or with matters of ethnic perspective. Like other intellectuals who influenced borderlands history, Castañeda worked within prescribed boundaries of the profession. Clearly, as he pioneered new territory in Spanish Texas history, he operated comfortably under the canopy of the Boltonian school because that was the trend at the height of his productivity. Unappreciative of that approach, Gilberto M. Hinojosa lambasted Castañeda for selecting "the official Church, rather than the faith community, as the core of his [scholarly] definition." A factor that troubled Hinojosa was an "absence" of any acknowledgment of "Mexicano religiosity" that misguided him and others "in the Mexican-American middle class" to identify with "the Church in time of crisis and change." Mario T. García, a critic inclined toward tolerance but familiar only with the broad outline of Castañeda's life, equated his productivity with middle-class success and relegated Don Carlos to an "elite" category. Unlike Hinojosa, García admired the broad scope of Carlos's scholarship, but he chided him for writing in the Boltonian style of grand pageantry instead of vigorously championing the human dignity of Indian cultures.[34]

Before the appearance of *Our Catholic Heritage*, the mission era was a virgin field waiting to be cultivated. Under Don Carlos's creative intellect, a lengthy history of Spanish Texas carefully evolved out of piles of uncataloged documents in Mexican archives. Six of the seven volumes of *Our Catholic Heritage* filled the gap in mission history; the last tome summarized the growth and development of dioceses in the Lone Star State since 1836. Almost four decades after his death, Carlos E. Castañeda, by virtue of his solid contributions to history, remains a giant among Hispanic scholars.

---

[34] Gilberto M. Hinojosa, "Mexican-American Faith Communities in Texas and the Southwest," in *Mexican Americans and the Catholic Church, 1900–1965*, ed. Jay P. Dolan and Gilberto M. Hinojosa (Notre Dame: University of Notre Dame Press, 1994), 91 (quotation); Mario T. Garcia, *Mexican Americans: Leadership, Ideology & Identiry, 1930–1960* (New Haven: Yale University Press, 1989), 232–251.

# The Borderlands of Culture:

## *Americo Paredes's George Washington Gómez*

In 1990, Américo Paredes published a splendid novel entitled *George Washington Gómez.*[1] Written over the 1935–1940 period, the pressures of everyday life delayed the novel's appearance
for fifty years. In *George Washington Gómez* we have a paradigmatic
instance of the state of Chicano letters at the end of the twentieth
century. The text speaks from the first part of this century to the
last; from the past to the present.[2] Paradoxically, it also expresses
from that past, the future in the present.

In an essay on "The Problem of Identity in a Changing Culture," Paredes maintains that "Conflict—cultural, economic, and
physical—has been a way of life along the border between Mexico and the United States." By the early twentieth century these

---

* Ramón Saldívar holds the Hoagland Family Chair in English and Comparative Literature at Stanford University. His teaching and research focuses on literary
criticism and theory, cultural studies, and Chicano studies. His major publications
include *Figural Language in the Novel: The Flowers of Speech from Cervantes to Joyce* and
*Chicano Narrative: The Dialectics of Difference.* Presently, Dr. Saldívar is working on a
book-length project on Chicano modernity and postmodernity.

[1] Américo Paredes, *George Washington Gómez: A Mexicotexan Novel* (Houston:
Arte Público Press, 1990).

[2] A note on the referents of self-identification: I will use *Chicano* as the popularly understood designator of the politicized generation of Mexican Americans
that emerged from the post-1965 Movement years; I will use Mexican and

175

patterns of conflict had become part of an entire discourse that has come to be known as "the culture of the border." In *With His Pistol in His Hand* Paredes studied the *corrido* (folk ballad) tradition that arose chronicling this history of border conflict in South Texas. Typically in the corrido of intercultural conflict, a hardworking, peace-loving Mexicano is goaded by Anglo outrages into violence, causing him to defend his rights and those of others in his community against the *rinches*, or Texas Rangers.[3]

*George Washington Gómez* is set against this history of cultural-political conflict. It takes especially as its moment the 1915 uprising in South Texas by Mexican Nationals and Mexican Americans attempting to create a Spanish-speaking republic of the Southwest. The *sediciosos* (seditionists), as they came to be known, were acting under the "Plan de San Diego." After the uprising, hundreds of innocent Mexican American farm workers were slaughtered by Texas Rangers, summarily executed without trial, at even the smallest hint of support or sympathy for the seditionists. Capitalist agribusiness thus overcame a major disruption in its development at the same time that Anglos were reinforcing anti-Mexican views to justify the exploitation of low-wage Mexican labor and the continuing transfer of land away from Mexican hands.[4]

Paredes's novel situates us in the midst of this historical scenario, taking its tonal key, however, not from the celebration of the tragic corrido hero, doomed to honorable but certain defeat, but from the pathos concerning the fate of the innocent on

Mexicano interchangeably to refer to Mexican national subjects, and Mexican American whenever U.S. nativity is important to my discussion of Paredes's text.

[3] Paredes, "The Problem of Identity in a Changing Culture: Popular Expressions of Culture Conflict Along the Lower Rio Grande Border," in *Views Across the Border: The U.S. and Mexico*, ed. Stanley R. Ross (Albuquerque: University of New Mexico Press, 1978), 68. Paredes is concerned generally with the South Texas border region, extending roughly from the Nueces River to the Lower Rio Grande. One of his contributions to the study of the cultural forms of this region has been his notion of a "Greater Mexico," that is, of a cultural zone extending across the political boundaries of both the United States and Mexico. Paredes, *With His Pistol in His Hand* (Austin: University of Texas Press, 1958).

[4] For this history of conflict, see David Montejano, *Anglos and Mexicans in the Making of Texas, 1836–1986* (Austin: University of Texas Press, 1987).

whom was exacted the cost of bitter defeat.

Paredes's story essentially begins with Gumersindo and María Gómez discussing with her mother, and her brother, Feliciano García, the naming of the child who has been born to them in the midst of the seditionist uprising and its bloody aftermath:

The baby . . . was feeding greedily at his mother's breast. Born a foreigner in his native land, he was fated to a life controlled by others. At that very moment his life was being shaped, people were already running his affairs, but he did not know it. Nobody considered whether he might like being baptized or not. Nobody had asked him whether he, a Mexican, had wanted to be born in Texas, or whether he had wanted to be born at all. The baby left the breast and María, his mother propped him up in a sitting position. She looked at him tenderly. "And what shall we name him?" she wondered aloud (p. 15).

Therein, of course, lies a tale. The answer to her question is one version of the histories of Mexican-American self-formation in the West and Southwest. We already know the literal answer to her question: the child is the title character. Positioned as a subject by the material actions and symbolic rituals of the community into which he has been born, the child also has a figural present and a prefigural future in the present already underwritten by the relations of class and race in which he will live his life. Indeed, the process of naming that we witness at the beginning of his story makes concrete the abstract process of categorization that has already configured the child even before his birth.

In response to María's question as to a proper name for the child, the other characters, her husband, mother, and brother, offer a variety of names, each indicative of an alternative narrative within which the child's destiny might be played out: first, "Crisósforo," a name of grandiose and idiosyncratic proportions, is considered as a sign of his singularity; "José Angel," serving as a sign of the continuity of traditional religious value, follows; "Venustiano" and "Cleto," names alluding to the Mexican revolutionary leader Venustiano Carranza and to one of the leaders of the ongoing sedition, are suggested perhaps as signs of revolutionary commitment. Even the father's own name, "Gumersindo," as a sign of genealogical continuity, is considered but, oddly, rejected like the rest. Finally, the child's mother speaks:

"I would like my son . . ." she began. She faltered and reddened. "I would like him to have a great man's name. Because he's going to grow up to be a great man who will help his people" (p. 16).

Gumersindo responds playfully, saying, "My son . . . is going to be a great man among the Gringos." He then adds in sudden inspiration, "A Gringo name he shall have!" "Is he not as fair as any of them?" (p. 16). Paredes thus introduces into this moment of subject formation the issues of race and color. We might see this instant as an example of the process whereby an "individual" is "appointed as a subject in and by the specific familial ideological configuration in which it is 'expected' once it has been conceived."[5] At issue immediately in the novel, then, are questions of identity, subjectivity and consciousness, especially as these concepts relate to culture.

Trying to recall what "great men" the Gringos have had, Gumersindo considers before exclaiming: "I remember . . . Wachinton. Jorge Wachinton." The grandmother's attempt to say the strange name "Washington" comes out as "Gualinto . . . Gualinto Gómez" (p. 16). And so the name sticks.

The clash of identities that is the substance of Gualinto Gómez's life is instantiated at this originary moment where Paredes signals the various discourses that might have ordered his life. A "foreigner in his native land," the child's story will follow out the commandments implicit in the ideologies unconsciously projected in his "very good name," ideologies that will position him as a subjected representation of the imaginary relations to the real conditions of existence in the early twentieth-century borderlands of South Texas.

Each of the names, those considered and rejected, as well as the one chosen and immediately transformed into its dialectal equivalent, signals a different set of speech genres, and promises to inscribe the child into a particular discursive history. Speech

---

[5] Louis Althusser, "Ideology and Ideological State Apparatuses: (Notes Toward an Investigation)," in *Lenin and Philosophy and Other Essays* (New York: Monthly Review Press, 1971), 176.

genres serve as normative restraints on our most intimate intentions; they form the legitimate borders of what we can say and not say.[6] The textual instance at hand represents two sets of such speech genres at work. On the one hand, they represent the utopian hopes and dreams of the father and mother who optimistically project a future of reconciled differences under the crossed references to the child's promised Mexican and American destinies. On the other hand, they are the historically validated misgivings of the child's uncle concerning these crossed destinies. As he leaves the scene of ritual naming, Feliciano, soon to be the child's surrogate father, sings some verses from one of the most famous of the corridos of border conflict, "El Corrido de Jacinto Treviño." Prefiguring the violent murder of Gumersindo by Texas Rangers in the very next chapter, the song activates an entirely different speech genre to guide the interaction between the child's Mexican nurturing and American enculturing.

The instability of this opposition is signalled throughout the remainder of the novel by the continuing impermanence of the title character's name. In crucial early scenes, before he enters the American schools, the child is Gualinto Gómez, a name he and his uncle like to explain is "Indian." These idyllic pre-school years will later serve as the edenic counterpoint, the largely untroubled duration of no-time before the fall into history, that might ironically reemerge to save him for history. In the narrated present, however, once the child enters school, his heart and mind become the battleground for cultural control:

[Gualinto] began to acquire an Angloamerican self, and as the years passed . . . he developed simultaneously in two widely divergent paths. In the schoolroom he was an American; at home and on the playground he was a Mexican. Throughout his early childhood these two selves grew within him without much conflict, each an exponent of a different tongue and a different way of living. The boy nurtured these two selves within him, each radically different and antagonistic to the other, without realizing their separate existences.

---

[6] Mikhail Bakhtin, *Speech Genres & Other Late Essays*, trans. Vern W. McGee, ed. Caryl Emerson and Michael Holquist (Austin: University of Texas Press, 1986), xv.

It would be several years before he fully realized that there was not one single Gualinto Gómez. That in fact there were many Gualinto Gómezes, each of them double like images reflected on two glass surfaces of a show window. The eternal conflict between two clashing forces within him produced a divided personality, made up of tight little cells independent and almost entirely ignorant of each other, spread out over his consciousness, mixed with one another like squares on a checkerboard (p. 147).

To raise the question of identity as this passage does is not to celebrate it or fix it as something that is essential, knowable, and a priori. What follows instead in the course of the narrative of Gualinto's history is a systematic exploration of the attempted standardization of the notion of identity, fully as much by the American school system that attempts to pass off ideology in the guise of truth, as by the economic system that commodifies the complex differences of identity by reflecting it as a catachrestic, specular image on the "glass surfaces of a show window" in the marketplace. Equally operative, even if repressed from the conscious levels of the narrative, is the fixation of Mexican gender ideology that also identifies Gualinto as a belated heir to the tradition of armed resistance represented most starkly by his uncle Feliciano. Given this interplay of determining discourses, figured in this passage by the cubistic image of the "checkerboard" of consciousness, identity will not be available from this point on except in the form of a mediation, one that includes the existential materials of daily life along with those psychological ones in which the identity-form is imprinted in the early versions of twentieth-century mass culture. The catoptric theatre of showcase windows is not accidental but symbolic; a representational stratagem. The magic mirrors of the marketplace are contrived to confound your identity and your relation to the object-world between you and the commodities that are mingled with your reflected selves.

As Paredes's narrator later puts it:

Consciously . . . [Gualinto] considered himself a Mexican. He was ashamed of the name his dead father had given him, George Washington Gómez. He was grateful to his Uncle Feliciano for having registered him in school as "Gualinto" and having said that it was an Indian name. . . .

The Mexican national hymn brought tears to his eyes, and when he said "we" he meant the Mexican people. . . . Of such matter were made the basic cells in the honeycomb that made up his personality (p. 147).

This initial characterization turns out to be romantically, not to say sentimentally, incomplete. It implies that we might be able later to read off the "real" identity of the subject by virtue of its relations to the experience of the Mexican object world that fills the private world of his affective life. From this view, to determine the position of the subject in the real is to recognize both the content of ideology and its source: a particular experience of reality determines the content of ideology. Paredes denies, however, that the identity of the subject may be understood solely by virtue of its conscious positioning for, as we learn:

[T]here was also George Washington Gómez, the American. He was secretly proud of the name his more conscious twin, Gualinto, was ashamed to avow publicly. George Washington Gómez secretly desired to be a fullfledged, complete American without the shameful encumberment of his Mexican race. He was the product of his Anglo teachers and the books he read in school, which were all in English. . . . Books had made him so (pp. 147–148).

This passage furthers the point about identity and the constitution of the subject as a social construct. Still, Gualinto's American self is not to be read simply as a latent repression of the Other ready to break through from unconscious levels of the psyche to overwhelm the manifest Mexican identity of his conscious self. The mediation between the terms is infinitely more complex than the classical scenario of "true" and "false" consciousness might imagine.

Without the security of the knowledge or even of the feeling that he will encounter what he already knows, Gualinto, like other Mexican children, does not have the advantage of his parents who as combatants in a racial and class struggle against an invariable enemy knew who they were. The narrative of their identity, troubled and painful as it might be, is nonetheless a determinate one, available in all the icons of Mexican material culture but especially in the expressions of folklore: jokes, popular sayings, legends, and songs. In the traditional corrido, for example, the most formalized expression of the organic patriarchal discourse that names this identity, the fate of the individual and of the community are not separate. Rather, they are bound together in an almost unitary structure as are the various stanzas of the song.

For the children, however, now "gently prodded toward complete Americanization," rather than violently repressed for being Mexican, identity both is and is not what it seems to be. Standing in the borderlands of culture, they exist on an unstable ground of double negations:

Hating the Gringo one moment with an unreasoning hatred, admiring his literature, his music, his material goods the next. Loving the Mexican with a blind fierceness, then almost despising him for his slow progress in the world (p. 150).

What it would take, materially and psychologically, to imagine a new identity, to imagine how one would go about conceptualizing what you cannot, by definition, yet imagine since it has no equivalent in your current experience, that is the substance of the remainder of Gualinto's story. It attempts to imagine what it would take to conceptualize the identity of identity, the affirmation that is contained in every negation, in short, the future in the present. The conceptualization of identity that we are offered at novel's end is not a precritically ideal one, even though it does remain historically, dialectically problematic to a disturbing degree.

Straddling the multicultural ground proves to be too much for Gualinto Gómez who, near the end of the novel, finally changes his name legally, forsaking the bewildering unreality of his former composite names, both the American "George Washington," with all of its now mixed ethnic signals, and the Indian "Gualinto," with all of its associations with familial and cultural history. He adopts the simpler "George G. Gómez." Now an officer in army counterintelligence whose job is, ironically, border security, Gualinto is curiously troubled by his recurring dream, which itself is a return of repressed boyhood daydreams. In the dream, he imagines himself leading a victorious counterattack against Sam Houston's army at the decisive battle of San Jacinto.

With Santa Anna hung and all traitors dispatched, in the dream "Texas and the Southwest will remain forever Mexican."

> He would imagine he was living in his greatgrandfather's time, when the Americans first began to encroach on the northern provinces of the new Republic of Mexico. Reacting against the central government's inefficiency and corruption, he would organize rancheros into a fighting militia and train them by using them to exterminate the Comanches. . . . In his daydreams he built a modern arms factory at Laredo, doing it all in great detail, until he had an enormous, well-trained army that included Irishmen and escaped American Negro slaves (p. 282).

On the verge of quite self-consciously losing himself as a pre-movement Mexicano into the American melting pot, Gualinto's political unconscious in the form of the collective memory instantiated by the sense of self offered by his father's, uncle's, and mother's lives, returns to offer an alternative ideology and self-formation.

The discursive speech genres of birth certificates, educational degrees, career dossiers, service records, or legal court records bind Gualinto institutionally to a formidable identity discourse. But now the simpler structures of a precritical utopian dream emerge to trouble the stability of his newfound bourgeois self. Gualinto's self-formation is powerfully formed by the public American sphere he has chosen to embrace. He continues to be authored as well, however, by experiences and discourses of experience that by now have retreated into the unconscious fantasy structures of his life. At the point of complete denial of his Mexican past, Gualinto can thus in the aftermath of his daydreams and fantasies

> . . . end up with a feeling of emptiness, of futility. Somehow, he was not comfortable with the way things ended. There was something missing that made any kind of ending fail to satisfy. And he would stop there, to begin from the beginning a few days later. But he had outgrown those childish daydreams long ago. Lately, however, now that he was a grown man, married and with a successful career before him, scenes from the silly imaginings of his youth kept popping up when he was asleep. He always woke with a feeling of irritation. Why? he would ask himself. Why

do I keep doing this? Why do I keep on fighting battles that were won and lost a long time ago? Lost by me and won by me too? They have no meaning now (p. 282).

Juan Flores and George Yudice have made the case that in times of crisis, such as in the crisis of stability indicated by the name "postmodernity," "'private' identity factors or subject positions may become unmoored from institutionally bound generic structures."[7]

But in this case perhaps the issue has less to do with the stylistics and formalisms implied by the term "postmodernity" than with the configurations of identity put at stake by shifting relations of material and cultural production on the U.S.-Mexico border in the first decades of this century. This unmooring of the subject position from the bonds of institutional ideology could explain why Gualinto's present "childish daydreams" and "silly imaginings" leave him "with a feeling of emptiness, of futility." It is for good reason that Adorno has claimed that "Identity is the primal form of ideology."[8] Situated in the sphere of intimacy, these daydreams fuel a decidedly discomfiting primal, utopian, self-formation that stands against the one that he has consciously chosen under the various signs of his interpellation. That is to say, the fantasy structures of the unconscious return bringing a historical memory that has the practical function of designating an alternative, even if deeply latent, content to the formed subject of history. As Jameson has noted, "Fantasy," in this sense

is no longer felt to be a private and compensatory reaction against public situations, but rather a way of reading those situations, of thinking and mapping them, of intervening in them, albeit in a very different form from the abstract reflections of traditional philosophy or politics.[9]

These alternative public spheres remain potential for Gualinto, situated as they are as knowledges formed by the anxiety of the clash between the everyday real and utopian fantasy.

---

[7] Juan Flores and George Yudice, "Living Borders/Buscando America: Languages of Latino Self-formation," *Social Text*, 24 (1990), 57–84.

[8] Theodor Adorno, *Negative Dialectics* (New York: Continuum, 1973), 148.

[9] Frederic Jameson, "On Negt and Kluge," *October*, 46 (Fall, 1988), 171.

Formulated as a potential for a future reconstruction in more self-consciously gendered narratives, this present undoing of the apparently stable subject-position that "George G. Gómez" has momentarily constructed at novel's end, serves as the marker for the boundaries of the borderlands of culture that Chicano literature is at times problematically in the process of traversing. In *George Washington Gómez*, this potential remains precariously fragile. Fantasy might as easily serve to dissipate practice and undermine its intent; gender remains latent and repressed, the traces of its course deferred and displaced. Still, the sublimation of the possibility of historical agency into the political unconscious at novel's end is only a first expression of the present reconsideration of the contradictory complexities of contemporary Latino identity. As such an expression, Paredes's novel works powerfully as a sign of the state of Chicano literature at the end of the twentieth century. It depicts the possibility of wresting from within the realm of necessity, the hope of freedom, that is to say, the possibility of attaining a future liberation in the present.

# Part Four:
# Bibliographies

Although historians have made laudable gains in the production of works on Chicana and Chicano history since the early 1970s, the lack of current and reliable reference sources continues to hamper the development of the field. Moreover, Mexican American history still awaits full integration into U.S. history textbooks and university titles during the 1990s. Some electronic information sources, however, are available. Historians should be aware of the Chicano Database, the *Handbook of Latin American Studies*, and the *Hispanic American Periodical Index* (HAPI). We offer the following bibliographies to demonstrate the impressive level of productivity in the history of Mexicans in Texas and to encourage its development and integration.

Arnoldo De León's bibliography includes selected major books, dissertations, theses, and journal articles that have appeared since 1970. It is the most complete and updated Tejano history bibliography. There is no such bibliography in book form. Cynthia E. Orozco's selective bibliography is intended for teachers, researchers, and students. It is a guide to academic sources useful for the study and teaching of Mexican American history in the United States.

# Estudios Tejanos:

## A List of Historical Literature on Mexican Americans in Texas

ARNOLDO DE LEÓN*

Allsup, Carl. *The American G.I. Forum: Origins and Evolution.* Austin: Center for Mexican American Studies, University of Texas Press, 1982.

———. "Education is Our Freedom: The American G.I. Forum and the Mexican American School Segregation in Texas, 1948–1957." *Aztlán,* 8 (Spring, Summer, Fall, 1977).

Almaráz, Félix D. Jr. "Carlos E. Castañeda, Mexican American Historian: The Formative Years, 1896—1927." *Pacific Historical Review,* 42 (Aug., 1973).

———. "Carlos E. Castañeda and Our Catholic Heritage: The Initial Volumes (1933–1943)." *Social Science Journal.* 13 (Apr., 1976).

———. "Carlos E. Castañeda's Rendezvous With a Library: The Latin American Collection, 1920–1927—The Final Phase." *Journal of Library History,* 16 (1981).

---

*Arnoldo De León holds the C. J. "Red" Davidson Endowed Professor-ship in History at Angelo State University. Some of his major works include: *The History of Texas* (with co-author Robert A. Calvert), *Mexican Americans in Texas,* and *The Tejano Community.* This bibliography originally appeared in the Southwestern Historical Quarterly, 98 (Jan., 1995).

———. "Contributions of Mexican Americans to Texas Historiography." In Light Townsend Cummins and Alvin R. Bailey Jr., *A Guide to the History of Texas.* New York: Greenwood Press, 1988.

———. "The Making of a Boltonian: Carlos E. Castañeda of Texas—The Early Years." *Red River Valley Historical Review,* 1 (Winter, 1974).

Alonzo, Armando C. "Tejano Rancheros and Changes in Land Tenure, Hidalgo County, Texas, 1850–1900." Ph.D. Diss., Indiana University, 1991.

———. *Tejano Legacy: Rancheros and Settlers in South Texas, 1734–1900.* Albuquerque: University of New Mexico Press, 1998.

Anders, Evan. *Boss Rule in South Texas: The Progressive Era..* Austin: University of Texas Press, 1982.

Arreola, Daniel D. "The Mexican American Cultural Capital." *Geographical Review,* 77 (Jan., 1987).

———. "Mexican Origins of South Texas Mexican Americans, 1930." *Journal of Historical Geography,* 19 (1993).

Austerman, Wayne R. "José Policarpo Rodríguez: Chicano Plainsman." *West Texas Historical Association Yearbook,* 59 (1983).

Ayala-Scheuneman, María de Jesús. "A Brief History of Three Presbyterian Educational Institutions in South Texas." *Journal of South Texas,* 4 (Spring, 1991).

Baeza, Abelardo. "La Escuela de Don Clemente: History of the Madero Ward Elementary School in Alpine, Texas, 1910—1936." *Journal of Big Bend Studies,* 7 (Jan., 1995).

Baeza, Abelardo. "La Escuela Del Barrio: A History of Alpine's Centennial School, 1936–1969." *Journal of Big Bend Studies,* 4 (Jan., 1992).

Bailey, Richard R. "The Starr County Strike." *Red River Valley Historical Review,* 4 (Winter, 1976).

Barbash, Louis, and Frederick P. Close. "Lydia Mendoza: The Voice of a People." *Texas Humanist* (Nov., Dec., 1983).

Barr, Alwyn. "Occupation and Geographic Mobility in San Antonio, 1870–1900." *Social Science Quarterly,* 51 (Sept., 1970).

Barton, Josef J. "Land, Labor, and Community in Nueces County: Czech Farmers and Mexican Laborers in South Texas, 1880–1930." In *Ethnicity on the Great Plains*, ed., Frederick C. Luebke. Lincoln: University of Nebraska Press, 1980.

Baulch, Joe. "The Murder of Stanley Welch and the 1906 Starr County Election." *Journal of South Texas*, 4 (Spring, 1991).

Binder, Norman and Frank J. García. "Winning Political Office in Cameron County, 1876–1988: The Mexican American Case." in *More Studies in Brownsville History*, ed. Milo Kearny. Brownsville: Pan American University, 1989.

Blackburn, George M., and Sherman L. Richards. "A Demographic History of the West: Nueces County, Texas, 1850." *Prologue*, 4 (Spring, 1972).

Blackwelder, Julia Kirk. *Women of the Depression: Caste and Culture in San Antonio, 1929–1939*. College Station: Texas A&M University Press, 1984.

Brackenridge, R. Douglas. "Presbyterian Missions to Mexican Americans in Texas in the Nineteenth Century." *Journal of Presbyterian History*, 49 (Summer, 1971).

———— and Francisco O. García-Treto. *Iglesia Presbiteriana: A History of Presbyterians and Mexican Americans of the Southwest*. San Antonio: Trinity University Press, 1974.

Buenger, Walter L. "Orthodoxy and Ethnicity." In Walter L. Buenger, *Secession and the Union in Texas*. Austin: University of Texas Press, 1984.

Calderón, Roberto R.. "Mexican Politics in the American Era, 1846–1900: Laredo, Texas." Ph.D. Diss., University of California at Los Angeles, 1993.

———— (comp. and ed.). *South Texas Coal Mining: A Community History*. Eagle Pass, Tex.: Privately printed, 1984.

Carlson, Paul H. "The Panhandle Pastores," in Paul H. Carlson, *Texas Woolybacks: The Range Sheep and Goat Industry*. College Station: Texas A&M University Press, 1982.

Carroll, Patrick J. "Tejano Living and Educational Conditions in World War II South Texas." *South Texas Studies*, 5 (1994).

Castillo Crimm, Ana Carolina. "Success in Adversity: The Mexican Americans of Victoria County, Texas, 1800–1880." Ph.D.

Diss., University of Texas at Austin, 1994.

Christian, Carole E. "Joining the American Mainstream: Texas' Mexican Americans During World War I." *Southwestern Historical Quarterly*, 93 (Apr., 1989).

Cisneros, Victor B. Nelson. "La Clase Trabajadora en Tejas, 1920–1940." *Aztlán*, 6 (Summer, 1975).

———. "UCAPAWA Organizing Activities in Texas, 1935–1950." *Aztlán*, 9 (Spring and Summer, 1978).

Coyle, Laurie, Gail Hershatter, and Emily Honig. "Women at Farrah: An Unfinished Story." in *Mexican Women in the United States: Struggles Past and Present*, ed. Magdalena Mora and Adelaida R. del Castillo. Los Angeles: Chicano Studies Research Center, 1980.

Croxdale, Richard. "The 1938 San Antonio Pecan Shellers' Strike." In Richard Croxdale and Melissa Hield, *Women in the Texas Workforce: Yesterday and Today*. Austin: People's History in Texas, 1979.

Cruz, Gilberto R., and Marta Cruz. *A Century of Service: The History of the Catholic Church in the Lower Rio Grande Valley*. Harlingen, Tex.: United Printers and Publishers, 1979.

Cuthbertson, Gilbert M. "Catarino E. Garza and the Garza War." *Texana*, 12, No. 4 (n.d.).

de la Teja, Jesús F. "Tejano and Texian: Seguín and Houston in the Making of Texas." *South Texas Studies*, 2 (1992).

De León, Arnoldo. *Apuntes San Angeleños: An Index of Newspaper Items Extracted from the San Angelo Standard Times, 1884–1984*. San Angelo: Fort Concho Museum Press, 1987.

———. *Apuntes Tejanos*, 2 vols. Austin: Texas State Historical Association, 1978.

———. *Benavides: The Town and Its Founder*. Benavides: Benavides Centennial Committee, 1980.

———. "Blowout 1910 Style: A Chicano School Boycott in West Texas, 1910." *Texana*, 12 (1974).

———. *Ethnicity in the Sunbelt: A History of Mexican Americans in Houston*. Houston: Mexican American Studies Program, University of Houston, 1989.

———. *Las Fiestas Patrias: Biographic Notes on the Hispanic Presence in San Angelo, Texas*. San Antonio: Caravel Press, 1978.

―――. *In Re Ricardo Rodríguez: An Attempt at Chicano Disfranchisement in San Antonio, Texas*. San Antonio: Caravel Press, 1978.

―――. *Mexican Americans in Texas: A Brief History*. Arlington Heights, Ill.: Harlan Davidson, 1993.

―――. *The Mexican Image in Nineteenth-Century Texas*. Boston: American Press, 1982.

―――. "Our Gringo Amigos: Anglo Americans and the Tejano Experience." *East Texas Historical Journal*, 32 (Fall 1993).

―――. "Rancheros, Comerciantes, and Trabajadores in South Texas, 1848–1900." In *Reflections of the Mexican Experience in Texas*, ed. Margarita B. Melville. Houston: Mexican American Studies Center, University of Houston, 1979.

―――. *San Angeleños: Mexican Americans in San Angelo, Texas*. San Angelo: Fort Concho Museum Press, 1985.

―――. *A Social History of Mexican Americans in Nineteenth-Century Duval County*. San Diego, Tex.: County Commissioners' Court, 1978.

―――. "Los Tasinques and the Sheep Shearers' Union of North America: A Strike in West Texas, 1934." *West Texas Historical Association Yearbook*, 55 (1979).

―――. *The Tejano Community, 1836–1900*. Albuquerque: University of New Mexico Press, 1982.

―――. "The Tejano Experience in Six Texas Regions." *West Texas Historical Association Yearbook*, 65 (1989).

―――. "Tejano History Scholarship: A Review of the Recent Literature." *West Texas Historical Association Yearbook*, 61 (1985).

―――. "Los Tejanos: An Overview of Their History." In Archie P. McDonald and Ben H. Procter, *The Texas Heritage*. St. Louis: Forum Press, 1980.

―――. "Texas Mexicans: Twentieth Century Interpretations." In *Texas Through Time: Evolving Interpretations*, ed. Walter L. Buenger and Robert A. Calvert. College Station: Texas A&M University Press, 1991.

―――. *They Called Them Greasers: Anglo Attitudes Toward Mexicans in Texas, 1821–1900*. Austin: University of Texas Press, 1983.

————. "Wresting a Competence in Nineteenth-Century Texas: The Case of the Chicanos." *Red River Valley Historical Review*, 4 (Fall 1979).

———— and Kenneth L. Stewart. "Lost Dreams and Found Fortunes: Mexican and Anglo Immigrants to South Texas, 1850–1900." *Western Historical Quarterly*, 14 (July, 1983).

———— and Kenneth L. Stewart. "A Tale of Three Cities: A Comparative Analysis of the Socio-Economic Conditions of Mexican Americans in Los Angeles, Tucson, and San Antonio, 1850–1900." *Journal of the West*, 24 (Apr., 1985).

———— and Kenneth L. Stewart. "Tejano Demographic Patterns and Socio-Economic Development." *Borderlands Journal*, 7 (Fall, 1983).

———— and Kenneth L. Stewart. *Tejanos and the Numbers Game: A Socio-Historical Profile from the Federal Censuses, 1850–1900.* Albuquerque: University of New Mexico Press, 1989.

Dickens, E. Larry. "Mestizaje in Nineteenth-Century Texas." *Journal of Mexican American History*, 2 (Spring, 1972).

Dinger, Adeline Short. *Folk Life and Folklore of the Mexican Border.* Edinburg, Tex.: Hidalgo County Historical Society, 1974.

di Stefano, Onofre. "'Venimos a Luchar': A Brief History of La Prensa's Founding." *Aztlán*, 16 (1985).

————. "La Prensa of San Antonio and Its Literary Pages, 1913–1915." Ph.D. Diss., University of California at Los Angeles, 1983.

Douglas, James Ridley. "Juan Cortina: El Caudillo de la Frontera." M.A. thesis, University of Texas at Austin, 1987.

Dyer, Stanford P., and Merrell A. Knighten. "Discrimination After Death: Lyndon Johnson and Félix Longoria." *Southern Studies*, 17 (Winter, 1978).

Dysart, Jane. "Mexican Women in San Antonio, 1830–1860: The Assimilation Process." *Western Historical Quarterly*, 7 (Oct., 1976).

Fisch, Louise Ann. *All Rise: Reynaldo G. Garza: The First Mexican American Federal Judge.* College Station: Texas A&M University Press, 1996.

Foley, Douglas E. "The Legacy of the Partido Raza Unida in

South Texas: A Class Analysis." *Ethnic Affairs*, No. 2 (Spring, 1988).

————, et al. *From Peones to Politicos: Class and Ethnicity in a South Texas Town*, rev. ed. Austin: University of Texas Press, 1988.

————, et al. *From Peones to Politicos: Ethnic Relations in a South Texas Town, 1900–1977.* Austin: Center for Mexican American Studies, University of Texas Press, 1977.

Foley, Neil F. "Chicanos and the Culture of Cotton in Central Texas, 1880–1900: Reshaping Class Relations in the South." In *Community Empowerment and Chicano Scholarship*, ed. Mary Romero and Cordelia Candelaria. Berkeley, Calif.: National Association for Chicano Studies, 1992.

————. "Mexican Migrant and Tenant Labor in Central Texas Cotton Counties, 1880–1930: Social and Economic Transformation in a Multi-Cultural Society." *Wooster Review*, No. 9 (Spring, 1989).

————. "The New South in the Southwest: Anglos, Blacks, and Mexicans in Central Texas, 1880–1930." Ph.D. Diss., University of Michigan, 1990.

————. *The White Scourge: Mexicans, Blacks, and Poor Whites in Texas Cotton Culture.* Berkeley: University of California Press, 1997.

García, Ignacio. *Mexican American Youth Organization: Precursor of Change in Texas.* Tucson: Mexican American Studies and Research Center, University of Arizona, 1987.

————. *United We Win: The Rise and Fall of the Raza Unida Party.* Tucson: Mexican American Studies and Research Center, University of Arizona Press, 1989.

García, Mario T. "The Chicana in American History: The Mexican Women of El Paso, 1880–1920." *Pacific Historical Review*, 49 (May, 1980).

————. *Desert Immigrants: The Mexicans of El Paso, 1880–1920.* New Haven: Yale University Press, 1981.

————. "In Search of History: Carlos E. Castañeda and the Mexican American Generation." Renato Rosaldo Lecture Series Monographs, no. 4, ed. Ignacio García. Tucson: Mexican American Studies and Research Center, University of Arizona, 1988.

————. "Mexican Americans and the Politics of Citizenship: The Case of El Paso, 1936." *New Mexico Historical Review*, 59 (Apr., 1984).

————. *Mexican Americans: Leadership, Ideology, and Identity, 1930–1960*. New Haven: Yale University Press, 1989.

————. "Porfirian Diplomacy and the Administration of Justice in Texas, 1877–1900." *Aztlán*, 16 (1985).

————. "Racial Dualism in the El Paso Labor Market, 1880–1920." *Aztlán*, 6 (Summer, 1975).

García, Richard A., "Class, Consciousness, and Ideology—The Mexican Community in San Antonio, Texas: 1930–1940." *Aztlán*, 9 (Fall, 1978).

————. "The Making of the Mexican American Mind, San Antonio, Texas, 1929–1941: A Social and Intellectual History of an Ethnic Community," 2 vols. Ph.D. Diss., University of California at Irvine, 1980.

————. "The Mexican American Mind: A Product of the 1930s." In Mario T. García, *History, Culture, and Society: Chicano Studies in the 1980s*. Ypsilanti, Mich.: Bilingual Press/Editorial Bilingüe, 1983.

————. *Rise of the Mexican American Middle Class: San Antonio, 1929–1941*. College Station: Texas A&M University Press, 1991.

Garza-Falcón, Leticia. *Gente Decente: A Borderlands Response to the Rhetoric of Dominance*. Austin: University of Texas Press, 1998.

Gil, Carlos B. "Lydia Mendoza: Houstonian and First Lady of Mexican American Song." *Houston Review*, 3 (Summer, 1981).

Gómez-Quiñones, Juan. "The Plan de San Diego Reviewed." *Aztlán*, 1 (Spring, 1970).

Graham, Joe S. *El Rancho in South Texas: Continuity and Change From 1750*. Denton: University of North Texas Press, 1994.

Greaser, Galen D., and Jesús F. de la Teja. "Quieting Title to Spanish and Mexican Land Grants in the Trans-Nueces: The Bourland and Miller Commission, 1850–1852." *Southwestern Historical Quarterly*, 95 (Apr., 1992).

Green, George N. "The Félix Longoria Affair," *Journal of Ethnic Studies*, 19 (Fall, 1991).

————. "The Good Neighbor Commission and Texas Mexicans." In *Ethnic Minorities in Gulf Coast Society*, ed. Jerrell H. Shofner and Linda V. Ellsworth. Pensacola, Fla.: Gulf Coast History and Humanities Conference, 1979.

————. "ILGWU in Texas, 1930—1970." *Journal of Mexican American History*, 1 (Spring, 1971).

Grijalva, Joshua. *A History of Mexican Baptists in Texas*. Waco: Baylor University. Texas Baptists Oral History Project, 1982.

Griswold del Castillo, Richard. "Literacy in San Antonio." *Latin American Research Review*, 15 (1980).

————. "'Only for My Family': Historical Dimensions of Chicano Family Solidarity—The Case of San Antonio in 1860." *Aztlán*, 16 (1985).

Harris, Charles H., and Louis R. Sadler. "The Plan of San Diego and the Mexican-United States Crisis of 1916: A Reexamination." *Hispanic American Historical Review*, 58 (Aug., 1978).

Hernández, José A. "The Proliferation of Mutual Aid Societies in the Chicano Community and the Attempt to Integrate Them: The Primer Congreso Mexicanista de Texas." In José A. Hernández, *Mutual Aid for Survival: The Case of the Mexican American*. Malabar, Fla.: Robert E. Krieger Publishing Co., 1983.

Hinojosa, Gilberto M. *A Borderlands Town in Transition: Laredo, Texas, 1755–1870*. College Station: Texas A&M University Press, 1983.

————. "Mexican-American Faith Communities in Texas and the Southwest." In *Mexican Americans and the Catholic Church, 1900–1965*, ed. Jay P. Dolan and Gilberto M. Hinojosa. Notre Dame, Ind.: University of Notre Dame Press, 1994.

————. "Texas Mexico Border: A Turbulent History." *Texas Humanist*, 6 (Mar., Apr., 1984).

Hunter, Cecilia Aros and Leslie Gene Hunter. "'My Dear Friend': The J. T. Canales-Lyndon B. Johnson Correspondence." *Journal of South Texas*, 5 (Spring, 1992).

Jordan, Terry G. "The 1887 Census of Texas' Hispanic Population." *Aztlán*, 7 (Aug., 1981).

————. "Population Origins in Texas, 1850." *Geographical Review*,

59 (Jan., 1969).

Juárez, José Roberto. "La Iglesia Católica y el Chicano de Sud Tejas, 1836–1911." *Aztlán,* 4 (Fall, 1973).

Justice, Glenn. *Revolution on the Rio Grande: Mexican Raids and Army Pursuits, 1916–1919.* El Paso: Texas Western Press, 1992.

Kanellos, Nicolás. "San Antonio." In Nicolás Kanellos, *A History of Hispanic Theatre in the United States: Origins to 1940.* Austin: University of Texas Press, 1990.

Kreneck, Thomas H.. *Del Pueblo: A Pictorial History of Houston's Hispanic Community.* Houston: Houston International University, 1989.

———. "Jesse Murillo: Social Artist for the Houston-Galveston Region." *Houston Review* (Summer, 1983).

Lack, Paul D. "Los tejanos leales a México del este de Texas, 1838–1839." *Historia Mexicana,* 42 (abril-junio, 1993).

Larralde, Carlos. *Carlos Esparza: A Chicano Chronicle.* San Francisco: R&E Research Associates, 1977.

———. *Mexican Americans: Movements and Leaders.* Los Alamitos, Calif.: Hwong Publishing Co., 1976.

———. "Santa Teresa: A Chicana Mystic." *Grito del Sol,* 3 (Apr., June, 1978).

Leal, Ray Robert. "The 1966–1967 South Texas Farm Workers Strike." Ph.D. Diss., Indiana University, 1983.

Ledesma, Irene. "Texas Newspapers and Chicana Workers' Activism, 1919–1974." *Western Historical Quarterly,* 26 (Autumn, 1995).

———. "Unlikely Strikers: Mexican-American Women in Strike Activity in Texas, 1919–1974." Ph.D. Diss., Ohio State University, 1992.

Limón, José E. "Healing the Wounds: Folk Symbols and Historical Crisis." *Texas Humanist,* 6 (Mar., Apr., 1984).

———. "El Primer Congreso Mexicanista de 1911: A Precursor to Contemporary Chicanismo." *Aztlán,* 5 (Spring, Fall, 1974).

———. "Stereotyping and Chicano Resistance: An Historical Dimension." *Aztlán,* 4 (Fall, 1973).

Lindsay, Marcia. "A Study of the Hispanic Population of Tom

Green County, Texas, in 1910." *Fort Concho Report,* 19 (Fall, 1987).

Longoria, Mario D. "Revolution, Visionary Plan, and Market-place: A San Antonio Incident." *Aztlán,* 12 (Autumn, 1981).

McKay, R. Reynolds. "Mexican Repatriation from South Texas During the Great Depression." *Journal of South Texas,* 3 (Spring, 1990).

————. "The Federal Deportation Campaign in Texas: Mexican Deportation from the Lower Rio Grande Valley During the Great Depression." *Borderlands Journal,* 5 (Fall, 1981).

————. "The Impact of the Great Depression on Immigrant Mexican Labor: Repatriation of the Bridgeport, Texas, Coalminers." *Social Science Quarterly,* 65 (June, 1984).

————. "The Texas Cotton Acreage Control Law of 1931 and Mexican Repatriation." *West Texas Historical Association Yearbook,* 59 (1983).

————. "Texas Mexican Repatriation During the Great Depression." Ph.D. Diss., University of Oklahoma at Norman, 1982.

Márquez, Benjamín. "League of United Latin American Citizens and the Politics of Ethnicity." In Roberto E. Villarreal, et al., *Latino Empowerment.* New York: Greenwood Press, 1988.

————. *LULAC: The Evolution of a Mexican American Political Organization.* Austin: University of Texas Press, 1993.

————. "Organizing Mexican-American Women in the Garment Industry: La Mujer Obrera." *Women and Politics,* 15 (1995).

————. "The Politics of Race and Assimilation: The League of United Latin American Citizens, 1929–1940." *Western Political Quarterly,* 42 (June, 1989).

————. "The Politics of Race and Class: The League of United Latin American Citizens in the Post-World War II Period." *Social Science Quarterly,* 68 (Mar., 1987).

Martínez, Camilo. "The Mexican and Mexican American Labor Contributions to the Economic Development of the Lower Rio Grande Valley of Texas, 1870–1930." Ph.D. Diss., Texas A&M University, 1987.

————. "Labor in the Valley: The Development of Texas' Citrus Industry." *Journal of South Texas,* 7 (1994).

————. "Vamos Pal West: Let's Go West." *West Texas Historical Association Yearbook*, 70 (1994).

Martínez, Oscar J., *The Chicanos of El Paso: An Assessment of Progress.* El Paso: Texas Western Press, 1980.

————. "On the Size of the Chicano Population: New Estimates, 1850–1900." *Aztlán*, 6 (Spring, 1975).

Matovina, Timothy M. *Tejano Religion and Ethnicity: San Antonio, 1821–1860.* Austin: University of Texas Press, 1995.

Mertz, Richard J., "'No One Can Arrest Me': The Story of Gregorio Cortez." *Journal of South Texas*, 1 (1974).

Miller, Hubert J. "Mexican Migrations to the United States, 1900–1920: With a Focus on the Texas Lower Rio Grande Valley." *Borderlands Journal*, 7 (Spring, 1984).

Montejano, David. *Anglos and Mexicans in the Making of Texas, 1836–1986.* Austin: University of Texas Press, 1987.

————. "The Decline of Jim Crow for Texas Mexicans, 1940–1970." *Aztlán*, 16 (1985).

————. "Frustrated Apartheid: Race, Repression, and Capitalist Agriculture in South Texas, 1920–1930." In *The World System of Capitalism: Past and Present*, ed. Walter Goldfrank. Beverly Hills, Calif.: Sage Publications, 1979.

————. "A Journey Through Mexican Texas, 1900–1930: The Making of a Segregated Society." Ph.D. Diss., Yale University, 1982.

————. *Race, Labor Repression, and Capitalist Agriculture: Notes from South Texas, 1920–1930.* Berkeley, Calif.: Institute for the Study of Social Change, 1977.

Morgan, George R., and Omer C. Stewart. "Peyote Trade in South Texas." *Southwestern Historical Quarterly*, 87 (Jan., 1984).

Navarro, Armando. *The Cristal Experiment: A Chicano Struggle for Community Control.* Madison: University of Wisconsin Press, 1999.

Nixon-Méndez, Nina L. "Los Fundadores Urbanos (Urban Pioneers): The Hispanics of Dallas, 1850–1940." *Journal of the West*, 32 (Oct., 1993).

Orozco, Cynthia E. "Alice Dickerson Montemayor: Feminism and Mexican American Politics in the 1930s." In *Writing the*

*Range: Race, Class, and Culture in the Women's West,* ed. Elizabeth Jameson and Susan Armitage Norman: University of Oklahoma Press, 1997.

―――. "Beyond Machismo, Ladies Auxiliaries, and La Familia: A Historiography of Mexican-Origin Women's Participation in Voluntary Associations and Politics in the United States," Renato Rosaldo Lecture Series. Tucson: Mexican American Studies & Research Center, University of Arizona, 1994.

―――. "The Origins of the League of United Latin American Citizens (LULAC) and the Mexican American Civil Rights Movement in Texas with an Analysis of Women's Political Participation in a Gendered Context, 1910–1929." Ph.D. Diss., University of California at Los Angeles, 1992.

Ortego, Philip D., and Arnoldo De León. *The Tejano Yearbook, 1519–1978: A Selective Chronicle of the Hispanic Presence in Texas.* San Antonio: Caravel Press, 1978.

Paredes, Américo. "José Mosqueda and the Folklorization of Actual Events." *Aztlán,* 4 (Spring, 1973).

―――. *A Texas-Mexican Cancionero: Songs of the Lower Border.* Urbana: University of Illinois Press, 1976.

―――. *With His Pistol in His Hand: A Border Ballad and its Hero.* Austin: University of Texas Press, 1958; reprinted Austin: University of Texas Press, 1971.

Peña, Manuel. "The Emergence of Conjunto Music, 1935–1955." In *"And Other Neighborly Names": Social Process and Cultural Image in Texas Folklore,* ed. Richard Bauman and Roger Abrahams. Austin: University of Texas Press, 1981.

―――. "Folksongs and Social Change: Two Corridos as Interpretive Sources." *Aztlán,* 12 (Spring and Fall, 1982).

―――. "From Rancho to Jaitón: Ethnicity and Class in Texas-Mexican Music." *Ethnomusicology,* 29 (Winter, 1985).

―――. *The Texas Mexican Conjunto: A History of a Working-Class Music.* Austin: University of Texas Press, 1985.

Primera, Joe C. "Los Hermanos Torres: Early Settlers of Pecos County." *Permian Historical Annual,* 20 (1980).

Procter, Ben H. "The Modern Texas Rangers: A Law Enforcement Dilemma in the Rio Grande Valley." In Manuel P. Servín, *The*

*Mexican Americans: An Awakening Minority.* Beverly Hills, Calif.: Glencoe Press, 1970.

Pycior, Julie Leininger. "From Hope to Frustration: Mexican Americans and Lyndon Johnson in 1967." *Western Historical Quarterly,* 24 (Nov., 1993).

———. "Lyndon, La Raza, and the Paradox of Texas History." In *Lyndon Baines Johnson and the Exercise of Power,* ed. Bernard J. Firestone and Robert C. Vogt. Westport, Conn.: Greenwood Press, 1988.

———. "La Raza Organizes: Mexican American Life in San Antonio, 1915–1930, as Reflected in Mutualista Activities." Ph.D. Diss., University of Notre Dame, 1979.

Quezada, J. Gilberto. *Border Boss: Manuel B. Bravo and Zapata County.* College Station: Texas A&M University Press, 1999.

———. "Judge Manuel B. Bravo: A Political Leader in South Texas, 1937–1957." *Journal of South Texas,* 5 (Spring, 1992).

———. "Toward a Working Definition of Social Justice: Father Carmelo A. Tranchese, S.J., and Our Lady of Guadalupe Parish, 1932–1953." *Journal of Texas Catholic History and Culture,* 4 (1993).

Ramírez, Elizabeth Cantú. *Footlights Across the Border: A History of Spanish-Language Professional Theatre on the Texas Stage.* New York: Peter Lang, 1989.

———. "Hispanics and Mexican Women on the Texas Stage, 1875–1900." In *Women and Texas History: Selected Essays,* ed. Fane Downs and Nancy Baker Jones. Austin: Texas State Historical Association, 1993.

———. "A History of Mexican American Professional Theatre in Texas: 1875–1935." Ph.D. Diss., University of Texas at Austin, 1982.

———. "A History of Mexican American Professional Theatre in Texas Prior to 1900." *Theatre Survey,* 24 (1983).

Ramírez, Emilia Schunior. *Ranch Life in Hidalgo County after 1850.* Edinburg, Tex.: New Santander Press, 1971.

Ramos, Henry A. J. *A People Forgotten, A Dream Pursued: The History of the American G.I. Forum, 1948–1972.* Corpus Christi: American G.I. Forum of the United States, 1982.

Raun, Gerald G. "Seventeen Days in November: The Lynching of Antonio Rodríguez and American-Mexican Relations, November 3–19, 1910." *Journal of Big Bend Studies*, 7 (Jan., 1995).

Rangel, Jorge C., and Carlos M. Alcalá. "Project Report: De Jure Segregation of Chicanos in Texas Schools." *Harvard Civil Rights-Civil Liberties Law Review*, 7 (Mar., 1972).

Reily, John Denny. "Santos Benavides: His Influence on the Lower Rio Grande, 1823–1891." Ph.D. Diss., Texas Christian University, 1976.

Reyna, José R.. "Notes on Tejano Music." *Aztlán*, 13 (Spring and Fall, 1982).

Rhinehart, Marilyn, and Thomas H. Kreneck. "'In the Shadow of Uncertainty': Texas Mexicans and Repatriation in Houston During the Great Depression." *Houston Review*, 10 (1988).

———. "The Minimum Wage March of 1966: A Case Study in Mexican American Politics, Labor, and Identity." *Houston Review*, 11 (1989).

Richmond, Douglas W. "La Guerra en Tejas se Renova: Mexican Insurrection and Carrancista Ambitions, 1900–1920." *Aztlán*, 11 (Spring, 1980).

Rios McMillan, Nora. "The Immigration Issue Between 1929 and 1954 as Seen Through *La Prensa*." *South Texas Studies*, 6 (1995).

Rocha, Rodolfo. "Banditry in the Lower Rio Grande Valley of Texas, 1915." *Studies in History*, 6 (1976).

———. "The Influence of the Mexican Revolution on the Mexico-Texas Border, 1910–1916." Ph.D. Diss., Texas Tech University, 1981.

———. "The Sting and Power of Rebellion." *Texas Humanist*, 6 (Mar., Apr., 1984).

———. "The Tejano Experience." In *The Texas Heritage*, ed. Ben H. Procter and Archie P. McDonald, 2nd ed. Arlington Heights, Ill.: Harlan Davidson, 1992.

———. "The Tejanos of Texas." In *Texas: A Sesquicentennial Celebration*, ed. Donald W. Whisenhunt. Austin: Eakin Press, 1984.

Romero, Mary. "El Paso Salt War: Mob Action or Political Struggle." *Aztlán*, 16 (1985).

Romero, Yolanda G. "Adelante Compañeros: The Sanitation Workers' Struggle in Lubbock, Texas, 1968–1972." *West Texas Historical Association Yearbook*, 69 (1993).

———. "The Mexican American Frontier Experience in Twentieth Century Northwest Texas." Ph.D. Diss. Texas Tech University, 1993.

———. "Los Socios del Sementerio [sic]: A Mexican American Burial Society in Early Lubbock, Texas." *West Texas Historical Association Yearbook*, 63 (1987).

Romo, Ricardo. "George I. Sánchez and the Civil Rights Movement: 1940–1960." *La Raza Law Journal*, 1 (1986).

Rosales, Francisco Arturo. "The Mexican Experience in Chicago, Houston, and Tucson: Comparisons and Contrasts." In Francisco A. Rosales and Barry J. Kaplan, *Houston: A Twentieth-Century Urban Frontier*. Port Washington, New York: Associated Faculty Press, 1983.

———. "Mexicans in Houston: The Struggle to Survive, 1908–1975." *Houston Review*, 3 (Summer, 1981).

———. "La Música en Houston: Fifty Years of Mexican American Music." *Americas Review*, 16 (Spring, 1988).

———. "Shifting Self-Perceptions and Ethnic Consciousness Among Mexicans in Houston, 1908–1946." *Aztlán*, 16 (1985).

Rosales, Rodolfo. "The Rise of Chicano Middle Class Politics in San Antonio, 1951–1985." Ph.D. Diss., University of Michigan, 1991.

Rozek, Barbara J.. "The Entry of Mexican Women into Urban Based Industries: Experiences in Texas During the Twentieth Century." In *Women and Texas History: Selected Essays*, ed. Fane Downs and Nancy Baker Jones. Austin: Texas State Historical Association, 1993.

Rubio, Abel G. *Stolen Heritage: A Mexican-American's Rediscovery of His Family's Lost Land*, ed. and with foreword by Thomas H. Kreneck. Austin: Eakin Press, 1986.

Salmón, Roberto Mario. "Don José San Ramón as Brownsville Capitalist, 1822–1879." *South Texas Studies*, 1 (1990).

Samora, Julian, et al. *Gunpowder Justice: A Reassessment of the Texas*

*Rangers*. Notre Dame, Ind.: University of Notre Dame Press, 1979.

Sánchez, Juan O. "Walkout Cabrones: The Uvalde School Walkout of 1970." *West Texas Historical Association Yearbook*, 68 (1992).

Sandos, James A. "The Plan of San Diego: War and Diplomacy on the Texas Border, 1915–1916." *Arizona and the West*, 14 (Summer, 1972).

————. *Rebellion in the Borderlands: Anarchism and the Plan of San Diego, 1904–1923*. Norman: University of Oklahoma Press, 1992.

San Miguel, Guadalupe, Jr. "Bitter Struggles: Mexican Americans and the Revision of the Texas Bilingual Education Bill of 1981." In National Association for Chicano Studies, *The Chicano Struggle: Analyses of Past and Present Efforts*. Binghampton, N.Y.: Bilingual Press/Editorial Bilingue, 1984.

————. "'The Community is Beginning to Rumble': The Origins of Chicano Educational Protest in Houston, 1965—1970." *Houston Review*, 13 (1991).

————. "Endless Pursuits: The Chicano Educational Experience in Corpus Christi, Texas, 1880–1960." Ph.D. Diss., Stanford University, 1979.

————. "From a Dual to a Tripartite School System: The Origins and Development of Education Segregation in Corpus Christi, Texas." *Integrated Education*, 17 (Sept., Dec., 1979).

————. *"Let All of Them Take Heed": Mexican Americans and the Campaign for Educational Equality in Texas, 1910–1981*. Austin: University of Texas Press, 1987.

————. "Mexican American Organizations and the Changing Politics of School Desegregation in Texas, 1945–1980." *Social Science Quarterly*, 63 (Dec., 1982).

————. "The Struggle Against Separate and Unequal Schools: Middle Class Mexican Americans in the Desegregation Campaign in Texas, 1929–1957." *History of Education Quarterly*, 23 (Fall, 1983).

Santos, Richard G. "Chicanos of Jewish Descent in Texas." *Western States Jewish Historical Quarterly*, 15 (1983).

Schneider, Ellen, and Paul H. Carlson. "Gunnysackers, Car-

reteros, and Teamsters: The South Texas Cart War of 1857."
*Journal of South Texas*, 1 (Spring, 1988).

Schlossman, Steven. "Self-Evident Remedy? George I. Sánchez,
Segregation, and Enduring Dilemmas in Bilingual Education."
*Teachers College Record*, 84 (Summer, 1983).

Schement, Jorge Reina, and Ricardo Flores. "The Origins of
Spanish Language Radio: The Case of San Antonio." *Journalism History*, 4 (Summer, 1977).

Shockley, John S. *Chicano Revolt in a Texas Town*. Notre Dame.:
University of Notre Dame Press, 1974.

Sloss-Vento, Adela. *Alonso S. Perales: His Struggle for the Rights of
Mexican Americans*. ed. and intro. by Arnold C. Vento. San
Antonio: Artes Gráficas, 1977.

Smith, Anita Torres. "Praxedis Mata Torres: The First Mexican
American Teacher in the Public Schools in Uvalde County,
Texas." *Journal of Big Bend Studies*, 3 (Jan., 1991).

Smith, Walter E. "Mexican Resistance to Schooled Ethnicity: Ethnic Student Power in South Texas, 1930–1970." Ph.D. Diss.,
University of Texas, 1978.

Smith, W. Elwood, and Douglas E. Foley. "Mexicano Resistance to
Schooling in a South Texas Colony." *Education and Urban Society*, 10 (1978).

Smylie, Vernon. *A Noose for Chipita*. Corpus Christi: New Syndicate
Press, 1970.

Stewart, Kenneth L., and Arnoldo De León. "Education is the
Gateway: Comparative Patterns of School Attendance and Literacy Between Anglos and Tejanos in Three Texas Regions,
1850–1900." *Aztlán*, 16 (1985).

———. "Education, Literacy, and Occupational Structure in West
Texas, 1860–1900." *West Texas Historical Association Yearbook*,
60 (1984).

———. "Fertility Among Mexican Americans and Anglos in
Texas, 1900." *Borderlands Journal*, 9 (Spring, 1986).

———. "Literacy Among Immigrants in Texas." *Latin American
Research Review*, 20 (Fall, 1985).

———. *Not Room Enough: Mexicans, Anglos, and Socioeconomic
Change in Texas, 1850–1900*. Albuquerque: University of New

Mexico Press, 1993.

———. "Work Force Participation Among Mexican Immigrant Women in Texas, 1900." *Borderlands Journal*, 9 (Spring, 1986).

Taylor, A. J.. "New Mexican Pastores and Priests in the Texas Panhandle, 1887–1915." *Panhandle Plains Historical Review*, 56 (1984).

Thompson, Jerry Don. "The Many Faces of Juan Nepomuceno Cortina." *South Texas Studies*, 2 (1991).

———. *Mexican Texans in the Union Army*. El Paso: Texas Western Press, 1986.

———. "Mutiny and Desertion on the Rio Grande: The Strange Saga of Captain Adrían J. Vidal." *Military History*, 12, No. 3.

———. *Sabers on the Rio Grande*. Austin: Presidial Press, 1974.

———. "A Stand Along the Border: Santos Benavides and the Battle of Laredo." *Civil War Illustrated* (Aug., 1980).

———. *Vaqueros in Blue and Gray*. Austin: Presidial Press, 1974.

———. *Warm Weather and Bad Whiskey: The 1886 Laredo Election Riot*. El Paso: Texas Western Press, 1991.

———, ed. *Juan Cortina and the Texas-Mexico Frontier, 1859–1877*. El Paso: University of Texas at El Paso, 1994.

Tijerina, Andrés A. *The History of Mexican Americans in Lubbock County*. Lubbock: Texas Tech University, 1977.

———. *Tejanos and Texas Under the Mexican Flag, 1821–1836*. College Station. Texas A&M University Press, 1994.

———. *Tejano Empire: Life on the South Texas Ranchos*. College Station. Texas A&M University Press, 1998.

Torres Smith, Anita. "Shearing: La Trasquila in the First Half of the Twentieth Century." *Journal of Big Bend Studies*, 6 (Jan., 1994).

Tovar, Ines H. "Sara Estela Ramírez: The Early Twentieth-Century Texas Mexican Poet." Ph.D. Diss., University of Houston, 1984.

Treviño, Roberto R.. "La Fe: Catholicism and Mexican Americans in Houston, 1911–1972." Ph.D. Diss., Stanford University, 1993.

———. "Prensa y Patria: The Spanish Language Press and the Biculturation of the Tejano Middle Class, 1920–1940."

*Western Historical Quarterly*, 22 (Nov., 1991).

Trotter, Robert T., II and Juan Antonio Chavira. *Curanderismo: Mexican American Folk Healing.* Athens: University of Georgia Press, 1981.

Vargas, Zaragosa. "Tejana Radical: Emma Tenayuca and the San Antonio Labor Movement During the Great Depression," *Pacific Historical Review*, 66 (Nov., 1998).

Wilson, James. Tejanos, *Chicanos, and Mexicanos: A Partially Annotated Historical Bibliography for Texas Public School Teachers.* San Marcos: Bilingual Bicultural Education Program, 1974.

Winn, Charles. "Mexican Americans in the Texas Labor Movement." Ph.D. Diss., Texas Christian University, 1972.

Wright, Paul. "Population Patterns in Presidio County in 1880: Evidence from the Census." *Journal of Big Bend Studies*, 7 (Jan., 1995).

Young, Elliott. "Deconstructing La Raza: Identifying the Gente Decente of Laredo, 1904–1994." *Southwestern Historical Quarterly*, 98 (Oct., 1994).

Zamora, Emilio, Jr.. "Chicano Socialist Labor Activity in Texas, 1900–1920." *Aztlán*, 6 (Summer, 1975).

————. "The Failed Promise of Wartime Opportunity for Mexicans in the Texas Oil Industry." *Southwestern Historical Quarterly*, 95 (Jan. 1992).

————. "Las Escuelitas: A Texas-Mexican Search for Educational Excellence." In *Los Tejanos: Children of Two Cultures*, Proceedings of the South Texas Head Start Bilingual-Bicultural Conference. Edinburg: South Texas Regional Training Office, 1978.

————. "Mexican Labor Activity in South Texas, 1900–1920." Ph.D. Diss., University of Texas at Austin, 1983.

————. *El Movimiento Obrero Mexicano en el Sur de Texas, 1900–1920.* México, D.F.: Secretaría de Educación Pública, 1986.

————. "Sara Estela Ramírez: A Note on Research in Progress." In *Hembra: Hermanas en Movimiento Brotando Raíces de Aztlán.* Austin: Center for Mexican American Studies, University of Texas, 1976.

————. "Sara Estela Ramírez: Una Rosa en el Movimiento." In *Mexican Women in the United States: Struggles Past and Present,* ed. Magdalena Mora and Adelaida R. Del Castillo. Los Angeles: Chicano Studies Research Center, 1980.

————. "Sindicalismo Socialista de los Chicanos en Texas, 1900–1920." In *Orígenes del Movimiento Obrero Chicano,* ed. Luis Arroyo and Juan Gómez-Quiñones. México, D. F.: La Serie Popular ERA, No. 64, 1978.

————. *The World of the Mexican Worker in Texas.* College Station: Texas A&M University Press, 1993.

———— and Roberto Calderón, "Manuela Solís Sager and Emma Tenayuca: A Tribute." In *Chicana Voices: Intersections of Class, Race, and Gender,* Proceedings of the National Association for Chicano Studies, ed. Teresa Córdova, et.al. Austin: The Center for Mexican American Studies, University of Texas at Austin, 1986.

Zelman, Donald L. "Alazan-Apache Courts: A New Deal Response to Mexican American Housing Conditions in San Antonio." *Southwestern Historical Quarterly,* 87 (Oct., 1983).

# Mexican American, Tejana, and Tejano History:

## An Instructional Bibliography

CYNTHIA E. OROZCO*

## I. Chicano History Surveys

Acuña, Rodolfo. *Occupied America: A History of Chicanos.* 3rd ed. New York: Harper and Row, 1988.

Cortés, Carlos E. "Mexicans." *Harvard Encyclopedia of American Ethnic Groups*, ed. Stephan Thernstrom. Cambridge, Mass.: Belknap Press of Harvard University Press, 1980.

Gonzales, Manuel G. *Mexicanos: A History of Mexicans in the United States.* Bloomington: Indiana University Press, 1999.

Griswold del Castillo, Richard and Arnoldo De León. *North to Aztlan: A History of Mexican Americans in the United States.* New York: Twayne Publishers, 1996.

Rosales, Arturo. *Chicano!: The History of the Mexican American Civil Rights Movement.* Houston: Arte Publico Press, 1996.

*Cynthia E. Orozco received her Ph.D. from the University of California, Los Angeles, and is currently a visiting assistant in history and Chicana studies at the University of New Mexico. She is a two-time Ford Foundation fellowship recipient and a founder and past chair of the Chicana Caucus of the National Association of Chicana and Chicano Studies. Dr. Orozco's forthcoming book is "No Mexicans, Women, or Dogs Allowed: The Rise of the Mexican American Civil Rights Movement."

———. "Mexican Americans." In *The Hispanic-American Almanac*, ed. Nicolas Kanellos. Detroit: Gale Research, Inc., 1993.

## II. Chicano History Bibliographies

Camarillo, Albert (ed.). *Latinos in the United States: A Historical Bibliography*. Santa Barbara: ABC-CLIO, 1986.

Etulain, Jacqueline J. *Mexican Americans in the Twentieth Century American West: A Bibliography*. Albuquerque: University of New Mexico Press, 1990.

Gómez-Quiñones, Juan. "Pre-Twentieth Century Mexicans North of the Rio Bravo: Selected Social and Economic Sources." In Juan Gómez-Quiñones, *Development of the Mexican Working Class North of the Rio Bravo: Work and Culture Among Laborers and Artisans, 1600–1900*. Los Angeles: UCLA Chicano Studies Research Center, 1982.

McDonald, Dedra S., Evelyn A. Schlatter, and Juneal Leversee. "Selected Bibliographies, Latinas/Hispanas." In *Writing the Range, Class, and Culture in the Women's West*, ed. Elizabeth Jameson and Susan Armitage. Norman: University of Oklahoma Press, 1997.

Meier, Matt S. (comp.). *Bibliography of Mexican American History*. Westport, Conn.: Greenwood Press, 1984.

## III. Chicana History Surveys

Cotera, Martha P. *Diosa y Hembra: The History and Heritage of Chicanas in the United States*. Austin: Information Systems Development, 1976.

Ruiz, Vicki L. *From Out of the Shadows: A History of Mexican Women in the United States, 1900–1995*. New York: Oxford University Press, 1998.

## IV. Chicana History Bibliographies

González, Rosalinda M. "The Chicana in Southwest Labor History, 1900–1975 (a Preliminary Bibliographic Analysis)." *Critical Perspectives*, 2 (Fall, 1984).

Ruiz, Vicki L. "Mexican Women in the United States: A Bibliography." In *Selected Reading Lists and Course Outlines from American*

*Colleges and Universities, Women's History*, ed. Annette K. Baxter and Louise L. Stevenson. New York: Markus Wiener Publishing, Inc., 1987.

Soto, Shirlene Ann. "Scholar's Exchange: Mexican Women in Historical Perspective: A Bibliography." *Conference Group on Women's History Newsletter*, 15 (Summer, 1984).

## V. Chicana Historiography

Castaneda, Antonia I. "Women of Color and the Rewriting of Western History: The Discourse, Politics, and Decolonization of History." *Pacific Historical Review*, 61 (Nov., 1992).

Del Castillo, Adelaida R., ed. *Between Borders: Essays on Mexicana/Chicana History*. Encino: Floricanto Press, 1990.

Leyva, Yolanda, "Listening to the Silences in Chicana Lesbian History," In *Living Chicana Theory*. Berkeley: Third Woman Press, 1998.

Orozco, Cynthia E. "Beyond Machismo, La Familia, and Ladies Auxiliaries: A Historiography of Mexican-Origin Women's Participation in Voluntary Associations and Politics in the United States, 1870–1990." In *Perspectives in Mexican American Studies*, 5. Tucson: Mexican American Studies & Research Center, University of Arizona, 1995.

Perez, Emma. *The Decolonial Imaginary: Writing Chicanas into History*. Bloomington: Indiana University Press, 1999.

Sweeney, Judith. "Chicana History: A Review of the Literature." *Essays on La Mujer*, ed. Rosaura Sanchez and Rosa Martínez Cruz. Los Angeles: UCLA Chicano Studies Center Publications, 1977.

## VI. Tejano History Surveys

De León, Arnoldo. "Los Tejanos: An Overview of Their History." *The Texas Heritage*, ed. Ben Procter and Archie P. McDonald. St. Louis, Missouri: Forum Press, 1980.

———. *Mexican Americans in Texas: A Brief History*. 2nd edition. Arlington Heights, Ill.: Harlan Davidson, 1999.

———. "Mexican Americans." In *New Handbook of Texas*, ed. Ron Tyler et al. Austin: Texas State Historical Association, 1996.

————. "A People with Many Histories: Mexican Americans in Texas." In *The Texas Heritage*, ed. Ben Proctor and Archie P. McDonald, 3rd ed. St. Louis: Forum Press, 1997.

————. *The Tejano Community, 1836–1900*. Albuquerque: University of New Mexico Press, 1982.

Montejano, David. *Anglos and Mexicans in the Making of Texas, 1836–1986*. Austin: University of Texas Press, 1987.

Rocha, Rodolfo. "The Tejano Experience." In *The Texas Experience*, ed. Ben H. Procter and Archie P. McDonald, 2nd ed. Arlington Heights: Harlan Davidson, Inc., 1992.

————. "The Tejanos of Texas." In *Texas: A Sesquicentennial Celebration*, ed. Donald Whisenhunt. Austin: Eakin Press, 1984.

## VII. Tejano History Bibliographies

Cruz, Gilberto Rafael and James Arthur Irby (eds. and comps.). *Texas Bibliography, A Manual on History Research Materials.* Austin: Eakin Press, 1982.

De León, Arnoldo. "Estudios Tejanos: A List of Historical Literature on Mexican Americans in Texas." *Southwestern Historical Quarterly*, 98 (Jan., 1995).

Wilson, James A. (comp.). *Tejanos, Chicanos and Mexicanos: A Partially Annotated, Historical Bibliography for Texas Public Schools.* San Marcos: Bilingual-Bicultural Education Program in cooperation with the Department of Education and the Department of History, 1974.

## VIII. Tejano Historiographical Essays

Almaráz, Félix D., Jr. "Contributions of Mexican Americans to Texas Historiography." In *A Guide to the History of Texas*, ed. Light Townsend Cummins and Alvin R. Bailey Jr. New York: Greenwood Press, 1988.

De León, Arnoldo. "Tejano History Scholarship: A Review of the Recent Literature." *West Texas Historical Association Year Book*, 61 (1985).

————. "The Tejano Experience in Six Texas Regions," *West Texas Historical Association Yearbook.* 15 (1989).

————. "Texas Mexicans: Twentieth-Century Interpretations." In *Texas Through Time, Evolving Interpretations*, ed. Walter L. Buenger and Robert A. Calvert. College Station: Texas A&M University Press, 1991.

Poyo, Gerald E. and Gilberto M. Hinojosa, "Spanish Texas and Borderlands Historiography in Transition: Implications for United States History," *Journal of American History*, 75 (Sept., 1988).

## IX. Tejana History Surveys

Orozco, Cynthia E. "Mexican American Women." In *New Handbook of Texas*, ed. Ron Tyler et al. Austin: Texas State Historical Association, 1996.

Ruiz, Vicki L. "Mexican Women." In *Encyclopedia of Southern History*. Chapel Hill: University of North Carolina Press, 1989.

## X. Tejana History Bibliographies

Malone, Ann Patton, "Women in Texas History." In *A Guide to the History of Texas*, ed. Light Townsend Cummings and Alvin R. Bailey Jr. New York: Greenwood Press, 1988.

Snapp, Elizabeth and Harry F. Snapp. "Mexican American Women." In *Read All About Her! Texas Women's History: A Working Bibliography*. Denton: Texas Woman's University, 1995.

Winegarten, Ruthe, ed. *Texas Women's History Project Bibliography*. Austin: Texas Foundation for Women's Resources, 1980.

## XI. Tejano and Chicano History Chronologies

García, Richard A. *The Chicanos in America, 1540–1974: A Chronology & Fact Book*. Dobbs Ferry, New York: Oceana Publications, Inc., 1977.

Kanellos, Nicolas with Cristelia Perez. *Chronology of Hispanic-American History from Pre-Columbian Times to the Present*. New York: Gale Research, 1990.

Ortega y Gasca, Philip and Arnoldo De León, comps. *The Tejano Yearbook, 1519–1978: A Selective Chronicle of the Hispanic Presence in Texas*. San Antonio: Caravel Press, 1978.

## XII. Borderlands Sources

Cooke, Jacob Ernest, ed. *Encyclopedia of the North American Colonies.* 3 vols.; New York: Charles Scribner's Sons, 1993.

Fernandez-Shaw, Carlos M. *The Hispanic Presence in North America from 1492 to Today.* New York: Facts on File, 1991.

Jimenez, Alfredo, ed. *Handbook of Hispanic Cultures in the United States: History.* Houston: Arte Publico Press, 1994.

Martínez, Oscar J. "A History of Chicanos/Mexicanos Along the U.S. Mexico Border." In *Handbook of Hispanic Cultures in the United States,* ed. Nicolas Kanellos and Claudio Esteva-Fabregat. Houston: Arte Público Press and Instituto de Cooperación Iberoamericana, 1994.

"Selective Bibliography on Spanish Texas, 1685–1821." In *Tejano Origins in Eighteenth-Century San Antonio,* ed. Gerald E. Poyo and Gilberto M. Hinojosa. Austin: University of Texas, 1991.

*Spanish Borderlands Sourcebooks.* 27 vols.; New York: Garland Publishing, Inc., 1991.

Stoddard, Ellwyn R., Richard L. Nostrand, and Jonathan P. West, eds. *Borderlands Sourcebook: A Guide to the Literature on Northern Mexico and the American Southwest.* Norman: University of Oklahoma Press, 1983.

Valk, Barbara G. *Borderline, A Bibliography of the United States-Mexico Borderlands.* Los Angeles: UCLA Latin American Center Publications, 1988.

## XIII. Chicana and Chicano Fact Sources

Chabran, Richard and Rafael Chabran. *The Latino Encyclopedia.* 6 vols.; New York: Marshall Cavendisch Corp., 1996.

Gonzales, Sylvia. *Hispanic American Voluntary Associations.* Westport, Conn.: Greenwood Press, 1985.

Meier, Matt S. *Mexican American Biographies: A Historical Dictionary, 1836–1987.* New York: Greenwood Press, 1988.

———, Conchita Franco Serri, and Richard A. Garcia. *Notable Latino Americans: A Biographical Dictionary.* Westport, Conn.: Greenwood Press, 1997.

——— and Feliciano Rivera. *Dictionary of Mexican American History.* Westport, Conn.: Greenwood Press, 1981.

Telgen, Diane and Jim Kemp, eds. *Notable Hispanic American Women.* Detroit, Michigan: Gale Research Inc., 1993.

## XIV. Chicana and Chicano Indexes and Other Resources

Castillo-Speed, Lillian. *The Chicana Studies Index: Twenty Years of Gender Research, 1971–1991.* Berkeley: Chicano Studies Library Publications Unit, University of California, 1992.

*Chicano Periodical Index, 1967–1993.* Boston, Mass.: G. K. Hall: 1978–1990. (Replaced by the online Chicano Data Base.)

De León, Arnoldo, comp. *Apuntes Tejanos.* Ann Arbor, Michigan: University Microfilms International, 1978.

## XV. Chicana and Chicano History Syllabi

"American Stories." Collected by the Committee on Minority Historians. *Organization of American Historians Magazine.* Bloomington, Indiana: Organization of American Historians, 1998.

Keller, Gary D., Rafael J. Magallen, and Alma M. García, eds. *Curriculum Resources in Chicano Studies.* Tempe, Arizona: Bilingual Review Press, 1989.

Ruiz, Vicki L. "La Chicana." In *Selected Reading Lists and Course Outlines from American Colleges and Universities, Women's History,* ed. Annette K. Baxter and Louise L. Stevenson. New York: Markus Wiener Publishing, Inc., 1987.

# APPENDIX

## Mexican Americans in Texas History
*University of Texas Institute of Texan Cultures*
*San Antonio, May 2–4, 1991*

### SPONSORS

Center for Mexican American Studies, University of Texas at Austin
Center for Studies in Texas History, University of Texas at Austin
Texas Committee for the Humanities, A state program of the National Endowment for the Humanities
Texas State Historical Association, Austin
The University of Texas at San Antonio
The University of Texas Institute of Texan Cultures at San Antonio

### ADVISORY COMMITTEE

Teresa Palomo Acosta, Texas State Historical Association
Gilberto Cárdenas, University of Texas at Austin
Dora Guerra, University of Texas at Austin
James McNutt, University of Texas Institute of Texan Cultures at San Antonio
David Montejano, University of Texas at Austin
Cynthia Orozco, Texas State Historical Association
Rodolfo Rocha, University of Texas-Pan American
Emilio Zamora, University of Houston
Jesse Zapata, Hispanic Research Institute, University of Texas at San Antonio

### CONFERENCE BIENVENIDA

Mexican Americans are descendants of both the indigenous peoples of Mexico and the Spanish conquistadores. Our legacy as Tejanos and Tejanas is therefore a mixture of indigenous, Spanish, and Mexican heritages and our history in the state predates the arrival of Anglo settlers.

After the 1519 conquest of the Aztec nation, the territory which is now Texas became New Spain's frontier when Spanish explorers moved north. Mexico established its reign here from 1821 to 1836. Thereafter, Mexicans in Texas lived under Anglo occupation. According to historian Arnoldo De León, after the Texas revolution of 1836, Mexicans in Texas developed a bicultural Tejano society which gave them the means "to resist oppression" while living under Anglo domination.

Despite the lengthy history of Mexican Americans in Texas, our history and culture have only recently become the subjects of serious scholarly inquiry. Tamaulipas-born Carlos Castañeda initiated this study, especially of the Spanish past, in the 1920s. His seven-volume history *Our Catholic Heritage in Texas* (1938–1958) is a landmark. In the 1930s Jovita González claimed the Texas Mexican heritage in her studies of border folklore. Américo Paredes also linked our heritage to Mexico in the classic *With His Pistol in His Hand: A Border Ballad and Its Hero* (1958). The more recent emergence of Mexican American history as a recognizable field is due, however, to the efforts of Chicano historians trained at the nation's universities since the 1970s. Motivated by the cultural renaissance, the political tenets of the Chicano movement, and the establishment of programs for Mexican American studies throughout the country, these historians focused attention on the Mexican community.

Since the 1970s, these scholars have written numerous books, journal articles, and monographs about Mexican Americans. Their topics have included the visual and literary arts, folklore, labor, political history, and community organizations. They have also established Mexican American studies programs at the University of Texas at Austin, Texas A&I University, the University of Texas at El Paso, and the University of Houston. In Texas, scholars formed a regional group of the National Association for Chicano Studies in the mid-1970s to support research on Tejanos. In 1989, the first significant number of Tejana and Tejano historians attended the annual meeting of the Texas State Historical Association. These activities are important signals that a new field of inquiry has been created.

Significant scholarly works on Tejanos produced in the 1980s are Arnoldo De León's *The Tejano Community, 1836–1900* (1982) and David Montejano's *Anglos and Mexicans in the Making of Texas, 1836–1986* (1987), which received the Frederick Jackson Turner award from the Organization of American Historians. Manuel Peña's *The Texas-Mexican Conjunto: History of a Working Class Music* (1985) is another outstanding example of this scholarship. Other historians have brought attention to early borderlands history and its relationship to Chicanos. Gerald E. Poyo's and Gilberto Hinojosa's "Spanish Texas and Borderlands Historiography in Transition: Implications for United States history" in the *Journal of American History* (September 1988) is a major contribution in redefining the colonial heritage of the United States.

Chicana history is a new area which has brought a much needed focus on Mexican American women, Martha Cotera pioneered the field in the 1970s with her book *Diosa y Hembra; The History and Heritage of Chicanas in the United States* (1976). Early in the 1980s, Elizabeth C. Ramírez discussed women in her dissertation "A History of Mexican American Professional Theatre in Texas, 1875–1935." *Between Borders; Essays on Mexicana/Chicana History* (1990), which was edited by Adelaida del Castillo, constitutes the first anthology of Chicana history, and Emma Pérez's forthcoming monograph on women in the Houston Chicano community will add to the growing body of knowledge and insights into the lives of Tejanas. Moreover, Yolanda Romero, Irene Ledesma, and Cynthia Orozco are writing dissertations on Tejanas in West Texas, Tejana unionism, and the League of United Latin American Citizens, respectively.

Research on Tejanas and Tejanos is growing, but more is needed. This conference on Mexican Americans in Texas history is the first one of its kind and is the result of both a new stage of development in the field and a significant network of scholars. As a result, this conference will increase scholarly and public attention to the field.

The cooperation of key humanities organizations in presenting this conference is a major step in promoting the study of Mexican Americans. In 1983, Oscar J. Martínez noted that "ignorance and prejudice unfortunately permeate the perceptions concerning ethnic minorities found among many in the state's population." This conference will address these misperceptions by assessing research on Mexican Americans in Texas, especially recent works. With a special focus on the post-1836 period, the conference will also bring insights into new areas of research, such as the arts and women; generate a dialogue between scholars and lay researchers; generate a research agenda on new topics; and enhance the network of researchers.

BIENVENIDA. As participants in this important gathering on the occasion of El Cinco de Mayo, you will have the opportunity to hear discussions on the role of race, ethnicity, gender and class, Texas-Mexico relations, folklore, oral history, community history, religion, the arts, and the role of libraries and archives in historical research on Chicanos. It is our hope that you will learn much about Mexican American history and culture in Texas and the importance its study has for the state.

Teresa Palomo Acosta
Research Associate for Hispanic
Studies and Conference Coordinator
Texas State Historical Association
Cynthia E. Orozco
Research Associate for Hispanic Studies
Texas State Historical Association

## CONFERENCE PROGRAM

BIENVENIDA/WELCOME

Teresa Palomo Acosta, Texas State Historical Association
Cynthia Orozco, Research Associate for Hispanic Studies Texas State Historical Association

SESSION 1: Documenting the History of Mexicanos in Texas

"The Mexican American Library Program at the University of Texas at Austin," Margo Gutiérrez, University of Texas at Austin
"Mexican American Archives in Houston and Corpus Christi: Urban Examples," Thomas H. Kreneck, Corpus Christi State University
"Documenting the Mexicano/Chicano in the El Paso/Juárez Border Area," César Caballero, University of Texas at El Paso

SESSION 2: War and Conflict in Nineteenth-Century Texas

"Salineros, Merchants and Texas Rangers; The Trouble Over Salt," Manuel Callahan, University of Texas at Austin
"Texas Revolution Historiography and the Tejanos," Gilberto Hinojosa, University of Texas at San Antonio
"Los Mexicanos Durante la Guerra de Secesión," Miguel Gonzales Quiroga, Universidad Autónoma de Nuevo León, Monterrey, Nuevo León

SESSION 3: Community Studies: Galveston, San Felipe del Rio and Houston

"El Barrio de San Felipe del Rio; A Tejano Border Community," Robert Overfelt, Sul Ross State University
"Galveston and the Mexican Immigrant, 1836–1900," Edward Simmen, Universidad de las Américas, Puebla, Mexico
"Agents of Americanization; The Houston Settlement Association and the Mexicano Community, 1900–1950," María Cristina García, Texas A&M University

SESSION 4: Historiography: Reconstructing Texas History

"On Reading and Writing Texas history," David Montejano, University of Texas at Austin
"John Gregory Bourke and the Problem of Hegemony: On War, Identity and Ethnographic Authority," José E. Limón, University of Texas at Austin
"The Borderlands of Culture: Américo Paredes's George Washington Gómez," Ramón Saldívar, University of Texas at Austin

SESSION 5: Música Tejana: Popular Culture and Social Identity

"The Implication of Recent Changes in Chicano Music: The Constitution of the Popular," Avelardo Valdés and Jeffrey Halley, University of Texas at San Antonio

"Crossing Border: The Corrido and the Emergence of Texas-Mexican Social Identity," Richard R. Flores, University of Wisconsin-Madison

SESSION 6: San Antonio: Archival Research on Hispanics in Texas

"An Overview of San Antonio's Importance in the Collection of Hispanic History in Texas," Richard A. Gambitta, University of Texas at San Antonio

"Archival Repositories: An Assessment," David R. Johnson, University of Texas at San Antonio

"Documenting San Antonio: The Cassiano-Pérez Collection," Ann Fears Crawford, Daughters of the Republic of Texas Library

"Hispanic Influences in Texas Maps," Ann Graham Gaines, Daughters of the Republic of Texas Library

SESSION 7: Texas Mexican Work and Culture, 1890–1920

"Unión, Paz y Trabajo: Laredo's Mexican Mutual Aid Societies, 1890s," Roberto R. Calderón, University of California at Los Angeles

"Work, Culture and Struggle; Texas Mexican Workers at the Turn of the Century," Emilio Zamora, University of Houston

SESSION 8: After the Alamo: The Tejano/Tejana Struggle in a New Era

"A Revolution Remembered; The Juan Seguín Memoirs," Jesús F. de la Teja, Texas General Land Office

"Occupied Texas: Bexar and Goliad, 1835–1836," Paul D. Lack, McMurry College

"Ida y Venida: Segunda Entrada de la Familia De León," Ana Carolina Castillo-Crimm, University of Texas at Austin

SESSION 9: LBJ and Mexican Americans, South Texas and Mexico

"Lyndon Johnson and Mexico; Accommodation or Frustration," Arnold Zárate, Southwest Texas State University

"Judge Manuel B. Bravo; A Political Leader in South Texas, 1937–1957," Juan Gilberto Quezada, San Antonio Independent School District

SESSION 10: Tejanas in the South Plains, South Texas and Along the Border in the Twentieth Century

"Trini Gámez and the Texas Farm Workers: Toil and Trouble on the Texas South Plains," Yolanda García Romero, North Lake College

"Jovita Pérez: A Look at an Hispanic Businesswoman and Civic Leader in Laredo, 1907–1970," Lucy Cárdenas, Laredo Junior College

"Gender and Labor Activism in the Southwest; Mexican American Women's Strikes, 1919–1974," Irene Ledesma, Ohio State University

SESSION 11: Oral history: The Legacy of the Mexican Revolution

"Memories of the Mexican Revolution; The Pride of Don Juan García," Michelle M. Espinosa, Southwestern University

"Across the Border; Family Memories of Immigration to Texas After the Mexican Revolution," Scott Sandoval, Southwestern University

"Paying the Price; Leaving Property and Family in Mexico to Come to Texas at the Time of the Mexican Revolution," Brian Krysewski, Southwestern University

SESSION 12: Texas-Mexican Material Culture in South Texas: Continuity and Change

"Randado: A South Texas Ranch," Mary Anna Casstevens, Texas A&I University

"The Built Environment of Ranching in South Texas, 1750–Present," Joe S. Graham, Texas A&I University

"Texas-Mexican Religious Folk Art in South Texas," Cynthia Vidaurri, Texas A&I University

CONFERENCE DINNER

Keynote Presentation

"Old Roads, New Horizons: Texas History and the New World Order," David Montejano, University of Texas at Austin

Recognitions

The conference Advisory Committee acknowledged the signficant contributions to Chicano history by Professor Arnoldo De León. He was presented an award in recognition of his prolific work.

The Committee organized a special program, also held during the dinner, honoring the contributions of Don Américo Paredes and Doña Jovita González to Tejano and Tejana folklore, history, and literature.

SESSION 13: Three Perspectives: Biography, The Historiography of Religion and Military Oral History

"Carlos E. Castañeda and the Critics," Félix D. Almaráz Jr., University of Texas at San Antonio

"Reflections of the Cross; A Historiographical Sketch of Tejanos and Religion in Post-Mexican Texas," Roberto T. Treviño, Stanford University

"El Escuadrón 201," Jesús Luna, California State University

SESSION 14: Museum and Archives: Content and Issues and Their Utilization

"Mexican Americans in Museums: Issues in Exhibiting Ethnicity," Phyllis McKenzie, University of Texas Institute of Texan Cultures at San Antonio

"The Hector Pérez García Papers; Untapped Resource," Eugenia Landes, Southern Methodist University

SESSION 15: Perspectives on the Pecan Shellers' Strike of 1938: Labor Leaders, Women and the West Side

"Chicanas at the Forefront of Labor Organization; A Look at Emma Tenayuca's role as a Labor Activist," Dedra S. McDonald, Texas Lutheran College

"Political Transformation in the West Side; The Pecan Shellers' Strike of 1938," Raul Ramos, Yale University

SESSION 16: Racial Repression and Resistance in Southwest and South Texas in the 1910s

"The 1915 South Texas Bandit War: A Re-Examination," Rodolfo Rocha, University of Texas-Pan American University

"The Antonio Rodríguez Lynching in 1910; Repercussion on Both Sides of the Border," F. Arturo Rosales, Arizona State University

SESSION 17: Land and Labor in Central and South Texas, 1846–1930

"A Hornet's Nest: Tejano Landholding in the Lower Rio Grande Valley, 1846–1900," Armando C. Alonso, Southwest Texas State University

"The Little Brown Man in Gringo Land: Mexican Sharecroppers and Wage Hands in Central Texas, 1900–1930," Neil F. Foley, University of Michigan-Ann Arbor

SESSION 18: San Antonio: The Role of *La Prensa* and Chicano Middle Class Politics, 1913–1977

"The Making of Cultural Values; La sección del hogar in *La Prensa*,"

Juanita Luna Lawhn, San Antonio College

"Historical Research into *La Prensa*'s Educational Task," Nora E. Ríos McMillan, San Antonio

"Electoral Politics and Community Politics; The Establishment of Chicano Middle Class Politics in San Antonio, Texas, 1968–1977," Rodolfo Rosales, Palo Alto College, San Antonio

SESSION 19: Mexican Americans on the Texas Stage: The Nature, Scope, Materials and Methods of Historical Study

"The Nature and Scope of Theatre History," Oscar Brockett, University of Texas at Austin

"The Materials on Mexican American Theatre at the Benson Latin American Collection," Laura Gutiérrez-Witt, University of Texas at Austin

"The History of Mexican American Theatre in Texas; A Case Study," Elizabeth C. Ramírez, University of Arizona